The Moon and Flowers

The Moon and Flowers

A Woman's Path to Enlightenment

Edited by Kalyanavaca

WINDHORSE PUBLICATIONS

Published by Windhorse Publications
11 Park Road
Birmingham
B13 8AB

Reprinted 1999
Design Dhammarati
Cover photograph by Fleur Olby
Photograph of Santacitta by Robert Battersby
Other photographs courtesy of Vidyamala, Kalyanaprabha, Clear Vision Trust Picture
Archive, Varaghosa, Varasuri, Samata, Varabhadri, Dayanandi, Muditasri, Devamitra,
and Sinhadevi

Printed by The Cromwell Press

We quote by permission of the Pali Text Society which owns the copyright in the
following works:
On page 63: C.A.F. Rhys Davids (trans.), *Poems of Early Buddhist Nuns*, Oxford, 1989.
On page 171: E.M. Hare (trans.), *Book of Gradual Sayings I*, (An. i.1–2.), 1979.

The publishers also wish to acknowledge with gratitude permission to quote from the
following:
Ryokan, *One Robe, One Bowl*, John Stevens (trans.), Weatherhill, New York/Tokyo, 1977.
On page 203: Declaration of Geneva (1994 version), World Medical Association,
Ferney-Voltaire.

British Library Cataloguing in Publication Data
A catalogue record for this book is available from the British Library

ISBN 0 904766 89 6

PUBLISHER'S NOTE: Since this work is intended for a general readership, Pali and Sanskrit
words have been transliterated without the diacritical marks that would have been
appropriate in a work of a more scholarly nature. US spellings have been retained in the
contributions from US writers.

The rain has stopped, the clouds have drifted away, and the weather is clear again.
If your heart is pure, then all things in your world are pure.
Abandon this fleeting world, abandon yourself,
Then the moon and flowers will guide you along the Way.

Ryokan

contents

II BUDDHISM AND WOMANHOOD

III SKILFUL RELATIONSHIPS

IV AT WORK IN THE WORLD

acknowledgements

This book is the result of many people's generosity. My thanks go to all the contributors, who set aside time from their busy lives to work on their chapters, and have agreed that the royalties from the sales of this book be given to Taraloka to contribute to its future development; to Vidyadevi and Catherine Hopper for their help with the editing process and for making many useful and thoughtful suggestions; to Jan Parker for her enthusiasm and encouragement; and to the many women, and in particular my good friend Muditavati, who have very generously sponsored me financially to enable me to complete the book. And to Sangharakshita, without whom none of us would have had anything to write about, my gratitude has no end.

Kalyanavaca
Glasgow
January 1997

Kalyanavaca

Foreword

THE OTHER DAY I was shown a brand new book about Buddhism for very young children. I was struck by the colourful photograph on its cover, of young trainee monks with shaved heads and orange robes, carrying large alms-bowls. It was a good picture, but it did make me wonder whether Buddhism in the West will ever be free from this particular image. After all, within the past thirty years or so Buddhism has come to the West not just as an esoteric subject of study for academics but as a living experience for many thousands of people. Some Buddhists do, of course, live in monasteries and wear robes; but a lot of them don't. They come in all shapes and sizes, and many of them are women.

For several years I lived and worked at Taraloka, a Buddhist retreat centre for women, and I continue to be involved in retreats there, especially those for women new to Buddhism. Over and over again I have been moved by the honest and searching questions which are asked by women experiencing their first taste of meditation and Buddhism. How do you make meditation part of your life? Can you combine motherhood and Buddhism? Isn't Buddhism sexist and patriarchal? How can I be a Buddhist and carry on with my career? What is the Buddhist view on abortion? Can a Buddhist be a feminist? If I commit myself to Buddhism will I have to give up sex?

This book is dedicated to all those women, and to all women who seek answers to such questions. Of course, they are not easy to answer, and the answers sometimes give rise to further questions. Buddhism is not dogmatic; it is very much about the intelligent and sensitive application of principles to the many and varied situations we find ourselves in. This means that there is no one right answer: much depends on the experience of the woman replying, and the situation of the woman asking the question.

It also means that the ways these questions are tackled in this book, while founded on basic principles, are unique to the women writing. The contributors to this book are as diverse as those who I hope will read it. Some live in Europe, some in America, some in India, some in New Zealand. Some teach meditation and Buddhism full-time; some work with other women in team-based Right Livelihood businesses; some are following careers, or are at present occupied with bringing up their children. Some lead a relatively monastic life, living and working at retreat centres; some live with their families; some live alone; and others live in communities with other Buddhists. But they all have one thing in common: their full-time commitment to the Buddhist path, expressed through their membership of the Western Buddhist Order.

The Friends of the Western Buddhist Order (FWBO) is a movement which aims to establish Buddhism in the West in a form which takes into account the conditions of modern life. The Western Buddhist Order (Trailokya Bauddha Mahasangha in India) which is at the heart of the FWBO was founded in 1968 by Sangharakshita, an Englishman who spent some twenty years as a Buddhist monk in the East, studying with many teachers from different Buddhist traditions.

The Western Buddhist Order is made up of men and women who are wholeheartedly committed to the Three Jewels of Buddhism: the Buddha (who represents the possibility of Enlightenment for all human beings); the Dharma (the teachings of the Buddha); and the Sangha (all those who have followed the Buddha's teachings and gained their own spiritual insight). Ordination is the same for both women and men, and all Order members take the same set of ten ethical precepts when they are ordained. This ordination is neither monastic nor lay, in the sense that these words are usually applied to the Buddhist community. The important thing is Order members' commitment to Buddhist practice, not their lifestyle.

I hope this book goes some way towards dispelling the idea that to be a real Buddhist you have to be male and live in a monastery. Women have practised Buddhism since the time of the Buddha. It is no surprise, therefore, that many are still turning to this path of wisdom and compassion, which is as relevant today as ever, and very much needed in the modern world.

Vidyavati

Vidyavati is a New Zealander who was ordained as a member of the Western Buddhist Order in 1984. Her interest in meditation led her to live at Taraloka Retreat Centre in England for three years before moving to America. She now lives in a residential women's community near Aryaloka Retreat Center in New Hampshire. She teaches classes and leads retreats at Aryaloka (where she has recently become chairwoman) and the four main FWBO centres in the US.

Vidyavati

Introduction

Contemporary Buddhism for Western Women

As WINDOWS EXPLODED under the pressure of intense heat, and flames devoured a short lifetime of possessions, I sat in full lotus on the grass verge watching my house burn. On my face was a calm smile of inexplicable relief. I knew what it meant. I was now free to disentangle myself from the seductive tentacles of an escalating career and materialistic lifestyle, the dubious delights of four boyfriends, and the façade of being a successful, upwardly-mobile professional woman with almost all one could wish for. My outward achievements barely concealed an inner emptiness.

Ever since I had read that little book on reincarnation a few months earlier, I had been disturbed. Nowhere in my Western college-level education had I encountered such a concept, nor as a result felt such an imperative to act on a new understanding. My friends regarded me with bemused incomprehension as, with a newly fervent tone, I expressed a strong desire to give away my beautiful possessions, leave my stimulating university work, and perhaps even extricate myself from my complex romantic involvements, in search of something more meaningful and satisfying. There seemed to be no honourable solution to my existential dilemma – until the flames licked away the material manifestations of my acquisitive mind-set and gave me an opening to a path of freedom.

It was barely a week after the fire that I encountered Buddhism for the first time and experienced a resonance that felt in the same moment like a coming home and a terrible responsibility. The external implications were less challenging than the internal ones. It was easy enough to offer my resignation at the university. I did not mourn my lost possessions. I found an unfashionable integrity in ending the romantic relationships.

But to understand the true nature of existence and develop boundless love for all life was much more daunting.

However, the resounding note had been struck and I couldn't close my ears to it. A gnawing unfulfilment lay in stasis. The Buddha's teaching and example, challenging though it was to my views of myself and society's expectations of a life well-lived, was my only choice.

Western women are living through a revolution that is at once liberating and destabilizing. Education, training, and increased confidence make us free to move into different fields of employment and positions of greater social and economic influence. My own career rode this wave in the seventies and I found a world open to me that my mother could never have imagined for herself. As the first woman employed as a lecturer in marketing management at my local university I was at times overwhelmed by the encouragement and opportunities available to me.

These were exciting times for an ambitious educated woman in her twenties. Traditional expectations and values were disintegrating around me. There were new choices for our generation: whether or not to have children, how many children to have, whether or not to marry, live with a sexual partner, or remain 'single' but sexually active, choose higher education, a vocation, combine motherhood and a career – the possibilities were many. Even if we chose to remain in a traditional role, this was being transformed by technology and social pressures. For me, involvement in a stimulating career took precedence over marriage or motherhood, and while I rarely gave serious consideration to the latter, when I did so I saw it happening in harmonious conjunction with my career.

These rapid and wide-ranging changes were requiring everyone in society, men and women alike, to redefine themselves. Younger women now had broader horizons, and older women's roles had changed in their lifetimes. Rapid change can be destabilizing, but it can also give rise to more metaphysical questions: what is the meaning of my life? How should I live it? What is true fulfilment? On what basis do I make choices? It is not surprising that a religion like Buddhism, which has a goal of limitless self-transformation, a clear ethical basis, and an emphasis on thinking for oneself, is attracting Western women today. It attracted me when I encountered it in a seminar at the university where I worked, not least because my career successes had not brought me the happiness I assumed they would. Why, with my stimulating work, interesting colleagues, and numerous accolades, did a deep, unavoidable feeling of emptiness gnaw at my heart? Even more significantly, what could I do about it? Nothing and no one around me seemed able to provide a solution. The expectations and values I had imbibed from my culture had not led me to a greater sense of happiness and fulfilment, but I knew of no alternative.

Western Buddhism

I was twenty-nine when I first heard the word 'Buddhism'. In New Zealand in the seventies Buddhism was not an integral part of daily life or values, nor even taught in schools; it had to be pursued through 'Eastern' and 'alternative' circles. Attending a day course at Auckland University, I was intrigued rather than burningly interested, but quickly came alive to what I was hearing in lectures and experiencing on my meditation cushion. Despite my restless mind, I had a small glimpse of a different way of experiencing myself and my world.

Meditation as a method of concentrating and calming the mind was gaining credence with professionals, and attracting the interest of those seeking something different. But the means by which I reached the point of disillusionment with what society offered was untypical of my generation. I did not come to Buddhism through drug-induced visions of a different way of seeing, or because I wanted to drop out of conventional society. I had thrown myself into pursuing a career path and worldly gains only to find them empty of any real sense of achievement, let alone freedom. Buddhism was a mystery and a risk. My dilute Protestant upbringing had given me a taste of the positive effects of worship, but belief in God was not for me. Knowing no other belief and lacking any existential angst to drive me in pursuit of the meaning of life, I could see no philosophical or practical use for religion. In this, and the experience of the 'death of God', I was not alone – many people of my generation in the West felt the same. However, I did want to grow in some way, and I was intrigued by the human potential movement of the seventies with its grab-bag of diverse therapies, although not always impressed by its proponents. Meditation, and learning about an exotic Eastern religion, seemed interesting to me. Fortunately it came to my doorstep.

The Buddhism I stumbled upon was in the throes of its own revolution – a revolution of a geographical and transcultural nature. For almost the first time in history, it had moved west rather than east from its birthplace in India. A handful of Asian Buddhist teachers and Western scholars first brought Buddhism to the West in the late nineteenth century, but accessibility to Buddhist teachings and the range of schools has widened dramatically in the last couple of decades, partly due to the Chinese invasion of Tibet and the Vietnam war, which brought many teachers and teachings to Western audiences, including the Dalai Lama, Tarthang Tulku, Chogyam Trungpa, Lama Yeshe, and Thich Nhat Hanh. At the same time some Westerners were exploring Buddhism in the East. Lama Anagarika Govinda, a German writer and artist, travelled and lived in Tibet and northern India for several years before returning to the West. And an English monk, Sangharakshita, returned to his homeland after twenty years of practice and teaching in India. It was the movement he founded in London in 1967 that I encountered in Auckland, New Zealand, in 1982.

This movement, the Friends of the Western Buddhist Order, was his answer to the question of how Buddhism could work in the West. For in coming to the West, Buddhism has encountered a psyche different from those it encountered as it moved East. In the West it has to take root in cultures created by the Western rationalist, materialist mind, affected by two centuries of technological revolution and conditioned by two millennia of God-based values and fear-based beliefs. We are an individualized, atomized society which has lost the belief in a wider cosmology that used to provide the individual with a place and meaning in the universe. The profound truths of the Buddha's teaching (the Dharma) need to be communicated to Westerners in a way that appeals to the psychological complexity of the Western rational mind, yet takes us beyond the psychological. Spiritual receptivity and devotion must be cultivated in a climate of scepticism; and the truth must be communicated through Western cultural media, without concessions to non-Buddhist ideologies, however fashionable.

In the West we are very fortunate. Our standard of living is high. Our lives may be busy, but most of us still have time to meditate, study, and meet together, unlike many people in the world who struggle simply to survive. We have access to education, and now we have access to Buddhist literature and teachers. At the same time, our culture throws up views and values that are inimical to the Dharma: the seeking of power, power-based competition, cynicism and the denigration of idealism, the cultivation of emotional dependence on sexual partners, self-absorption, democratic values which deny spiritual hierarchy, consumerism, an emphasis on rights rather than on duties, and a prevailing sense of anxiety and insecurity. As Westerners begin to practise Buddhism, we need to develop new standards. Spiritual values and progress cannot be measured by worldly terms or goals. Physical appearance, wealth, even intellectual sophistication, are not the measure of a spiritually mature person. Indeed, these things, which are valued so highly in Western society, may be hindrances if we are too attached to them.

Initially, Eastern teachers offered Buddhism to Westerners in the form they had inherited. In most of the major cities in the West there is now a range of Buddhist groups offering evening and weekend classes: Zen, Theravada, Tibetan Vajrayana, South-east Asian Mahayana, Chinese Pure Land, and Western Buddhism, to name a few of the main traditions. The United States perhaps offers the widest choice, owing in part to its immigrant populations of ethnic Buddhists, as well as the efforts of some determined Eastern teachers who migrated at the turn of the twentieth century. In Europe, Buddhism has had a more Theravadin emphasis, though this has changed in recent years with the arrival of Tibetan teachers and more recently the emergence of Western movements.

The task today for both Eastern and Western teachers and their Western disciples is to distinguish what is merely cultural in their traditions from what is effective spiritual practice, not diluting the latter in the search for cultural comfort and compatibility of values. For Western women, with our new-found freedoms, there is the challenge of valuing and distinguishing deep inner faith (*shraddha*) from worldly confidence; humility and spiritual receptivity from passivity and compliance; and conviction based in direct experience from power-based assertion or emotional manipulation. Buddhism also brings the challenge to act ethically (skilfully). In lieu of an external authority or literal code, acting skilfully requires us to develop intelligent, aware consideration of our motivation and the consequences of our actions. When I encountered Buddhism I knew I had a lot to learn from the people I met. I also knew I had a great deal to unlearn. I had developed some very useful skills in the world, but they could not be employed with the same motivation in the spiritual life. To give just one example, in my marketing work, identifying, cultivating, and appealing to human desires brought profit. As a Buddhist I needed to recognize such states of craving, but only in order to let them go, cultivating instead a sense of contentment without grasping.

Choosing a Teacher

The variety and accessibility of Buddhist teachings, combined with Western standards of living and mobility, make it possible for a Western woman today not only to practise Buddhism but also to find a school or teacher that particularly appeals to her. Some practitioners choose not to be involved with a specific Buddhist community (*sangha*) but instead prefer to float between one group and another. Sooner or later, however, this tends to prove unsatisfactory. A broad range of experience does not conduce to depth. Depth is cultivated through commitment to a particular form of Buddhist practice, a specific teacher and spiritual community.

In the early eighties, especially in the United States, instances of male teachers (both Eastern and Western) not acting in accordance with the ethical precepts of Buddhism began to be made public: excessive consumption of alcohol, married teachers having affairs with female disciples, teachers carrying handguns, living luxurious lifestyles while their disciples lived simply and worked to finance their excesses, and in one instance knowingly spreading AIDS. Both men and women were shaken by these revelations of unskilful behaviour in the areas of sex, money, and power, and further confused by the secrecy and collusion that surrounded such behaviour in Buddhist sanghas. To have placed one's trust in such a teacher only to have it betrayed often had the effect of damaging their faith not just in the teacher but also in the spiritual community and sometimes in the efficacy of Buddhist practice.

There was a lot of soul-searching. Why had these behaviours been concealed, why had disciples not questioned them, how could a teacher act in such a way? Some gullibility and lack of discernment on the part of Western disciples had to be acknowledged. Idealizing the guru, entranced by the mystique of an Eastern master and a foreign religion with its cultural trappings, they had blindly accepted rationalizations for ethically aberrant behaviour. Despite feminism, women still looked to men as authority figures. Lack of open communication within sanghas perpetuated unskilful actions, and did disservice to the teachers themselves. Teachers from the East, unused to Western social codes, were not immune to the pull of sexual freedom, materialistic culture, and the perceived power of their position, and acted unwisely and unskilfully, as fallible human beings will. There were calls for public exposure, disciplinary measures, and even an intra-Buddhist ethics board. I think these demands were misplaced. The solution lay not with externally imposed morality, but within the Buddhist framework of ethics. Buddhists seek to transform their mental states through awareness. Within the context of spiritual friendship our blind spots are revealed to us, and once we have seen and acknowledged that it is harmful, we naturally confess unskilful behaviour to those who share our ideals, and resolve to cease such actions. Such moral transparency is cultivated within, not forced from outside.

Disciples have had to revise their perceptions of their teachers. Giving up one's personal authority and discernment to one's teacher is not the mark of a faithful disciple or transcendence of ego. Westerners are conditioned by a need for critical enquiry and informed argument. In order to build a foundation for insight into the true nature of Reality we need to cultivate what Buddhists would call Right View within the morass of wrong views, and this requires thought, questioning, and the pursuit of our views to their roots. We need to think more clearly and become less attached to our unhelpful desires. Personal integrity in thinking needs to be infused with receptivity to those more spiritually advanced than we are, from whom we can learn.

Rationalist scepticism is of course inherent in our culture, and recent events have made people understandably cautious about committing themselves to a particular teacher. Once we are reasonably convinced that a teacher's personal actions exemplify their teachings, however, we can benefit a great deal by being receptive to them. Perhaps the best thing is to think of the teacher as a spiritual friend who is further along the path than we are. If we are just setting out on the spiritual path, whether or not the teacher is Enlightened is not really relevant to us. Someone a little closer to us, with clearer vision but an understanding from their own experience of the kind of difficulties we encounter in practice, is likely to be able to help us more than anyone else.

Today there is a new generation of Western teachers who have taken over spiritual responsibilities from their Eastern mentors. Women are numbered amongst these, including Bobby Rhodes from Providence, Rhode Island, a Dharma Master in the Korean Zen Chogye lineage, and Ani Pema Chodron, who was born in New York City, and is now the spiritual director of the Dharmadhatu Retreat Center in Nova Scotia. Western women teachers like Thubten Chodron (Tibetan), Yvonne Rand (Zen), and Sharon Salzberg (Vipassana) have attracted a following. Some, like Ruth Denison who was born in East Prussia, Ayya Khema from

Berlin, and Tsultrim Allione, have established their own retreat centres. Many teachers, men and women, travel the world teaching groups rather than staying in one place and having disciples come to them. A Western woman can now choose not just the cultural origin but also the sex of her teacher.

Choosing a teacher by gender may feel safe, but a better criterion is the spiritual depth of the teacher – not, of course, that it is at all a simple matter to judge 'depth'. I was so concerned to make my own assessment that I travelled from New Zealand to the UK in order to meet Sangharakshita and find out for myself whether he was genuine. Did he exemplify his teachings? Was he to be trusted as a teacher who would encourage anyone, man or woman, who expressed an interest in practising the Buddhist path? After a particularly satisfying meeting with him, I was convinced that he was genuinely practising what he taught, and that his understanding came from direct experience of the Buddha's teachings.

Just as important as the teacher is the nature of the spiritual community around them. Although I didn't visit other Buddhist groups when I first encountered the FWBO, I was not unsceptical as I became more deeply involved with this movement. I wanted to be sure that the actions of the Buddhists I met were in accordance with their teachings. They said that women had the same potential for Enlightenment as men, but were their attitudes consistent with this? While they were far from perfect, I could see that people in the FWBO were sincere in their attempts to go for Refuge, practise the precepts, meditate, study the Dharma and apply it in their everyday lives, and develop spiritual friendships. Their teachings rested on basic Buddhist principles. I did not find any institutional discrimination against women; respect was accorded by merit, by personal qualities, rather than gender. I was also relieved to find much less positive discrimination towards women than I had encountered in the outside world. In my career as a research consultant and university lecturer, I had occasionally experienced pressure to be more visible in my field than my abilities or experience warranted.

It was also refreshing, although to my worldly mind a little embarrassing, that faults and failures were not concealed. In the early days of the movement, the team-based Right Livelihood businesses which were hailed as one of the foundations of the 'new society' were struggling, and sometimes the people working in them felt discouraged. But they aired their difficulties, and although sometimes there was no easy solution, people were ready to discuss their situation, and aware of what they were working towards.

Sangharakshita is the founder and main teacher of the FWBO, but any Order member may teach, and so clarification and inspiration can be gained from many sources. I have grown a great deal through my friendships particularly with women in our order. Through these friendships I have become more open and appreciative of others, as well as experiencing the delights of sharing myself with other people who understand what I am trying to do with my life. I feel immensely fortunate to have found such spiritual mentors.

Committing Ourselves

Related to finding a teacher and a spiritual community is another big question that faces Buddhist women today: what does it mean to be ordained? Women's expectations about what is now possible for them in society are encountering both perceived and real limits in some schools imported from the East. In the Theravadin and Tibetan traditions, for instance, it is not technically possible for a woman to be ordained as a *bhikkhuni* (nun), because the prescribed conditions required for women to be ordained (for example, having fifteen bhikkhunis present at the ordination, and the *vinaya* or monastic precepts of that school having been practised in an unbroken lineage) are now impossible to fulfil. In an attempt to revive the Theravadin bhikkhuni ordination, continuation of the lineage has been traced through the Chinese Mahayana, and several Eastern and some Western women have taken full bhikkhuni ordination. Controversy remains over whether these ordinations are orthodox, particularly as the vinaya practised in Mahayana schools is different from that of the Theravada.

Many Western women are pioneering a different path. For them, taking up Buddhist practice in a society that does not support full-time religious practitioners, the challenge is to find a way to deepen experience and understanding while remaining 'in the world'. Maintaining a daily meditation practice, attending a weekly Dharma class, and going on a week-long retreat once a year, are integrated into a lifestyle that requires working a forty-hour week and caring for children. In the Eastern model, this is seen as 'lay practice'. Many Westerners encountering Buddhism will not find it playing a very central role in their lives, but others, like myself, may experience a level of commitment more akin to that of men and women in the East who take the step of ordination. Our goal is Enlightenment, or at least Stream Entry (irreversible momentum on the path), not simply a better rebirth (a typically Eastern way of seeing things) or greater calm and contentment (which is what Westerners commonly seek). Our ethical practice may be equivalent to that of the ordained community. While supporting our local Buddhist centre, we may also try to create conditions conducive to spiritual practice – whether it be choosing to have a separate room for meditation in our homes, living with others who practise Buddhism, attending retreats, or taking time off work for extended retreat periods.

Serious Western practitioners are redefining what it means to be a lay disciple. They are people who want to find the truth, who have a radical concept of what they are doing with their lives, but who continue to follow their careers and live with their families. In this lifestyle the challenge is to cultivate activities that conduce to spiritual growth while fulfilling one's responsibilities in activities that are seemingly unrelated or even inimical to it. One attempts to act in a way that at least doesn't obstruct one's commitment to Buddhism and at best is a medium for it – that is, one attempts to turn all aspects of one's life into spiritual practice, not just the gaps between 'ordinary' activities. For example, one would use the precepts to provide an ethical environment in which to raise one's children. If one's occupation caused harm, one would seek work elsewhere. Within a neutral or ethically positive field of work, one could cultivate better communication and attempt to reduce stress.

Some Western women see traditional ordination, despite its difficulty of attainment, as signifying greater commitment, as providing more conducive conditions for practice, and perhaps even higher status. In some Buddhist schools, one does not have access to certain teachings or practices if one is not ordained. But in my view it would be more useful for women in both East and West to take up the debate starting from different premises. Just as the meaning of lay practice is being revised in the West, what it means to be ordained needs to be reviewed. Ordination in the East has come to represent a settled monastic lifestyle, supported by the laity. While this lifestyle can provide a strong context for ethical practice, study, and meditation, those ordained can also fall prey to lassitude, settling for spiritual life as a comfortable career. In the West support for full-time practitioners is not freely forthcoming, and full-timers have needed to rely increasingly on business income to supplement donations. But what does ordination really mean? How can it effectively support our practice as Westerners? What are the conditions that surround it, and do they support a woman wishing to take her practice deeper in our Western culture and society? Is the motivation of those seeking ordination to engage more deeply in their practice of Buddhism, to have access to teachings, or to achieve greater institutional status?

A key question to be considered is the taking of ethical precepts. With ordination one takes precepts that guide one's actions towards a more skilful, non-harmful way of being. While general principles of non-violence, compassion, mindfulness, and wisdom underlie these precepts, in some schools the list of prescribed ways of behaving is extensive, detailed, and literalistic. Even where a principle is intended, it is too often interpreted as an absolute way of behaving. If one is ordained within such schools one is expected to maintain precepts such as not handling money, not sleeping on high beds, not travelling in vehicles, not eating after midday, and keeping one's right shoulder uncovered. In cooler climates, in a society where one pays for services and where to communicate the Dharma one must travel, these precepts have proved limiting if not impossible to maintain. Frustration ensues, and the price to be paid is that of living with numerous unavoidable daily transgressions of the vinaya. One can adopt the spirit rather than the letter, but the letter is not wisely dismissed in some cases. How is one to choose? The very validity of these requirements needs to be questioned.

The choice I have made is to join an order which is neither monastic nor lay. As a Dharmacharini ('farer in the Truth') of the Western Buddhist Order, my commitment is essentially to place Going for Refuge to the Three Jewels – to use the traditional language – at the centre of my life. (The Three Jewels are: the Buddha, representing the ideal of Enlightenment, to which all men and women can aspire; the Dharma, the Buddha's teaching; and the Sangha, those men and women who have gained Enlightenment through following the Buddha's teaching.) My commitment to the Three Jewels is supported by the taking of ten ethical precepts or training principles taken from the earliest Theravada and Mahayana sources. All Order members, whatever their lifestyle, and whether they are men or women, take the same ordination and the same precepts (those who choose to be celibate simply observing a modified form of the precept relating to sexual conduct). When one has effectively oriented one's life in this way, one can be ordained. This commitment is then expressed through one's lifestyle, whether it be fulfilling family responsibilities, working in a vocation – as a doctor, for instance – teaching public classes, or maintaining retreat centre facilities. There is no wearing of robes or shaving of the head. One's inner commitment manifests in the world through one's actions of body, speech, and mind.

My own commitment has led me to leave my native country and come to live and work in the United States. I reached this decision through discussion with my spiritual friends and my teacher. When I first arrived at Aryaloka Retreat Center in New Hampshire in 1990, there were several male Order members, but no women teaching there. Having seen the potential for commitment to this path of radical transformation among the American women I met on a brief visit, I chose to return and play a part in helping them go for Refuge into our order. In 1993 the first of them was ordained, and in 1995 three more took that step.

To support myself I work part-time as a muralist and sign-writer. At weekends, and occasionally for a week, I lead retreats, mostly for women, but occasionally for both men and women. Two evenings a week I teach a Dharma class. My personal practice is stimulated by meditation and study and reflection on the Dharma. I very much value spiritual friendship as a means of sharing my spiritual life with others, in all its ups and downs. I have chosen to live with four other Buddhist women, creating a living environment that supports our practice. We meditate together in the mornings before work and spend our evenings either at classes at our local Buddhist centre, or deepening our friendships with one another or others in the nearby community.

A Greater Freedom

For Western women who choose a path such as Buddhism, recent changes in society can both facilitate and hinder spiritual growth. Greater social confidence, education, and higher expectations will benefit us, but we still need to cultivate greater confidence, a larger vision of our potential, the ability to speak out, and more emotional independence from men. In Buddhism we encounter an ideal more far-reaching and sublime than social, legal, and economic freedoms, valuable though these are. Buddhism offers a greater freedom within which these lesser –

though hard-won – freedoms find a new perspective. Social freedoms provide some of the fabric of the raft which will take us to the further shore of Enlightenment, but they need to be augmented by other kinds of freedom. Some of our social fabric may also need to be reviewed in the light of spiritual rather than mundane goals. Does our confidence survive drastic changes in our material, social, and personal circumstances? Can we stand our ground, confident in our own experience? What is true knowledge rather than mere learning or education? Do our expectations have an altruistic dimension?

Not since the first few hundred years after the life of the Buddha have women sought to commit themselves to this path in similar numbers to men. Never before has Buddhism encountered a society where women play such a public role outside the home. In Buddhism, attainment to the truth is indiscriminate of gender. Indeed, ultimately it transcends gender identification. While our roles have conditioned us, in Buddhism they need not define us. Nevertheless we are conditioned beings: our views, speech, and bodily actions are affected by many factors such as culture, class, upbringing, education, and biology. It is a challenging time for all Western women to find our way amid often conflicting options; but for those of us who take up Buddhist practice there is the additional challenge of recognizing our conditionings, transforming those that hinder us in the spiritual life, and reviewing those that have served us well until now but are only foundations, not ultimate ends, or will not translate to spiritual growth. I gained a lot from my experiences in my twenties. My achievements at work gave me confidence in my ability to present ideas, speak publicly, and tackle challenging projects. But these were external qualities. I had assimilated a Protestant work ethic from my upbringing which served me well in my career. But in trying to establish a daily meditation practice I found my restless mind a hindrance. For all my worldly achievements I had barely touched my inner being, where anxiety, uncontrolled mental activity, and an aching discontent reigned. I have needed to continue to work on cultivating and maintaining calm, centred states of mind.

All women experience biological conditioning – monthly cycles, hormonal changes, child-bearing, or menopause – and we are challenged to respond creatively to the physical discomfort and mood swings that these may cause. Associated with our ability to give birth comes a facility for nurture and harmonizing, but the need to establish a nest often narrows our concerns to a small sphere and the minutiae of life. For Buddhist women, the challenge is to cultivate the vastness of the Buddhist vision, and develop the clarity of thought and initiative required to break through such conditioning. As Western women choose either not to have children or, more commonly, to limit their family size, the direct effects on our lives of child-bearing and rearing will lessen – although the biological drive to have children will still of course affect us. Our atomized society and fractured nuclear family mean that many women find themselves isolated with overwhelming child-care responsibilities and economic concerns. Finding time to meditate may then seem an impossibility. It remains a demanding task for Buddhist communities in the West to find a satisfactory solution to the issue of child rearing.

Some Western women may wonder if their practice of Buddhism will look different from that of men. In my experience, the conditioning we have to work with as women is different, and therefore it is useful to experience ourselves in a women-only context, with women teachers who have worked successfully with their conditioning. These teachers will have greater understanding of issues like lack of confidence, conflicts in decisions about motherhood, and emotional over-investment, because of their own struggles. However, spiritual progress can be measured by the same criteria for both men and women: overcoming one's fixed view of oneself; practising the spiritual life in a creative rather than an automatic or reactive way; and doing what we know we need to do to grow spiritually, rather than wilfully ignoring it. And the taste of freedom we attain as we liberate ourselves from our wrong views and unskilful behaviour will have the same flavour as it has for men.

Personally, I have come very much to appreciate being part of a Buddhist movement in which women are fully involved with each other's spiritual lives. Women can be spiritual mentors to other women. Women are able to practise and develop spiritually in a women-only context, developing not only friendships but also those qualities we may ordinarily think of as being 'male' or 'masculine'. Women Order members teach at our city Buddhist centres and rural retreat centres, as well as at two retreat centres for women only. The ordinations of women are conferred by women. In this our order is revolutionary.

So far there are still considerably more men than women in the Western Buddhist Order. Why the imbalance? In my view, some factors relate to historical circumstances, some to biological and social conditionings, and others to the need for close spiritual friendship with Order members who can guide you. When, a few years after its inception, the movement began to experiment with single-sex activities, men adapted quickly to the new situation, while women took longer to find their direction and establish resources for themselves. The numbers of men joining the Order expanded faster, which of itself perpetuated faster growth – particularly owing to the significance placed on spiritual friendships as a means of growth, since there were more men to offer friendship to newcomers.

On average, women also seem to take longer to reach the point at which they are able effectively to place the Three Jewels at the centre of their lives and let that commitment guide their actions. This may be due to a combination of social, cultural, and biological conditionings. If increasing social and cultural freedoms for women in the West do not result in more women being able to reach a level of spiritual development where they can commit themselves wholeheartedly to the spiritual path, then our biological conditioning will need deeper exploration. Conditioning is complex and multidimensional, and it is useful to be open to change in all areas.

I was ordained only six weeks after I asked, and two years after I first came across Buddhism. My glimpse of the vision for growth that Buddhism offered had been significantly strengthened by a pilgrimage to the holy places of the Buddha's life in India which confirmed my conviction that this was the path to freedom. My meeting with Sangharakshita, and visits to FWBO centres, brought alive his vision of a community of men and women connected by their common commitment to the Three Jewels. I saw Western women responding to the radical nature of the Dharma, struggling to change themselves and their lives. Buddhism had come to the West, and I had come to Buddhism.

I Basic Buddhism

Kalyanavaca

Kalyanavaca was born in Scotland. After taking a degree in French, she worked in a press library in London for a few years. In 1974 she came across the FWBO, and in 1978 she travelled overland to Nepal and lived in India for fifteen months. On her return she joined the first Buddhist women's residential community in west London, and worked for over seven years in a wholefood business associated with the West London Buddhist Centre, before becoming secretary and press officer at Taraloka Retreat Centre for six years. Recently she moved back to Scotland to concentrate on writing, and now lives in a women's community in Glasgow. She also leads and supports retreats, particularly for women new to Buddhism. Kalyanavaca was ordained in 1992. Her name means 'Beautiful Speech'.

Kalyanavaca

Crossing the Rainbow Bridge

A Brief Look at Buddhist Ethics

PICTURE A WIDE, turbulent river, rushing along, crashing against rocks, whirling and eddying, making a tremendous noise. Now imagine yourself standing on the bank of this river. You know you have to cross it somehow. But how? It's too deep and turbulent to wade across – you might be swept away by the fast current. The rocks are too sharp and slippery to use as stepping-stones – you might slip and hurt yourself on their unyielding edges. What to do?

Then, over to your right, you see a bridge spanning the river: no ordinary bridge, but a bridge made of light. Looking a little more carefully, you see that the light is composed of several colours: a deep, rich red; a warm gold; a peaceful green; bright silver; and thousands of rainbows, dazzling the eye. Joyfully you step on to the bridge and cross over.

A few years ago I wrote a poem about ethics, and those were the images that came to me when writing it. Before I go into what the image of the bridge meant to me, perhaps the first thing to say is that it might seem odd for anyone to want to write a poem about ethics (although, of course, Wordsworth wrote his 'Ode to Duty', which begins 'Stern daughter of the voice of God!'). To many of us, the traditional morality of our culture can only seem dull and restrictive, a question of doing what we're told for reasons we don't understand by someone we don't believe in.[1] Over the last few decades the collision of the permissive society and political correctness with the Ten Commandments has produced an uneasy mixture of moral messages. In contrast to this muddle of moral values, Buddhist ethics provide clarity, vision, a breath of fresh air. In this short chapter I want to explore first what Buddhist ethics are not, and then what they are; then look at five ethical precepts fundamental to all Buddhist ethical traditions.

So, first, what ethics are not. Since Buddhists don't believe in a creator God who must be obeyed, Buddhist ethical precepts are not commandments laid down by an authority who must be placated by good behaviour. If our only reason for behaving ethically is to save ourselves from damnation, or indeed from being ostracized by the group to which we belong, our sense of morality is rooted in fear – no healthy basis upon which to build an ethical life.

But if our sense of morality is not based on fear, if there is no one to obey, we are still left with the question of what values should guide our behaviour. Although there is no God, we need not – perhaps cannot – live in a moral vacuum. The word ethics means 'rules of conduct, or moral principles', and 'moral' is derived from the Latin word for custom or behaviour. Ethics, then, are concerned with behaviour or action, and ethical principles are guidelines which help us to distinguish – not exactly between right and wrong, good and evil, but, to use more Buddhistic terminology, between skilful and unskilful. The words good and evil suggest absolutes judged by external criteria, and tend to reduce morality to the observance of rules. But morality is much more than this. It is about acting from what is best in us, from the depths of our understanding, from love and compassion. The use of the word 'skilful' in itself suggests that morality is very much a matter of intelligence, the intelligence needed to act skilfully, explore possibilities, and assess one's actions. This is true morality, natural morality, not to be confused with the conventional morality which is an aspect of cultural conditioning. Sometimes we may feel as though we have done something wrong simply because we are going against the expectations and norms of our cultural group. To avoid this kind of confusion, we need criteria to enable us to distinguish for ourselves what is truly ethical and what is not.

According to Buddhism, whether an action is skilful or unskilful depends on the state of mind with which it is performed. Any action arising from greed, hatred, or ignorance – the three poisonous roots – is unskilful. Any action arising from the opposite states of mind – generosity, love, and awareness – is skilful. This emphasis on motivation means that it may not be possible for an observer to determine whether or not someone's action is ethical, because their motivation is not always obvious.

Before we go any further, we need to look a little more closely at the definition of 'skilful' and 'unskilful'. An unskilful action is defined as an action arising from greed, hatred, and/or ignorance, while a skilful action is based on generosity, love, and/or wisdom. But from a Buddhist point of view, as we have seen, motivation is all-important. This means that one behaves in a skilful way not simply to be 'good', to secure one's place in heaven, so to speak – although to have that as a motivation is certainly a start. But the aim of the Buddhist life goes beyond this. This is the fundamental difference between Buddhist ethics and other systems of morality, and unless we take it into account, our practice of ethics will be limited. We may use different terms – skilful and unskilful instead of good and evil – but the change may be a superficial one rather than the deep and radical transformation of one's world view that Buddhist ethics make possible.

Let me say a bit more by way of explanation of this point. When the Buddha became Enlightened, he saw clearly that everything – and every-one – arises in dependence on conditions, and ceases when those conditions cease. From this fundamental insight, later Buddhist tradition developed the doctrine of *shunyata*, emptiness. This does not mean that the world does not exist, or that 'everything is void', although this has been a common misunderstanding. What it means is that everything – and everybody – is empty of 'own-being'. Each of us is a complex coming together of many conditions, an ever-changing flux of physical and mental characteristics. There is no 'I' that has these attributes; there is no fixed, unchanging 'me' – no soul or self – apart from my physical and mental states, which change all the time.

But, of course, we would not have it so. We are ruled by a stubborn clinging to a fixed sense of 'I'. This is basically what ignorance is: a refusal to recognize the true nature of how things really are. From this ignorance, from our clinging to a sense of 'me', come the other root poisons: craving, which grasps whatever will support a sense of 'me'; and hatred or aversion, which thrusts away whatever threatens 'me'. We can see this played out in every area of human life.

The point of Buddhist life and practice is to move towards an appre-ciation of the way things really are, a sense of egolessness. This is really the basis of Buddhist ethics. Anything that strengthens our sense of 'I' strengthens our ignorance; whatever attenuates it leads us closer to an awareness of reality. So morality is not just about being 'good' – or even 'skilful' – for its own sake, or even in the hope of getting to heaven. It can take us further than that. According to a traditional formulation, the practice of ethics is the first stage of a Threefold Path to Enlightenment: ethics, meditation, wisdom.

A 'Bodhisattva' – the word means 'Enlightenment-being' – is one who is determined to gain Enlightenment not just for their own sake, but for the benefit of all beings. They are motivated by an awareness that in reality there is no distinction between 'me' and 'the rest of the world'. Another aspect of the Buddha's insight was the perception that all things are interconnected. Everything in conditioned existence is intrinsically involved with everything else. John Donne glimpsed the truth of this when he wrote 'No man is an Island entire of itself'; the discoveries of today's scientists echo the same reality – 'when a butterfly flaps its wings, a breeze blows on the other side of the world'. Buddhist ethics and meditation both lead to the experience of this truth which is true wisdom. We are not separate, fixed individuals; we all affect one another all the time, and the effect we have can be either positive or negative. This is the heart of the matter.

Another way of putting this is that all actions have consequences. Any action which comes from a positive state of mind results, sooner or later, in an experience of happiness for the person acting in such a way. The opposite is also true: any action which comes from a negative state of mind will sooner or later result in pain for the person who has committed the action. This is the briefest possible expression of what is known as the law of karma.

Karma, in the Buddhist interpretation, simply means action – not just any old action, but action which is willed, intentional, an act of volition. The law of karma is not the Buddhist equivalent of divine retribution. It simply states that actions have consequences, that states of mind and actions are linked. In the opening verses of the *Dhammapada*, the Buddha says:

> *Unskilful mental states are preceded by mind, led by mind, and made up of mind. If one speaks or acts with an impure mind, suffering follows him even as the cart wheel follows the hoof of the ox.*
> *Skilful mental states are preceded by mind, led by mind, and made up of mind. If one speaks or acts with a pure mind, happiness follows him like his shadow.*[2]

The law of karma is frequently misunderstood. The fact that every willed action which springs from a negative mental state will bring you pain does not mean that everything painful that happens to you is a result of your unskilful behaviour. According to Buddhism karma is just one of five different levels of conditionality: physical inorganic; physical organic or biological; (non-volitional) mental or psychological; volitional (karmic); and transcendental. Any of these five orders of conditionality can 'cause' things to happen. To give a traditional illustration: suppose you are suffering from a fever. This could be due to a sudden chill (the physical inorganic level), to a germ (biological level), to mental strain or worry (psychological level), to the fact that you have caused harm to someone previously (volitional level), or to changes taking place in your body as a result of transcendental realization (transcendental level).

The word karma has become current in the English language, its usage tending to correspond roughly to the Hindu understanding of the term, which views karma as unalterable fate. But for the Buddhist karma is not some kind of predetermined destiny.[3] The Buddhist view is that we create our own karma – which means, in effect, that we have the power to make our lives happy, at least on the karmic level of conditionality. There is not much we can do about the other levels, but we can reduce our suffering considerably through choosing to act skilfully.

Buddhist ethics lead us to take responsibility for ourselves. We alone are responsible for our own actions, and there is nobody who can save us from their consequences. We cannot 'be washed in the blood of the lamb'; no one can take upon themselves the consequences of our unethical behaviour. So in a sense Buddhist ethics can be seen as a path of positive self-interest. Furthermore, a person acting skilfully has a very positive effect on their surroundings. This is reflected in the five basic ethical precepts common to all Buddhist traditions.

The Five Precepts
Precepts are not rules or commandments, but guidelines or training principles. They are said to reflect the natural behaviour of a fully Enlightened person – always skilful, always positive in its effect. However, we do not have to put off efforts to behave skilfully until a future time when it 'comes naturally'. Indeed, the point of skilful behaviour, as we have seen, is to help us to move towards Enlightenment. Through

following the guidelines of the precepts, we can gradually transform every aspect of ourselves: body, speech, and mind. (The first three precepts relate to acts of body, the fourth to speech, and the fifth to the mind.)

A traditional image of spiritual life depicts someone crossing a river by means of a raft, to reach the further shore of Enlightenment. But when I was writing my poem, I saw not a raft, but a bridge. The bridge, made up of different-coloured light, represents the five precepts: each precept is a different colour.

The first colour, representing the First Precept, is a deep rich red. Red is the colour of love – and love, of course, is a word with many meanings. Here I am using it in the sense of *metta*, a word from the ancient Indian language Pali which means something like 'loving-kindness' or 'universal friendliness'. Metta is not tepid, but, like the colour red, warm, fiery, and passionate – friendliness taken to its highest possible degree, friendliness towards all forms of life. Love, or metta, is the positive principle underpinning the First Precept, which is:

> *I undertake the training principle of abstention from killing living beings.*

The scope of this precept goes beyond simply refraining from killing people or animals. It means that wherever possible we refrain from using violence in any form, and from harming any living being – including ourselves – in any way. Putting this precept into practice has broad implications for our everyday lives. It means developing a passionate feeling of solidarity with all life, so that to harm another being becomes unthinkable. For most Buddhists it means becoming vegetarian, and for some, vegan.

The question of abortion arises in connection with this precept. There is a chapter on abortion in this book, so here I will simply say that in terms of this precept, abortion is a form of killing. According to Buddhist tradition, human life begins at conception; this needs to be taken into account when considering methods of contraception. The contraceptive coil, which does not prevent conception but prevents the implantation of the fertilized ovum in the uterine wall, is in effect an abortifacient. But the contraceptive pill can have harmful side-effects, and barrier methods such as the diaphragm or condom are unreliable. Perhaps the best we can do is to choose the method we think will cause the least harm.

It comes as a shock to many newcomers to Buddhism that the First Precept includes themselves. Women, especially, are taught from a very early age that we should put others first. We may even have the idea that it is somehow wrong to love ourselves. But we cannot love others if we do not also love ourselves. It is a common experience that while at least the grosser forms of harming others are relatively easy to avoid, not harming oneself is more difficult. Such habits as smoking and drinking, for example, are hard to change, however harmful to oneself one knows them to be.

We can also apply this precept of non-harming to the question of how we earn our living. Obvious forms of wrong livelihood are the making or selling of weapons, and butchery. Less obvious, perhaps, is involvement in the advertising industry, which makes its money by promoting craving. But for most of us the questions are going to be more subtle. What, for example, do we do when the company we work for is taken over by another company whose ethics we find questionable? Could we feel at ease working for a company manufacturing luxury items that waste the earth's resources? There are no easy answers.

If we have any money to invest, practising non-violence will mean investing in businesses that do not exploit others. This is easier than it used to be now that there is a range of ethical investment companies, although it's important to check out what they mean by 'ethical'. It is worth making the effort to avoid buying products that are made by companies that act unethically – although a company's ethical status is very difficult to ascertain. I used to work in a Buddhist wholefood business, and we found it very difficult indeed to apply this precept rigorously, although we did our best to promote vegetarian food supplements and cosmetics produced without cruelty to animals.

Yet another application of this precept is caring for our environment. One might, for example, consider joining campaigns to stop environmental depredations, and using a bicycle or walking rather than taking the car. Trying to live out this one precept can have very many effects on one's life; as with all ethical practice, there is much scope for imagination.

The next colour on the bridge is a beautiful, warm, glowing gold, the colour of ripe harvests and sunshine, the colour of abundance. This is the colour which represents the Second Precept:

I undertake the training principle of abstention from taking the
not-given.

The positive principle behind this precept is generosity, a generosity that
flows spontaneously from a feeling of inner abundance. Anything that
can be owned can be given. Giving need not be confined to material
things. We can give people our time, our energy, our understanding. We
can give them confidence, we can remind them of their positive qualities
when perhaps they have forgotten them. We can even give our lives, by
dedicating ourselves to helping others, giving them our talents, energy,
and enthusiasm. Giving helps us to go beyond our narrow boundaries,
to free ourselves from our petty wants and needs, our narrow self-
obsession.

Some instances of 'taking the not-given' include evading income tax;
taping or photocopying copyright material without asking; making un-
authorized copies of computer software; withholding payment when a
debt falls due; keeping things we borrow; not paying fares; stealing
envelopes from the office. It seems to be common for people to think that
because something is not owned by a particular person this gives them
the right to take it. People may even feel that they have a right to steal,
especially if they are poor and stealing from a body which they perceive
to be vastly wealthy. But such actions are still forms of taking the not-
given, even though there is no one person who suffers as a result.

But 'not taking the not-given' means more than just not stealing.
Anything we appropriate without the consent of another is the not-given.
Practising this precept means not draining people's energy by forcing our
company upon them; not taking someone's time unless it is freely given;
not trying to get what we want from others by subtly manipulating them.
Trying to get our own way by sulking, flirting, or using charm – all of
these are examples of manipulative behaviour, and as such, subtle forms
of taking the not-given.

The next colour making up the bridge is a soft, peaceful green, a
harmonious, healing, calming colour. This colour represents the Third
Precept:

I undertake the training principle of abstention from sexual misconduct.

The positive principle behind this precept is perhaps more subtle than
those underlying the first two. It is to cultivate a sense of stillness,

contentment, and simplicity. A healthy human being has sexual needs; traditional Buddhism makes no pronouncements about sexual orientation or particular forms of sexual activity. The principle to be borne in mind is that of not harming oneself or others through sexual activity. One needs to be very careful not to use deception in one's sexual relationships, even in small ways.

Many forms of sexual misconduct could be added to the three – rape, adultery, and abduction – explicitly mentioned by the Buddha. There is also sexual harassment; pornography; the sexual abuse of children; exploitation of sexuality, in particular that of women, to sell things, and so on.

Trying to get from sex something it can't give, trying to use it to satisfy neurotic craving, is harmful both to oneself and to the person, or persons, being used in this fashion. More broadly speaking, we need to aim to free ourselves from neurotic sexual attachments, to cultivate a sense of wholeness and contentment within ourselves which does not need to grasp at things outside for fulfilment. A lot is made of sex in our society, and very often our sexual relationships are the most important in our lives. Widening the sphere of our friendships can take the pressure off our sexual relationships.

To help to break any neurotic habits associated with sex, some Buddhists take the Third Precept in the following form, for short periods of time, or for life:

I undertake the training principle of abstention from non-chastity.

My own experience of experimenting with this precept has been a sense of feeling much more free to be myself in dealings with people who in other circumstances might have become sexual partners. It has given me peace of mind and contentment in this area of my life, which has in the past given me much suffering as well as, occasionally, joy.

The first three precepts are concerned with acts of body; with the fourth, we come to the realm of speech. Perhaps, when I was thinking of the colour to go with this precept, I was subtly influenced by the maxim 'speech is silver, silence is golden'. Silver seemed to me the appropriate colour for truthful speech, which is the positive principle underlying the Fourth Precept:

I undertake the training principle of abstention from false speech.

This doesn't just mean not telling lies, although at the very least we should try to be factually accurate in our speech. Examples of false speech include white lies, exaggeration, insincere compliments, saying no when we mean yes, or yes when we mean no. Even the most basic level of truthful speech is extremely difficult to practise. To speak the truth we have to know what it is: and how often can we claim to know the truth? Very often we don't really know what we're talking about; but rather than admit it, we carry on spinning a yarn to satisfy our own sense of self. Sometimes we end up believing our own tales. We need to get to know the truth about ourselves and then begin to communicate from this basis, being as open and honest as we can.

Sometimes, of course, we don't feel comfortable with the truth, especially the truth about how we really feel. Truthful speech can also be kindly; bearing the First Precept in mind, we need to learn to speak the truth without harming others. This can be difficult when we are feeling towards them an emotion we would rather not have, such as anger.

It is perhaps true to say that women are not generally encouraged to show anger. But repressing it can be destructive, leading to moodiness, depression, feelings of helplessness, or martyrdom. Clearly this is not very helpful. However, the emphasis in some psychotherapeutic circles on getting in touch with anger by letting it out needs to be approached with caution. Anger can so easily become hatred. It is worth considering whether one needs to express anger in order to become aware of it. Often anger covers hurt; once we know we feel hurt, we may be able to communicate this. Real communication is then more likely to happen, because we are expressing ourselves at a deeper level.

Anger is not the only mask for other emotions. When I began trying to practise truthful communication, one of the things I noticed was that I used to sigh a lot, although previously I had been unaware of it. I began to realize that sighing was for me an attempt to express my feelings without allowing myself to become fully aware of them. Usually they were feelings I did not want to acknowledge. Once I discovered this, whenever I heard myself sighing, I would stop what I was doing and try to get in touch with what I was feeling. This helped me to get to know myself a lot better quite quickly, and it was the first step towards transforming the feelings into more positive ones.

It is very important to believe someone when they are telling the truth.[4] If we do not, we are negating their very being, and committing an act of violence against them. This does not mean naïvely accepting what people say at face value; it means making an effort to develop discrimination and sensitivity, so that one can tell when people are really being truthful. At the very least one should be prepared to give others the benefit of the doubt.

All these precepts imply having a good deal of awareness, and it is this which is the concern of the final precept:

I undertake the training principle of abstention from intoxicants that cloud the mind.

The positive principle behind this precept is the development of mindfulness, or awareness. This is the final band of colour in the bridge, crystal light, from which blaze thousands of rainbows. Awareness in its full sense is being fully awake to the truth of things, seeing life with crystal clarity. At a very basic level, things are unlikely to be crystal clear if one is in any sense intoxicated. Most people find that drinking or taking drugs clouds their awareness; the principle to follow is not necessarily total abstinence, although for many committed Buddhists it does mean this, but complete honesty with oneself about their effect. Many people take drugs or drink to escape from the reality of their lives – a self-defeating process which obliterates consciousness rather than transforming it. Of course, drink and drugs are not the only intoxicants available to us. There are so many ways to escape from oneself: third-rate television, pulp fiction, computer games. Work, sex, even religion – all these can be used as a means of escaping awareness.

One of the most effective ways of developing mindfulness is meditation. A fundamental practice is the Mindfulness of Breathing, a way of progressively focusing one's attention on the rise and fall of the breath which, if practised regularly, helps one to become not only more aware but also more integrated. When I first started to practise this meditation, everything seemed to be bathed in a glorious technicolor light, and I felt literally as though my eyes had been opened to my surroundings.

These five precepts have brought about transformation in every area of my life, and I am fully confident that they will continue to do so, as long as I practise them.

In conclusion, here is my poem:
Spanning the restless river,
A shimmering rainbow bridge;

Heart's blood, love-red,
Glad, golden giving,
Green, still meadow,
Silver song of truth,
A thousand rainbows blaze
From the clear crystal of mindfulness.
Pure, I cross over,
Singing a song of freedom.

Ratnavandana

*After a childhood in Cornwall, Ratnavandana moved to
London at the age of 16 to work in the music industry. From
1958 to 1973 she had a high-flying career in England and
America; but in 1974 she gave it all up, wanting to be free of
a career spent involved with the destructive lives of rock
stars, wanting something purer. She moved to Cornwall with
a friend, and they tried out a life of self-sufficiency. Then, in
early 1977, having come across Buddhism in Cornwall, she
moved back to London, this time to become involved with
FWBO activities there. She was part of the first women's
community at the London Buddhist Centre, and founded
Jambala, a women's Right Livelihood business. She was
ordained in 1983. In 1992 she moved to Taraloka Retreat
Centre, where she has specialized in leading meditation
retreats, as well as tending the garden. She has recently
moved to Birmingham, England, as part of the community of
women preceptors.*

Ratnavandana

Journey to the Inner Realm

Discovering Meditation

The moon which rests reflected in the water of the pure heart
When the wave breaks, becomes light.[5]

In 1974 I was living in Cornwall, a remote county in the far west of England. For fifteen years I had been chasing my dreams in the rock-and-roll business. I was jaded and needed to renew myself. Together with a friend, I plunged into a different lifestyle. We experimented with hatha yoga, fasted, learned to cook vegetarian meals, and spent time generally unwinding in our beautiful surroundings. Still reeling from the effects of my life in London, I was intent on trying to purify my body and mind, hoping that I might discover a meaning to life that had eluded me until then.

I had been struck, a few years before, by a Buddha figure I had seen in a shop in the West End of London. This figure spoke to me in a way I didn't understand but which touched me deeply. The expression on its face, its cross-legged posture, seemed to speak of something other. Just looking at it produced a feeling of calm and stillness. I bought the figure, and now it sat in my room radiating a sense of inner space and calm.

Yoga also had a strong effect on me, making me more aware of my body and mind, producing a different state of consciousness in me which I was drawn to exploring further. I had read about yoga and meditation in a book which said you could develop higher states of consciousness without the aid of drugs. Another book gave instruction on how to meditate on a candle flame. I practised this method for a while, but I felt very unsure about what I was doing, whether I was approaching it in the right way, and what was supposed to happen.

So I was very excited to hear, through a chance remark, of an opportunity to learn to meditate properly. The man who was to teach meditation was a Buddhist, but I was not to worry, I didn't have to be a Buddhist or take up Buddhism to learn the meditation practices. I hadn't read or heard anything about Buddhism, but I knew it came from India or somewhere like that, so I was intrigued to discover what the person who was to teach meditation would be like. I expected him to be Indian, but he was a young Englishman with long hair.

After a brief introduction, we were invited to sit cross-legged on the floor, and began our first session of meditation. I still remember it clearly because, although I was extremely uncomfortable in that position, something happened to my consciousness. It expanded, and I felt as though I had entered another realm which was infinitely spacious, calm, and still. I learned later that I had indeed entered another realm, infinitely more vast than anything I had previously experienced, and that I had been fortunate to have this experience during my first 'proper' attempt to meditate. I had experienced beginner's mind. I had entered a higher state of consciousness at my first attempt, without knowing how or why.

Besides learning to meditate, I valued meeting and making friends with others who were doing the same. I quickly became friends with a couple of women, and enjoyed many hours of stimulating conversation over tea or coffee about meditation, Buddhism, and ourselves. Meditating was quite out of the ordinary at that time, and it helped me enormously to share my experiences with others in this way.

I knew I wanted to explore meditation and Buddhism further. It has led me a very long way from my days in the music business. At the time of writing I live and work at Taraloka, a Buddhist retreat centre for women set in the spacious countryside of Shropshire.

I continued to meditate because it had a tangible effect on me which I liked. Besides feeling calmer and clearer, I experienced myself in a new way. I felt as though I was at the beginning of a long road towards discovering myself. I was fortunate to be blessed with glimpses of what was possible in meditation which inspired me to carry on after my initial burst of good fortune ended.

What I remember about this time was the sense of having come home. This was such a relief, putting me in touch with deeper parts of myself that I had unsuccessfully struggled to express for years. Everything I heard about meditation and Buddhism resonated deeply in my being. It seemed to correspond to what I already knew deep down, but had never found or heard words to express. I had no real idea what those deep stirrings were about, other than that they were connected with a search for meaning in my life. I had a sense of setting out on a path of discovery.

For so many years my world had revolved around my work in the music industry, and my entire being had been saturated by it. My work had been my whole life, and I could see how narrow this had made my view of the world. Now I felt as though the world was opening up and broadening out, as though my eyes were opening for the first time.

I learned the two basic meditation practices taught in the FWBO, the Mindfulness of Breathing and the Metta Bhavana. Initially I was very taken by the Mindfulness of Breathing: a practice, in four stages, of ever-increasing concentration, using the breath as the focus. When I practised it, I felt a lovely sense of calm and spaciousness, and delighted in the process of the breath coming in and going out of my body. The very word 'mind-full-ness' gave me a feeling of what it might be like to be more present in each moment. I also loved the fact that you focused on something as natural as the breath. The Metta Bhavana was quite different, in that you were trying to contact and develop a feeling of loving-kindness for all that lives. This seemed radical. I wasn't sure I wanted to develop this feeling for *everyone*. The practice is in five stages: you begin by cultivating feelings of warmth and friendliness towards yourself, then a dear friend, then a neutral person, and then someone with whom you have difficulty. In the final stage, you bring all four people together, including yourself, and try to feel equal warmth towards each, before radiating it out, like a great sun, to shine on all living beings, wishing them happiness. As a result of doing this practice, I found myself taking people in much more. I remember really looking at people, trying to connect imaginatively with them, and feeling my heart open to them. I felt connected with the stream of life that was all around me, rather than remaining in my own little world.

I saw how beneficial these two practices were, and that they affected me in different ways. The Mindfulness of Breathing helped me become clearer and more tranquil, more aware of myself and the world. I sensed that this awareness would have implications, though I didn't yet know what they would be. Practising the Metta Bhavana made me much more aware of my emotions. I realized how much they 'just happened' to me in response to different triggers. I knew very little about my emotions, and it was uncomfortable to be so buffeted by them. I began dimly to glimpse the need to develop positive emotions and emotional clarity. I also began to understand what was meant by the word concentration: it conjured up images of something very whole and focused in my mind. According to the dictionary, 'to concentrate' is 'to bring together at one centre'. What you try to do in meditation is bring your energies together by focusing on a particular object.

Meditation is like a mirror; you begin to see yourself as you are, and sometimes that's hard to accept. I discovered that in many ways I didn't like myself. The kind of change I hoped for was to drop those unacceptable parts and exchange them for nicer ones. It took me a while to realize that the process of transformation brought about by meditation was not going to be like that.

Once my initial burst of beginner's luck was over, I found that it wasn't as easy as I thought to concentrate. My mind seemed to have a life of its own. I had always found it easy enough to concentrate when reading a book or doing some particular task. But sitting down, closing my eyes, trying to bring my awareness to the breath and letting it remain there seemed impossible. My mind seemed to fly off at a tangent, carrying me away from the breath hither and thither, involving me in all sorts of dramas and scenarios that demanded my attention right there and then. I was discovering the nature of mind – always commenting, judging, and planning. It felt limiting.

Learning to work creatively with the hindrances that stop me concentrating is a continuing process. Awareness and recognition are major keys. The mind can be trained in the same way as the body, to become supple and pliant rather than narrow and fixed. Years of habitually being in a certain way begin to untangle once you have this new awareness. This process is a source of deep enrichment, because you start to discover new aspects of yourself.

I was sure that if I plumbed the depths of my being I would find darkness and shadows. I was afraid to acknowledge these depths, afraid of what might happen if I allowed them to emerge. I haven't liked a lot of what I have found, of course, but it has been much better to know about it, so that I could begin the process of transforming it rather than having so much energy locked up 'down in the cellars', unavailable for the living of life. I have also discovered some precious jewels which have brought untold riches into my life. One of meditation's great gifts is this process of bringing to consciousness.

Traditionally there are five hindrances which prevent the deepening of concentration: sense desire, hatred and ill-will, restlessness and anxiety, sloth and torpor, and doubt. Sense desire is desire for pleasurable experience through the five physical senses, often through food or sex, but day-dreaming or mental fantasy also come high on the list. Hatred and ill-will include anger, jealousy, resentment, and associated negative mental states. These usually arise when one's desire for sense experience has been frustrated. Restlessness and anxiety is the inability to settle, to be still. It has mental and physical manifestations, a lot of scattered energy niggling and worrying about everything. Then there is the opposite tendency: sloth and torpor. This is inertia, stuck energy, and is often the result of resistance to experiencing oneself on a deeper level, or resistance to change. The fifth hindrance is doubt – not a healthy, questioning doubt, but indecision, an unwillingness to commit oneself, to make up one's mind, so that one does not allow the meditation to affect one deeply. Doubt is insidious, has many guises, and in a sense underlies all the other hindrances.

My experience seemed to be a mixture of these hindrances. Buddhist tradition suggests various antidotes to them,[6] and I found these a great help, but I also needed to learn to work in meditation in a receptive, positive way. It was no use giving myself a hard time because I was getting caught in a particular hindrance. I needed to recognize what was happening, have an attitude of kindness towards myself, understand what underlay the hindrance, reflect on it, and try to restore the balance.

There were times when I would break through these barriers to concentration. Suddenly I would feel as though I was free from restraints, and I could move forward with relative ease. At these times there would be a lovely sense of expansion, contentment, and enjoyment filling my body and mind. It was a bit like being in a boat dragging through the mud, and feeling the mud clearing and the boat gliding gently forward in the water. This experience is known as access concentration, so called because it's the doorway to concentration proper.

When we first begin to meditate we usually encounter our reactive mind quite strongly. We begin to see that what hinders us from becoming concentrated in our meditation is also present in our everyday life. These hindrances are not just little tricks of the mind that stop us meditating, but a major part of our mundane consciousness. Generally speaking we live most of the time in the grip of this reactive mind, a mind that reacts. It reacts to external stimuli experienced through the five sense-organs (eye, ear, nose, tongue, skin). Our attention is caught up in something we see or hear, which sets us off on a train of thought or pattern of behaviour that is repetitive, mechanical, and predictable. Reactive mind is limited, restricted, dependent, not free. It is mind conditioned by the circumstances of our lives from the cradle to the grave. Our ordinary mind can function in two ways: reactively or creatively. Meditation opens the door to developing this creative mind, a mind that acts spontaneously out of its own fullness and richness. This is a mind that responds, a mind that is not dependent, predictable, or mechanical, but free and unlimited. Creative mind developed to its highest possible level coincides with Absolute mind, or Enlightened mind, the goal of the Buddhist path.

After I had been meditating for a while, I began to notice the overall effect of meditation on my life. I was happier and clearer. Even if I hadn't managed to become very concentrated, I felt different at the end of a session. I liked to meditate first thing in the morning, noticing that it gave me a really good start to the day. I also began to notice that the way I lived my life affected my meditation. I saw that I needed a clear conscience to deepen my practice of meditation; more than that, I began to experience a natural sense of morality, which felt inherent rather than imposed. This morality was about acting from the best in myself, from a deeper understanding.

One of meditation's great gifts is integration, another word which captured my imagination. One dictionary definition is 'harmonious combination of elements into a complex whole'. I recognized this in my own experience, and greater possibilities for the future began to open up. So much more of me was now present and active, giving my life a depth and richness which is hard to put into words.

Through meditating we become aware, if we weren't already, that our personalities are multi-faceted, that they contain many paradoxes. Different, sometimes contradictory, sides of ourselves are expressed when we are with different people or in different situations. It can be confusing to experience the pushes and pulls of these different aspects of ourselves. Increased awareness through meditation leads to increased awareness in our daily lives, and this helps to bring about the integration of our contrary selves.

When we overcome the hindrances to meditation and begin to penetrate more deeply, we find ourselves in access concentration. All the different elements of our everyday consciousness become unified and concentrated, and we feel free from conflict and confusion, tranquil and clear, with a delightful sense of poise. We are still in the world of sensuous experience, but from here we can enter the gates of meditation proper, or full concentration, a series of states known as the *dhyanas* or absorptions. At this point vertical integration begins, bringing together the forces of our heights and depths, gradually uniting them with the superconscious. We are now contacting energies of a different quality altogether, energies which are purely spiritual. Sangharakshita says: 'Absorption [*dhyana*] represents the unification of the mind on higher and ever higher levels of consciousness and being.'[7]

This process of integration is intensely pleasurable. In the first level of dhyana we experience one-pointedness and rapture, the bodily pleasure that comes from the unification of our energies, along with a deeply pervading sense of bliss and calm. Thought is present in our experience, but it's clear, soft, and lucid. It has been said of the first dhyana that while it is a much higher level of consciousness than most of us ordinarily experience, it is a healthy human state that we could enjoy all the time. Everything that we experience in this dhyana – bodily pleasure, bliss and calm, clear thought – can be experienced, at least potentially, outside meditation. The seeds are there in our everyday life.

There are three more dhyanas or absorptions, each progressively more intense and refined. Put very simply, in the second dhyana thought drops away and rapture intensifies; in the third, the more physical element of rapture drops away, and a more refined experience of bliss intensifies in a deeply satisfying manner. In the fourth dhyana we are so completely absorbed that our concentration cannot be shaken. The main quality of this dhyana is equanimity, human consciousness journeying to the most sublime peaks imaginable. Was it of this that my Buddha figure spoke as he sat cross-legged, his eyes closed and that beautiful, ineffable expression on his face?

I feel very fortunate to live and work at Taraloka. One of my responsibilities is the development of our meditation retreats. Hundreds of women from all walks of life, all sorts of backgrounds, come on retreat here. It never ceases to delight and inspire me when I see the effect of a retreat on them, even if they only come for a weekend. Like flower buds exposed to the sun, they slowly start to open and blossom. I spend many weeks on retreat each year, and these are some of my happiest and most fulfilling times. Having the opportunity to meditate and being able to share my experience with others brings me much joy. Teaching meditation myself now, witnessing others responding, just as I did all those years ago, sets everything in perspective. Helping to open the door for others as they begin their journey is a way of expressing my own heartfelt devotion and gratitude to those who taught me.

In recent years I have especially enjoyed retreats which have focused on what is known in Buddhism as 'insight' meditation. Buddhist tradition outlines various practices whose purpose is to deepen reflection, in the context of meditation, on the truths the Buddha taught. The facts of life – that all things are impermanent, that we have no fixed self, that mundane existence is unsatisfactory – are challenging and hard to face. It is very important, therefore, to establish oneself in a calm and positive state of mind before beginning to reflect.

In Buddhism a distinction is made between *shamatha* ('calming') meditation – practices such as the Mindfulness of Breathing and the Metta Bhavana – and *vipashyana* ('insight') meditation. In Buddhist circles in recent years, *vipashyana* has come to be associated with a particular form of mindfulness practice taught by various teachers from the Burmese Buddhist tradition. More traditionally, though, the term *vipashyana* covers a broad range of meditation practices, all designed to help one to reflect on the nature of reality. On the insight retreats for Order members we run at Taraloka, we spend the first few days of the retreat deepening and strengthening our *shamatha* practice before beginning *vipashyana* practices such as reflections on impermanence and the *bardo* verses from *The Tibetan Book of the Dead*, reflections on conditionality, and on the elements of which all life is made up and to which all must return. It's a bit like stilling the waters of a lake so that they give a pure and clear reflection.

After twenty years I still have a strong sense of a journey in my own meditation practice. It is the most satisfying and fulfilling journey I have ever undertaken, and I still feel that this is only the beginning. It's like discovering a new country. When you turn your senses within, you need a new language to help you find the way, just as when you go on a journey to another country you need to know the language, or at least have some method of communication, and maps to make sure you are heading in the right direction.

There is nothing unnatural about meditation. All its elements are already within us. The seeds are there, and just like the gardener who carefully sows and tends the seeds, chooses the right time and place for planting, and provides water so that they will germinate, take root, and grow, so too will the seeds of our potential grow and flourish within us if we create the right conditions.

As I look at my Buddha figure, I have a strong sense of connecting with a tradition that is 2,500 years old, and I love the feeling that millions have followed this path. When I sit down to meditate, I know that I can attain what the Buddha attained. Little did I know where I was going when I started out; little, indeed, do I know now. But I do know that the goal of the spiritual life is not some sort of heaven, or union with God, but – with the help of meditation – to see things as they really are.

Kulaprabha

Kulaprabha lives in Glasgow with her partner and teenage daughter. Before her involvement with the FWBO she was a research chemist. She works at the Glasgow Buddhist Centre and has particular responsibility for developing facilities for women, especially those who have asked for ordination. She regularly leads meditation retreats, and more recently has led Dharma study seminars and courses in clear thinking for women. She has been ordained for nine years.

Vidyadevi is introduced at the beginning of the next chapter.

Kulaprabha and Vidyadevi

Searching for the Truth

The Study of Buddhism

AFTER THE BUDDHA gained Enlightenment, he spent seven weeks just walking up and down by the river among the trees, contemplating and absorbing what had happened. After many years of searching, after much effort and exertion, and much letting go, at last he knew what he had taken such pains to find out: how to go beyond suffering, how to go beyond old age, sickness, and death. He had become a Buddha, 'one who is awake'. And instinctively he knew that he was at present unique among human beings. No one else had seen what he had seen, or understood what he had understood.

As he strolled up and down, deep in thought, he came to realize that he had a problem. His innate compassion compelled him to share his experience with others. But how could he ever communicate to anyone else what he now knew? The truth he had discovered was subtle and hard to contact. Perhaps people were too immersed in the affairs of the world to be able to understand it. And in any case, how could he put into words the experience of Enlightenment? It was simply inexpressible.

At that point he almost decided that there was no point in trying. But then he had a vision. He saw all men and women as being like lotuses – some still buds deeply buried in the mud, some having found their way above the surface of the water, and some on the point of breaking into full bloom. In an instant he realized that there were people who would understand, people in whom wisdom would flower.

Understanding this, he set out to find five of his former disciples, resolved to find a way to communicate to them the path to Enlightenment. And when he had tracked them down, he discovered that his instinct had been right. After many hours of discussion, the truth the

Buddha was trying to express finally dawned on one of the five – his name was Kondanna – and his face lit up. The Buddha, delighted, exclaimed 'Kondanna knows! Kondanna knows!'[8]

From this decisive moment has unfolded the whole Buddhist tradition, the passing on of knowledge from one person to another. Each of the Buddha's first five disciples gained Enlightenment, and many others followed. The early scriptures contain dozens of accounts of the Buddha meeting and talking to people, describing the way to attain Enlightenment with great clarity and precision, presenting it in a way that was relevant to the person he was speaking to, whether it was a queen, a chief minister, a farmer's wife, a courtesan, or a merchant. If he succeeded in convincing someone – and he didn't always succeed – they would respond in astonishment at what had been revealed to them:

'It is amazing, Venerable Gotama, it is wonderful, Venerable Gotama! Just as if one might raise what has been overturned, or reveal what has been hidden, or point out the way to him who has gone astray, or hold a lamp in the dark so that those who have eyes may see objects, so likewise has the Truth been explained by Venerable Gotama in various ways.'[9]

As the order expanded, the Buddha's disciples also began to teach, and the tradition continued. In the different cultures that have embraced Buddhism, the passing on of knowledge has taken many different forms. Many students of the Dharma in its early days in India learned teachings by heart and passed them on orally; the Buddha's words were not written down until several hundred years after his death. Tibetan Buddhists, following the tradition of the great Buddhist university at Nalanda in India (which had its heyday in the third to fifth centuries CE), devised study courses which could take twenty years or more to complete, and developed a tradition of examinations and stylized debates. Zen Buddhists, meanwhile, struggled to win Enlightenment through wrestling with the paradoxical koans handed to them by their masters. All these methods, very different though they were, had – and have – the same purpose: to help the student on the path to Enlightenment, to communicate to him or her the essence of the Buddha's teaching in such a way that eventually not just intellectual understanding, but transcendental insight, might dawn.

Now, of course, Buddhism has come to the West. When the Buddha himself was teaching, truth-seeking was very much part of the culture in which he lived. His former disciples may have doubted at first whether he had found the way to the truth, but they didn't doubt that there was truth – the Truth, even – to be found, or that to attempt to find it was worth while. Today we are living in a very different climate. Materialism, scepticism, post-modernism, the new science, mingled with the philosophies and religions of all ages and cultures, are all potentially part of our world-view, mediated to us through television, radio, newspapers, the Internet. Living not in the forests of ancient India but in what the art critic Robert Hughes calls the 'forest of media', we find ourselves surrounded by many different world-views. Journalists often tend to adopt a position of 'ethical neutrality', presenting all views of whatever kind as being of equal value – or non-value. What really matters to us? Who can say? To declare oneself a truth-seeker in this world of uncertainties is to admit that one faces a tremendous challenge. But we also have a great opportunity. No longer bound to a rigid adherence to past traditions, we are free to think for ourselves – if we can learn to think clearly in the face of so much information.

Buddhist teachers from the East who have taken on the task of trying to communicate the Buddha's message in Western countries tend to take one of two approaches, depending on the tradition of which they are part. Some, mindful of the importance of right motivation in Buddhism, advocate learning what might be called the theory of Buddhism before taking any practical steps. Others go to the opposite extreme, teaching complex meditation practices and rituals without worrying too much about whether the student understands the context in which these practices are effective. As many teachers are finding, though, a balance of theory and practice seems most effective. Newcomers to Buddhism can begin to get an understanding of Buddhist teaching while at the same time learning the basics of meditation and ethical practice. A little has been said about ethics and meditation in previous chapters. In this chapter, the focus will be on the study of Buddhism.

A standard definition of study is that it is 'the devotion of time and attention to acquiring information or knowledge'. The first part of this is helpful in the context of studying Buddhism, in that it suggests that study is going to involve long and careful consideration – an idea which runs counter to the ideal of instant gratification characteristic of modern life. But the second part of the definition, 'acquiring information or knowledge', implies something academic, intellectual. Today many people are wary of a too-rational approach to life, to the extent that how we feel has come to matter more than what we think. And, of course, it is right to be wary of a too cerebral, even anthropological approach to Buddhism, in which knowledge is acquired with no sense of needing to apply the teachings to one's own life.

To study the Dharma, no academic qualifications are needed. The intellect has an important function – we will come back to this later – but this is a question of being reasonable, using one's natural intelligence, not of being intellectual. Although one can study Buddhism as an academic subject, and Buddhists are very much indebted to the scholars and translators who over the years have made so many texts available to us, this is not the only – or the best – way to study Buddhism. In *A Survey of Buddhism*, Sangharakshita remarks, 'The only possible Right Motive with which the study of Buddhism can be undertaken is the hope that through such study Enlightenment may ultimately be attained.'[10] The study of Buddhism is not separate from Buddhist practice, from the leading of a Buddhist life; it can itself be a transforming spiritual practice.

The study of Buddhism in this sense includes a commitment to trying to live in accordance with what that study reveals. Buddhism is pragmatic. One need not feel that one has to accept its teachings as a revelation of divine authority. For a Buddhist, the truth is not revealed by God or any other authority, not imposed, and not to be accepted in blind faith. The nature of Buddhist belief is evoked by the description of the Dharma (the Buddha's teaching) given in the *Ti Ratana Vandana*, a set of devotional verses chanted by Buddhists all over the world. They describe the Dharma as 'well-communicated, visible, timeless, verifiable, fruitful, and to be understood individually by the wise'.[11]

If this is an indication of what our experience of practising the Dharma could be, then it seems we can expect something that is visible and apparent, not hidden; something we can verify for ourselves if we are prepared to try it out; and something that will be fruitful in the sense of helping us to develop clarity, positivity, and, eventually, understanding of reality. In addition we are told that the relevance of the Buddha's teaching is not limited to a particular place or time, and that it can be understood by each one of us – if we practise it wisely. Here, 'wisely' means with discrimination and a readiness to take the advice of more experienced practitioners.

So the point of studying Buddhism is to 'understand reality', to 'gain Enlightenment', to 'develop wisdom'. But what does this really mean?

As we have seen, the Buddha himself, having gained Enlightenment, could hardly imagine how to describe it. But over the years the Buddhist tradition has come up with various descriptions of the development of wisdom. Indeed, there is far too much to say about wisdom to do it justice in a short essay; but one straightforward way to think of it is in terms of views.

'Views' here are not simply opinions, but very deeply rooted ways of seeing the world. When he became Enlightened, the Buddha saw that everything – including the individual human being – is in a state of flux, impermanent, changing. There is nothing, he saw, that is not subject to change; there is no aspect of what we think of as 'me' that remains the same, no fixed, unchanging self or soul. He saw that everything is interconnected, that everything has an effect on everything else. And he saw that whatever happens in the world does so in dependence upon certain conditions. 'This being, that becomes, from the arising of this, that arises; this not becoming, that does not become; from the ceasing of this, that ceases.'[12] Seeing this, he saw that all our actions have consequences.

We may perhaps be able to assent to all this, just as – to take one aspect of it – all of us 'know' that one day we will die. But to uncover our true views, we need to look to our behaviour. Do we behave as though we know and accept that we and everyone we love will die? Do we live in the world in full awareness that everything is impermanent? Most of us do not, cannot, because we hold what the Buddha described as the four 'topsy-turvy views' or 'mental perversities'.[13] We imagine to be permanent and substantial what is really impermanent and insubstantial; and because we put our faith in, even give our hearts to, what cannot last in the form it now has, we perceive as pleasant and beautiful what in the long term can only be painful and ugly.

This assessment of our predicament has led many people in the West to think of Buddhism as a pessimistic teaching. In fact, however, it is a hopeful one; the universal principle of change, together with the truth that actions have consequences, is what makes it possible for us to change ourselves – and even the world – for the better. This teaching is not a theory, but simply a description of how things really are. If we can learn to live in harmony with this basic truth, really accepting that things are impermanent and insubstantial, and that we can find no refuge or lasting happiness in mundane existence, we will find true freedom, because, whatever circumstances we meet, the slings and arrows of outrageous fortune will not be able to hurt us. We will be able to enjoy pleasure while we can and let it go when it's over; bear pain while we must, knowing that it will pass.

The purpose of Buddhist study is to reveal our wrong views, these perceptions of whose truth we are so convinced, and gradually replace them with a clearer, truer vision. As well as the topsy-turvy views, there is our tendency towards either eternalism (the desire somehow to live for ever) or nihilism (the desire for oblivion). There is also the sense of separate selfhood, the idea that our lives do not impinge on the rest of the world, that we have no effect. These are among the classic wrong views which the Buddha identified – and which have a strong effect on the way we live.

These existential wrong views find expression in many ways. Women today are on the receiving end of a torrent of views about what we are and what we can do. The liberating realizations of the past century have helped us to become confident in our potential; but this sense of liberation is all too often harnessed to materialism. Magazines and television programmes are eager to tell us that we can all have – are entitled to have – a place at the top of the career ladder, loving relationships with children and partners, a great sex life, economic freedom, a 'designer lifestyle',… whatever we want.

The question is not whether it is realistic to think that we can have, do, and be all these things, but whether they are ultimately worthwhile goals. The Buddha made a distinction between the 'ignoble quest' for material happiness and the 'noble quest' for Enlightenment. (This does not imply, incidentally, that the Buddha thought there was anything noble about poverty. He advocated a middle way between extravagance on the one hand and ascetic self-denial on the other.) We need to make sure that our quest is a noble one, and to do this we need to become aware of the views and values we have imbibed from our culture, and examine them in the light of the Dharma.

Wrong views are not just mistaken ideas, but have a lot of emotional weight behind them; so the process of uncovering and changing our views is one in which our emotions are very much engaged. However, intellectual activity also has its place in the process of self-discovery. Knowing oneself involves becoming clearer and more objective about one's life, and in this intellectual curiosity, discernment, and debate as well as emotional honesty and commitment play a part. True wisdom, in other words, encompasses both reason and emotion.

According to the Buddhist tradition, the development of wisdom has three stages: listening, reflecting, and meditating (or becoming). In the rest of this chapter we will consider the contribution of studying the Dharma to the development of each of these stages or levels of wisdom.

Listening

This stage simply involves the taking in of information. For most of us 'listening' is likely to involve reading books as much as or perhaps more than literally listening to the teachings through lectures and so on. So the first question is: what to read?

Buddhist spiritual literature is not contained – or containable – in one small volume the size of the Bible or the Koran, although some texts, like the *Dhammapada* and the *White Lotus Sutra*, hold a special place in many hearts. The Buddhist canon amounts to quite a substantial library. Having been passed on by word of mouth for hundreds of years, the teachings were written down and over the years translated into many languages. There are biographies of the Buddha; accounts of his teachings to the many people he encountered as he wandered over northern India for the fifty years between his Enlightenment and his death; and precepts, meditation practices, and rituals around which his followers could shape their lives. In periods and places in which the written Dharma was in danger of being interpreted from too narrow a perspective, later texts added the language of myth and parable, which encouraged an appreciation of the universal scope of the Buddha's teaching.

Given this large depository of advice, from a wide variety of Buddhist cultures and traditions, it can be difficult to know where to start. Here are just a few ideas. One can find out a lot about Buddhism by reading about the life of the Buddha himself. Bhikkhu Nanamoli's *Life of the Buddha* is a biography compiled from traditional accounts which includes many of the essential episodes and teachings, while Marie Beuzeville-Byles's *Footprints of Gautama the Buddha* is a more impressionistic account of the Buddha's life, almost like a historical novel. For a poetic and devotional account, one might turn to *The Light of Asia*, a long poem written by Sir Edwin Arnold in Victorian England (he was the editor of the *Daily Telegraph*, as well as one of the first writers to bring Buddhism to a Western readership). Much inspiration and encouragement can also be drawn from the lives of early Buddhist women. The *Therigatha*, or 'Songs of the Sisters', is available in translation in *Poems of Early Buddhist Nuns*, translated by Mrs C.A.F. Rhys Davids and K.R. Norman; and further accounts are given in *The First Buddhist Women* by Susan Murcott.

One might also turn one's attention to some of the texts which express the Buddha's basic teachings. To get a broad idea of these, one might consult the anthology called *Buddhist Texts Through the Ages* compiled by Edward Conze et al., which gives a useful introduction, as does a more recent work, *Teachings of the Buddha*, compiled by Jack Kornfield. For complete works, one might read the *Dhammapada* or the *Sutta-nipata*, both being short and fairly accessible texts from the Pali Canon, which contains the oldest accounts of the Buddha's teaching; while from the next phase of Buddhist history, the Mahayana, the *White Lotus Sutra* is perhaps the best-known work, while Shantideva's *Entering the Path of Enlightenment* is quite accessible, and gives a strong sense of the devotional side of Buddhism. For a glimpse of the dizzying world of Buddhist metaphysics, one can look to texts such as the *Diamond Sutra* and the *Heart Sutra*; while of Tibetan teachings one might perhaps consider the famous *Tibetan Book of the Dead*.

Sampling a few of these texts – which are among the more accessible of the hundreds available to us – would be enough to give a sense of the authentic flavour of Buddhist teaching. But even these works – especially those of the later phases of Buddhist history – plunge us into a world which is very unfamiliar to the Western mind or imagination. In such strange country, one really needs a guide. As well as translations like these, many commentaries have been published; of these, some are essentially scholarly works, while others are more useful and practical, written for people who want to learn about Buddhism with a view to putting the teaching into practice.

Of all the books on Buddhism now available in the West, many – perhaps most – present the author's own interpretation of the original teachings. How to choose which to read? To gain an understanding of the Buddha's teaching, it makes sense to take a systematic approach and keep things simple, resisting the temptation to go for 'advanced' teachings, books which seem to promise too much too quickly, or which aim to make the reader feel good, but which have little substance and are therefore often unsatisfying and quickly forgotten. One might want to read a general overview of the Buddhist tradition, or a history of its development, to have a sense of how the different teachings fit together.

But although one can learn a lot about Buddhism from books, one learns most about the Buddhist life from getting to know other people who are trying to live it. This is why the 'sangha', which at its broadest means all those people who are living a Buddhist life, is as important to Buddhists as the Buddha and the Dharma. It is through the lives and practices of Buddhists down the ages that Buddhism is available to us today. An important consideration is whether one is going to pay special attention to the advice of one particular teacher or tradition. While some of the original texts are quite accessible, many of them – even in translation – may be all but meaningless without the guidance of a teacher who can shed light on them and distinguish their essential meaning for Western Buddhists.

The question of having a teacher raises what is a difficult issue for many people, that of spiritual hierarchy. In our egalitarian culture, many people are loath to accept that there are some people with more wisdom than others; 'everyone is wise in their own way', we say. In a sense this is true; and certainly there is no place in the spiritual life for hierarchies based on power or status. But if we take our sense of equality too far, so that we find ourselves unwilling to respect another person as being further along the spiritual path than we are ourselves, this is a wrong view we will have to tackle if we are to make progress.

Spiritual friendship is often the key to understanding. We find recognition of the role others can play in one's spiritual life in some of the stories of the very first women Buddhists, as recorded in the ancient Indian text called the *Therigatha*. For example, here is the account of a nun called Uttama, who met and learned from another woman, a disciple of the Buddha called Patachara:

Four or five times
I left my cell.
I had no peace of mind,
no control over my mind.

I went to a nun
I thought I could trust.
She taught me the Dharma,
the elements of body and mind,

the nature of perception,
and earth, water, fire, and wind.

I heard what she said
and sat cross-legged
seven days full
of joy.

When, on the eighth
I stretched my feet out,
the great dark was torn apart.[14]

Uttama's simple statement – 'I heard what she said' – is a reminder that, having considered what to listen to, one needs also to consider *how* to listen. Gampopa, a Tibetan teacher born in the eleventh century CE, used the image of a pot to elucidate the best approach to listening to the Dharma. A pot is an appropriate symbol of receptivity and openness. But suppose the pot is upside down? That might mean that one's mind is too caught up with other things to allow one to give one's attention to taking in anything new. Or suppose the pot is leaky? That suggests that although one is taking in the words, one's emotions are not engaged, so that the teachings can have no lasting effect, but seep away from awareness. And suppose the pot is poisonous? One's mind may be so full of negative emotions and wrong views that even the truth affects one like poison.

So it's important to be open-minded and receptive. But this does not mean being gullible. As we have seen, faith in Buddhism is not blind faith; 'test my words as a goldsmith tests gold in the fire,' the Buddha said. In listening to and reading about the Dharma we need to discriminate, to develop discernment and keenness of intellectual perception. Some of what we hear is going to go against the grain, of course, because we see the world in the topsy-turvy way we do; we need to accept that our vision is at present limited. What if we come across a teaching that just doesn't ring true, doesn't seem to accord with our experience? Often the best thing is to accept it provisionally – neither rejecting it without further thought nor accepting it despite one's misgivings, but putting it to one side, so to speak, to be thought about again at some future time. Sometimes one might accept it for the time being, until one has some experience of it, because one trusts the person who has said it.

One might question the value of studying a number of Buddhist teachings. The Buddha gave some very clear accounts of the path to Enlightenment – accounts which are both succinct and comprehensive, like the Noble Eightfold Path. Once one has the general idea, what's the point of continuing to study? One answer is that fresh approaches stimulate our continued interest. Also, gaining knowledge about the Dharma is not like adding a pebble to a heap of pebbles. When we come across a new expression of the Buddha's teaching, it completely changes everything we thought we already knew about it. And engaging with an ongoing course of study is valuable for another reason: the process of study itself transforms us, as we move from the stage of receptive and attentive listening to the next stage: reflecting.

Reflecting

This stage of the development of wisdom involves making what one has heard one's own. Reflection brings the Dharma alive, establishes one's emotional connections with it, shows how it applies to one's own life. 'Reflection' implies careful and long consideration, musing, wondering. It suggests also the need to calm and clarify one's mind through meditation. Just as the world is perfectly reflected in clear, calm water, so reality is reflected in a clear, calm mind.

One can begin with one simple thought – for example, 'All things are impermanent.' Keeping the thought in mind as undistractedly as possible, mulling it over, one gradually becomes more aware of its effect on one's life. One can reflect by thinking associatively, seeing what the original subject of one's reflections brings to mind; and one can learn to think directedly, focusing on the topic in hand and returning to it when one's mind wanders, trying to see all its possible consequences and any related assumptions.

One may find oneself returning to the same thought or question for many years. It's as though each of us discovers our own personal koan, whether it is 'Why do people suffer?' or 'What is the meaning of my life?' We don't usually have to go looking for questions; life itself presents us with paradoxes and conflicts which challenge and confuse us. And in conflict is the seed of transcendence. The teachings of Buddhism, brought clearly and courageously to mind, may suggest new ways in which to contemplate our situation.

Solitary reflection can be very valuable. Even in the busiest life, one can take a few minutes here and there to reflect. Something simple like spending a short while each day looking at the tree outside one's window, observing its changes through the seasons, can be very effective. One can study Buddhism on one's own; this gives the opportunity to follow one's own interests at one's own pace. However, as already mentioned, most of us benefit from some kind of guidance or direction in our explorations, and this is where contact with other Buddhists comes in.

If one can arrange to study with someone who has more experience of the spiritual life than oneself, as Uttama did with Patachara, that is a great opportunity, a chance to explore one's thoughts and feelings, doubts, inspirations, and insights, in company with someone who can help one make sense of them, and provide guidance and stimulation.

Another way to study, which is used to good effect in some Buddhist circles, is with a group of people. In a study group, in which perhaps six or eight people regularly meet to discuss the Dharma, a topic can be approached from a number of different points of view, according to the temperaments and experience of the participants. A good study group – led, where possible, by someone with experience of studying and practising the Dharma – can provide the conditions in which reflections can ripen and bear fruit.

Reflection is difficult and requires effort in any circumstances. It is more difficult when we ourselves are the subject of our reflections, when we are trying to clarify our thoughts and emotions, and particularly when we are trying to uncover our own wrong views. Wrong views are invariably underpinned by strong emotional preferences and prejudices, which themselves arise from psychological factors of whose origins we may be completely unaware. A study group helps us to discover our unhelpful views; it is often easier to observe someone else's views at work than it is to recognize one's own. But for that to happen, people in the group need to be able to trust one another and know that everyone there is committed to practising the Dharma, and to helping one another to understand it more deeply. This sense of trust and friendship seems to arise more readily in the context of a single-sex study group.

There are certain tendencies we need to look out for in studying the Dharma with others. It is a strength to be able to contact and, when appropriate, express one's emotions, but this can go too far, so that one becomes too emotional and subjective, confining the subject of study to one's own experience to the extent that one may be restricting oneself, not allowing for the possibility that one's experience may change in response to the teaching one is studying.

We need also to be careful not to be too 'psychological' in our approach to the Dharma, but to open ourselves to its transcendental perspective. And we need not be afraid of conceptual thinking; nor should we dismiss mental clarity as being 'in one's head'. While, as we have seen, one needs to distinguish between an intellectual appreciation of a truth or principle and a deeper understanding based in experience, a clear intellectual understanding is a necessary starting point from which deeper knowledge can arise. On the other hand, some people need to watch out for a tendency to become preoccupied with abstract ideas and avoid seeing their implications for everyday life. Our realizations are unlikely – at least for some time – to be as radical as those of the Buddha's early disciples, but if they spring up within the sphere of influence of an active study group, we only need to carry on putting in effort and listening to the advice of our spiritual friends for our reflections to mature further.

One way to make the connection between study and practice is to come up with 'personal precepts'. A personal precept comes out of the experience of studying and reflecting: it's an aspect of the teaching that you decide to apply to your own life – or that friends you study with suggest you could try. To take a simple example, you might have been contemplating or discussing the principle of generosity. You might have considered that it springs from an awareness of the interconnectedness of all life, and that it is a positive counterpart of non-violence; and you might have thought about the many ways in which one can be generous. Then you might decide to make a particular practice of being generous – perhaps for a week or longer. You might even decide to focus on a particular aspect of generosity. This you would take as your personal precept. Having tried to practise this particular precept for the time you decided on, you could evaluate the experience, either thinking it over yourself or discussing it with a friend or with those with whom you study. Did you encounter any inner resistance? Did you notice that trying to practise generosity had any particular effect on your mental states? Did anything unexpected happen as a result of your commitment to this new emphasis? Taking this experimental approach, one can test the teaching 'as gold in the fire'.

A distinction can be drawn between method and doctrine – that is, between those teachings which are to do with practice and those which focus on theory. The precept relating to generosity, to use that example, is an aspect of method; while the principle of interconnectedness is an example of doctrine. The purpose of studying methods is to gain an understanding of what Buddhist practices are and what part they play in spiritual life. Basically, one needs to know why one is doing what one is doing in order to be able to do it wholeheartedly and for the right reasons.

On the other hand, studying doctrine lifts us beyond our present experience and gives us a glimpse of the nature of life as seen from a higher level. It is important not to dismiss doctrines as dealing in abstract principles that have little relevance to our present level of experience; however baffling they may sometimes be, they have a crucial part to play in expanding our vision, inspiring us with a new sense of what is possible. Dharma study acts in all sorts of ways. Sometimes it suddenly reveals a stunning panorama of ideas and images, all woven together in a harmonious pattern; sometimes it throws up just a single idea that mysteriously manages to shed light on parts of ourselves that have been hidden in vague twilight. And sometimes it reveals images or concepts that call forth energy and confidence from our own hearts. Such revelations eventually lead us towards the third level of the development of wisdom: becoming.

Becoming

With the third level of wisdom we come to something very different from the other two. The Pali word for this level is *bhavana*, which means simply becoming, developing, bringing into being. When one has developed this level of wisdom to its fullest extent, one completely embodies the truths which one has heard and upon which one has reflected. For example, if one could listen with complete receptivity and attention to, say, the precept concerning truthful speech, and then reflected with utter lucidity of mind and openness of heart on the negative consequences of speaking untruthfully, and the positive consequences of speaking truthfully, from then on one's every word would be wholly and completely truthful.

Of course, one is unlikely to be able to listen with undivided attention, or to reflect with a completely open heart and unprejudiced mind, and it follows that one cannot all at once embody the truth. However, when we listen, at least something sinks in, and when we reflect, we see at least a glimmer of the truth, so that we are changed, even if only a little. And so we progress, little by little. The *Dhammapada* says:

> *Do not belittle your virtues,*
> *Saying, 'They are nothing.'*
> *A jug fills drop by drop.*
> *So the wise become brimful of virtue.*[15]

As we gradually clarify our views and give our hearts to understanding the truth, so eventually our reflections flower into insight into the truth. At least, that's one way of putting it. But in a sense it's rather misleading. When one gains insight into reality, one's apprehension of and relationship with the world is completely different. This is not just another level of wisdom, but a new dimension of being. In a sense there is a continuity; through developing the first two levels of wisdom, we set up the conditions in which this third level can arise. It isn't that the arising of insight is completely random, like lightning striking. But thinking of this third level as a slow and steady haul towards wisdom doesn't do justice to the real magic of experiencing the world in a completely different way.

So there's a paradox here. In a sense we need to move towards Enlightenment slowly, step by step, drop by drop. And yet the actual experience is said to be a sudden and complete transformation, a new perception for which no previous experience has prepared us. The Buddhist tradition – following from the Buddha's own sense of the mysterious and inexpressible nature of Enlightenment – often expresses it not in rational language, but in terms of poetry and symbolism. The Buddha himself, trying to put his experience into words, said it was like being freed from prison, or like putting down a burden, or like being released from a heavy debt.

This culminating stage of the development of wisdom is sometimes translated as 'meditating'. In the still silent depths of deep meditation, one brings to mind one's reflections on the truth, and – like Kondanna – one is suddenly one day flooded with the joyful knowledge that one has realized the truth for oneself. At least, this is one situation in which the third level of wisdom may arise, and some would say that this is the most likely context in which it will happen – a life lived in a retreat centre or monastery, devoted to meditation. It could be said, however, that what really makes the difference is whether one is living one's life with reference to the Dharma.

It has even been suggested that perhaps a life in which one tries to deal with the objective challenges of work or family on the basis of an understanding of the Dharma is a surer route to wisdom for many people. Not many of us, perhaps, would be able to make the most of having the opportunity to meditate all day every day; it takes great courage and commitment to make that into a truly challenging lifestyle. Perhaps coming up against objective difficulties is in a way easier. But whatever our situation, our task is the same. Whether we are deep in meditation, or brokering a business deal, or changing the baby's nappy, we can try to do so in a context of awareness of the true nature of life.

Many of us have had experiences of a very different way of perceiving the world, in childhood perhaps, or illness, or even through drug-induced states; mostly such experiences are quickly forgotten, though some people suffer the horror of being trapped in states they don't understand, which can lead to mental breakdown or psychosis. To set out on the path to Enlightenment is to step into the unknown. Studying Buddhism is important because, as well as giving us guidelines for everyday living, it gives us a way of making sense of our experience, even a way of preparing for the totally different experience which is the dawning of insight into the way things really are. Without such a framework, our insights and struggles may be frightening or bewildering.

Conclusion

The effect of studying the Dharma is, in a sense, cumulative. As one persists in trying to understand the teachings, weeding out unhelpful views and uncovering personal preferences and prejudices, one increasingly discovers a sense of faith in the Buddha's vision. The image of 'spiritual detective' comes to mind. The trail to be followed is clearly laid out in the Buddha's teaching; it only remains to track down any villainous wrong views which prevent us from progressing along that trail. The clues are there somewhere in our own minds. All we need to remember is that some villains are very plausible and persuasive indeed, not to mention highly attractive and intelligent in their own dastardly fashion!

In the eighth century CE, the Buddhist poet Shantideva wrote a work called *Entering the Path of Enlightenment*. He ends the chapter on 'Full Acceptance of the Thought of Enlightenment' with these words:

> *For the caravan of humanity, moving along the road of being,*
> *hungering for the enjoyment of happiness, this happiness banquet is*
> *prepared for the complete refreshment of every being who comes to it.*
> *Now I invite the world to Buddhahood, and, incidentally, to happiness.*[16]

Shantideva's image of the caravan of humanity evokes a sense of searching and longing for something that can be completely relied on, that can provide a true home and a truly human existence, a wish to have done with emotional superficiality and limited understanding. Those who have chosen to follow the Buddha's teaching have all experienced this kind of dissatisfaction to some extent. Such longing, together with the confidence to search for a spiritual home, and the acceptance that we will have to change in the process, is what constitutes Buddhist faith. And it is such faith that Dharma study can awaken within us.

To take up the study of the Dharma, to declare oneself a seeker after the truth, one needs to be prepared to put all one's views and personal preferences into the crucible of the Buddha's insight into reality and his advice on how to attain that insight. If in the process one comes across dearly-held views that are not conducive to attaining Enlightenment, one needs to be prepared to set them aside for the sake of that great attainment. If we can do this, someday, whether in this lifetime or a future one, our hearts will thrill with full understanding of the truth, and we will join the lineage of Enlightened women; like Mettika, a brahmin's daughter, who, on attaining full Enlightenment in her old age, exclaimed:

> *Though I be suffering and weak, and all*
> *My youthful spring be gone, yet have I come,*
> *Leaning upon my staff, and climbed aloft*
> *The mountain peak.*
> *My cloak thrown off,*
> *My little bowl o'erturned; so sit I here*
> *Upon the rock. And o'er my spirit sweeps*
> *The breath of Liberty! I win, I win*
> *The triple Lore! The Buddha's will is done!*[17]

Vidyadevi

Vidyadevi was brought up in the north of England, and studied English literature at Cambridge. She began editing for Windhorse Publications very soon after her first contact with Buddhism. Over the last few years she has been involved in a project dedicated to bringing Sangharakshita's talks and seminars into print. She was ordained in 1993.

Vidyadevi

The Great Miracle

Faith in Buddhism

ONE WINTER, unhappy and wanting to avoid the usual Christmas celebration, I happened to meet someone who suggested an alternative. Why didn't I try a Buddhist retreat? A few days later I found myself in a draughty old school building with seventy other people, all there to learn meditation and find out something about Buddhism. My first impression of Buddhists was that they wore blankets and slippers. I was too withdrawn and miserable to respond to the friendly atmosphere, although I managed to notice that the people I met were kind. But something did get through the haze of self-preoccupation that shrouded me. We were given a talk about an incident from the life of the Buddha. On this occasion, the Buddha met a woman (her name was Kisa-Gotami) whose child had just died. When she pleaded with the Buddha to restore her child to life, he didn't say yes or no. He told her to go to the village and ask for a mustard seed. This, he said, would give her what she wanted. As she leapt up, ready to dash away and find the precious mustard seed, the Buddha said just one more thing: that the seed must come from a household where there had been no death. As Kisa-Gotami went from house to house, finding people all too willing to give her the mustard seed, but each time discovering that someone from the household had died, the truth began to dawn on her: that all must die. Now able to grieve for her child, she went back to the Buddha, and asked him to teach her more.[18]

What struck me was how very sensible the Buddha was. He didn't try to persuade Kisa-Gotami to be rational. Nor did he perform a miracle. He found a way of communicating with her that led her to greater understanding. I couldn't help thinking of the miracles of Jesus, which, when I thought about it, seemed only to encourage a shying away from the truth. Faith in the Buddha, I realized – for I knew already that I was going to be a Buddhist – would be something very different from the faith in Jesus I had struggled to find.

I discovered later that the Buddha, while acknowledging that minor miracles – things like walking on water, raising the dead, or flying through the air – could be performed by those with sufficient spiritual attainments, used to discourage his disciples from working them. The great miracle, he said, happened when a man or woman made a commitment to discovering the truth. That's a strong statement which acknowledges the tremendous struggle that goes on in us between 'life as it is' and 'life as it could be'. Except on those occasions when the flow of our life is disrupted by some tragic event, as Kisa-Gotami's was, we tend to accept life at face value. At the same time, each of us at times experiences a yearning for something beyond life as we know it. It's as though archetypal forces are at war within us, although we rarely become aware of them.

Buddhism is sometimes thought to be about the eradication of desire, but its teachings suggest that it is more about rechannelling it. Buddhist tradition speaks of *kamachanda* and *dharmachanda* – the first being 'desire for sense experience' and the second 'desire for the truth'. The implication is that we need not give up being creatures of desire; our passion can gradually be redirected from sense experience, which is inevitably fleeting, to become a passion for the truth. Having faith in Buddhism, one could say, is about gradually shifting our emotional life from *kamachanda* to *dharmachanda*. In this essay I want to consider how we identify 'desire for the truth' in ourselves, and what we can do to strengthen that desire.

I made some more discoveries on my first retreat. So far I knew about Buddhism only what I had heard in the talk and the brief but effective introduction to meditation that newcomers such as myself had been given. But in the evenings the whole retreat would gather together and perform a puja. Everyone repeated the words spoken by the leader; mantras were chanted; people bowed and offered incense. I had never seen anything like it; certainly nothing in my Methodist upbringing had prepared me for it. Somehow that didn't seem to matter. Indeed, the aspects of the ceremony that were the most obscure – the chanting of strange syllables, the bowing before the Buddha-image, and the recitation of something called the *Heart Sutra*, which included such baffling pronouncements as 'Form is only emptiness, emptiness only form' – were the things that somehow thrilled me with a strange sense of understanding.

Mine was quite a common response, I think. Also common is the other extreme: a recoil, a sense even that this mumbo-jumbo this bowing and scraping, is not really Buddhism – Buddhism being characterized more by the reasonableness the Buddha showed in his encounter with Kisa-Gotami. But devotional practices are a crucial aspect of Buddhist life, and we need to find a way to make them make sense to both our minds and our hearts, whether our starting point is credulous or sceptical – and perhaps especially if we have a Western background. I'll come back to this.

When I found myself on that Christmas retreat, I was suffering from a sense that my life had no meaning. I was twenty-four. I had got my degree; I had married a kind man. I had done what I thought I wanted to do. No one had ever suggested it wouldn't be enough. But I felt empty; it seemed I had no life of my own. Perhaps a sense of pointlessness is close to the surface of many people's lives. One can go for years scarcely noticing it, but then – often because of some traumatic or moving event – suddenly a desire to find meaning surges up. We can't bear it any longer. But what can we do? Often then something happens to assuage the pain of this feeling; the grief subsides; life must go on.

If, however, we don't just resign ourselves to our fate, we begin to ask questions. What is really important in life? What do we want from it? What, even, is our heart's desire? We have an innate love of truth and beauty – much exploited by the advertising industry, which ties our unformed longings to cars and clothes and holidays. If we can resist the temptation to smother our longing for a different kind of life in the life we already have, new possibilities open up.

I am reminded of this every day by the name I was given when I was ordained: Vidyadevi. Your ordination name is usually chosen by the preceptor who ordains you; it is said both to reflect your potential and to give you a challenge. With this in mind, on the night of my ordination I was bracing myself for a shock. Typically, I imagined that my name would be hard work, a burden I'd have to shoulder. Actually 'Vidyadevi' came into my mind, but I dismissed it as being too beautiful for me. When it turned out that this was the very name chosen for me, it certainly was a shock – and a challenge, though not of the kind I'd resigned myself to. *Vidya* is wisdom or knowledge, but not intellectual knowledge. It's more an aesthetic appreciation, a seeing of things as they are without any utilitarian sense of appropriation. *Devi* means 'female shining one'. As I saw it my name was challenging me to relate to the world in a completely different way. If I could become 'Vidyadevi' my experience would be both meaningful and beautiful, because I would learn to see the essence, the heart of things. A beautiful challenge – but still a challenge.

To go forth from materialism is to put one's faith in the intangible, the invisible, that which is beyond the reach of the physical senses. However, this is not at all the same thing as belief in 'immortal, invisible, God only wise'. The difference is that the Christian God is by popular definition (as distinct from mystical experience) eternally separate from humanity. But Buddhist faith is confidence in humankind's innate potential for Buddhahood. The Buddha was a human being who became Enlightened; intrinsic to his teaching is the encouragement that all human beings – *with sufficient effort* – can also become Enlightened.

Even amid the selfishness and foolishness that so often characterize my behaviour I can identify at least some capacity to be kind and clear-sighted. An Enlightened person is someone who has developed these qualities of kindness and clear-sightedness to perfection; he or she *is* great compassion and perfect wisdom. So there is a continuum of experience between 'me as I am now' and the Enlightened being I can become. As we meditate, try to live more ethically, reflect, and so on, we can observe ourselves changing and growing, however slowly, gradually tipping the balance in ourselves so that the positive qualities become stronger and the negative qualities dwindle. (It's often easier to spot such changes by looking back on what you used to be like – if you can stand it! – or by asking a friend.)

It is clear that the nature of things – and people – is to change. We also need to develop the confidence that we can change ourselves for the better, can take life in our own hands. Any sense we have that it is sinful, hubristic, or simply impossible to do so is an expression of what Buddhism graphically describes as a fetter, one of ten that are said to hold us back from spiritual progress: the fetter of fixed self-view. This is the attitude that 'there is a core of selfhood in you which is never going to change, and which is the real "you". Such an attitude blocks change and inhibits growth, because you think that as you are now so you will be forever. It is very difficult to break this fetter, and imagine oneself as different from what one is now. But it can be done.'[19]

The Buddhist idea of self-transformation also goes beyond a humanist perspective. The pope John Paul II apparently once brushed off Buddhism with the pronouncement that it was 'an excellent human teaching'; but an Enlightened being, though having become Enlightened as a human being, is completely different from an ordinary person. Their experience has leapt beyond the psychological, beyond the mundane, to a transcendental dimension. It is this that distinguishes Buddhism from humanism. So the question is, how far will we let our imaginations go? We may be able to envisage change up to a certain point, but if we settle for a psychological reading of our situation, missing out the transcendental perspective, we are going to limit ourselves.

Something that concerns all of us, consciously or unconsciously, is the question of what will happen to us when we die. And this has an effect on our faith in the possibility of transforming ourselves in accordance with our vision. Is one lifetime enough? We may feel a resonance with the Buddha's life story, which shows that his spiritual quest began with an awareness of suffering and a determination to find a way beyond it. He too set out to find the meaning of life. And he managed it in one lifetime. But Buddhist tradition generally puts that one life in the context of many other lives before it, all dedicated to the same purpose.

A belief in a continuity of lives may be foreign to us, but to me the idea makes sense. It was once put to me that one has four choices about what to believe: that we began at birth and will end at death (the materialist view); that we come from nowhere and will continue into eternity after death (the Christian view); that we came from eternity and will end at death (nobody's view, as far as I'm aware); and that this life was preceded by many other lives, and will be followed by many more (the Buddhist and Hindu view). One cannot know the truth of this, perhaps, but for me the most helpful option is a belief in a continuity of lives. This reassures me that the positive effort I make in this lifetime will not be lost, but will influence and affect my next life; and, on the other hand, that this one life does not determine an eternal future.

It has been said that we need only a very little intellectual knowledge to gain Enlightenment. On the strength of the Buddha's essential teachings – such as that actions have consequences; that mundane life is impermanent, insubstantial, and unsatisfactory; that there is a way beyond suffering – we can go a long way. The challenge is to find a way of making emotional – as well as rational – sense of this. I may be rationally convinced of the truth of the Buddha's teaching, but what does my heart say – not just when I am feeling inspired, but the rest of the time? We all have occasional experiences – while meditating, or when out in the countryside, or seized by the power of a great play or symphony, or moved by a heartfelt communication – that hint that a richer experience is open to us. These glimpses are to be cherished; it is all too easy to forget about them because they are not part of the 'real world' in which we live day to day. But there are many other times when, if we're honest, we're too caught up in ordinary life to care very much about spiritual matters.

But we need not rely on spontaneous moments of inspiration to strengthen our feeling for spiritual life. Buddhism is in all things methodical; and this is what Buddhist devotional practice is for. It is not to propitiate a God or gods. Neither is it to conjure up material prosperity, although some people think so. It is designed to remind us of what we can become, and to develop our feeling for that possibility. When Buddhists bow before an image of the Buddha, it is not idol worship, but a grateful acknowledgement to the one who showed the way, and a gesture of determination to follow that way. In a sense, it is our own future self that we are acknowledging.

Since the time of the historical Buddha, Buddhist tradition has produced a great number of archetypal Buddhas and Bodhisattvas (Buddhas-to-be, we could call them in this context), each exemplifying the qualities of Enlightenment: compassion, healing, wisdom, energy. An obvious question is: are these Buddhas and Bodhisattvas outside oneself, or within oneself? It's easy to get tangled up in this one – at least I find it so. If I think of them as being outside me, I am in danger of setting up a static relationship with them – they are over there and I am here – which makes their qualities unattainable to me; they become like God, in other words. If they are archetypes within me – because I have the potential to develop their qualities – I may limit my idea of what is possible according to my view of myself as I am at present. I may even fall for the idea that 'I am Buddha already; I just have to realize it' – which fails to do justice to, and may get in the way of, the process of self-transformation that 'just realizing it' is going to involve.

The Tibetan Buddhist tradition has come up with a way of resolving the inside/outside question in the form of the visualization practice. In these practices, you visualize the form of a particular Buddha or Bodhisattva, and also recite their mantra. (A mantra is a 'sound symbol', representing in sound what the form of the figure represents in imagery.) In doing this you develop a personal connection with the figure. The form of the practice usually involves both a sense of separateness from the Buddha or Bodhisattva and a sense of identification with them, so that it is an imaginative enactment of the process of growing towards Enlightenment, a bridging of the gap between inside and outside. These practices help to draw out the part of us that loves myth and symbol and ritual – the part of us that liked to hear stories when we were children. As we can tell from our dream life, we function not just in terms of ideas and concepts, but also in terms of symbols and images. When I was given a visualization practice (as part of my ordination) I knew it was an opportunity I would only gradually learn to take, so much of my adult life being bound up with the surfaces of things.[20]

The classic situation in which our feeling for our ideals can flower is what is called in Buddhism a puja. (The word means 'worship'.) A puja is a powerful antidote to any sense that life is meaningless, because in performing one we enter a world in which everything is full of meaning. Usually the focus of attention is a shrine – simple or elaborate, and as beautiful as the materials available allow. Everything on the shrine has meaning. The Buddha image symbolizes Enlightenment and our own potential to become Enlightened. The candles stand for the truth; the flowers for beauty and impermanence; the incense for the way the truth perfumes – influences – the world; the offering-bowls for offerings to an honoured guest (the Buddha being the guest); and so on. Everything is there for a reason.

To perform a puja is to engage in an archetype of purposeful action. Everything you do with your body – bowing, folding your hands, offering incense – has meaning. Everything you say with your voice – chanting mantras, reciting verses – has meaning. On a good day, when you feel connected with what you are doing and manage to avoid getting distracted, even everything you do with your mind has meaning. Our interactions with other people in this context – chanting together, making offerings together, listening to one another – are also deeply meaningful.[21]

Living for a brief time in this symbolic world has an effect on the rest of our lives. A little reflection shows that really everything we do, say, and think, every communication we have, and everything we see in the world, has meaning. The haiku of Zen poets give a sense of this; so, in a different way, do the poems of William Carlos Williams. Puja is a specific practice of mindfulness or awareness, a quality which is very much part of Buddhist life: awareness of oneself, one's feelings, thoughts, and emotions; awareness of other people; awareness of one's environment; and awareness of reality. Performing a puja reminds us of who we are, of what we are doing. At least, ideally it does – but it only works if we bring enough awareness to it. At times we are sure to be beset by another of the fetters which prevent us from being ourselves at our best. This one is traditionally known as 'dependence on moral rules and religious observances'; it has also been called, more simply, 'superficiality'.[22]

This is not at all to say that moral rules and religious observances are in any way a bad thing. It ain't what we do, it's the way that we do it. Going through the motions, wanting to be seen to behave in the right way, looking for approval, while it is characteristic of much religious observance, is clearly not going to do us or anybody else any good. In Buddhism there's an expression, 'beginner's mind'; it means trying to approach everything we do with the freshness and open-mindedness we had the first time we did it. This fetter is the opposite of that, a weary, perhaps dutiful, sense of being a good girl, doing the right thing – perhaps feeling virtuous, pious, even proud of our devotion to duty. We may even become rather a martyr to it. (Or we rebel against it, to be a bad girl instead.)

This is difficult to deal with. There is definitely a virtue in doing the same practices again and again, building up positive habits, going beyond ourselves when we 'don't feel like' doing something. The key, the way to keep the initiative in what we are doing, is to keep on remembering why we are doing it (this is known as 'mindfulness of purpose'), recommitting ourselves to our vision.

The kind of reminder we are given by the puja – and other devotional practices, such as reciting traditional texts (*sutras*) and chanting mantras – is very precious. The Buddhist view of our predicament is not that we are evil sinners but that we are foolish and forgetful – forgetful of our true nature, forgetful of the possibilities of human existence. It is ignorance, not evil, that binds us. Like so many fairy-tale characters, we have fallen asleep and forgotten who we really are. The purpose of Buddhism, as many have said, is simply to say 'Wake up!' (The word 'Buddha' means 'one who is awake'.)

Many people have been awakened to the truth of Buddhism by the sight – perhaps in a museum or shop or in an Eastern country – of a Buddha image. A serene posture, a compassionate smile, a sense of vibrant alertness … something subtle yet powerful, communicates itself, intrigues us. What we are responding to is the meeting of truth with beauty; and it is not just Buddha images that evoke this response. Some people are plunged into the spiritual life by a painful experience, but others are drawn to it by an experience of transcendent beauty that reveals life's deeper meaning.

Once we have committed ourselves to the Buddhist life, all of us need pleasure and enjoyment, at least sometimes, to keep us going. Some people find it purely in Buddhist practice – in the pleasures of their meditation, say. But for others, this is where nature and the arts come in. As I've said, to commit ourselves wholeheartedly we need to make an emotional shift. The leap from 'everyday me', beset by all the distractions twentieth-century flesh is heir to, to 'Buddhist me' may be too much; a bridge is needed. We can find this in our love of our native landscape; or our feeling for the words, music, and images of our culture; or our admiration for the heroes and heroines of our history. Home is where the heart is. True, our culture has produced much that is ugly, power-driven, distracted, utilitarian. But it has also produced seekers after truth: poets, philosophers, explorers, scientists. Once we have studied the Dharma and begun to get a feeling for the truth the Buddha experienced, we can recognize that truth as reflected in our own culture, and our spiritual lives will be nourished and enriched.

Buddhism is not just an Eastern religion. It is not even really a religion; nor is it just a philosophy or a system of ethics. It is a seeking after truth. 'Poet' means 'maker'; 'philosopher' means 'lover of wisdom'. Personally I hope that one day the term 'Buddhist' will have the breadth and freedom of 'poet' or 'philosopher', will be thoroughly at home in our Western context. This integration will take some time, no doubt. As Buddhism has spread from one culture to another, it has been integrated into local culture rather than imposing its own. This process took 500 years in China; who knows how long it will take here? The Buddha's own attitude – as when, for example, he urged his disciples to pass on his teachings to people in their own local dialects – hints that such integration was part of his vision.

There are, I should add, many aspects of Buddhism as practised in the East which are becoming part of Western Buddhist culture. For example, when I visited Buddhist friends in India, I was glad that the ancient languages of Pali and Sanskrit are used universally as part of Buddhist ritual, because the verses we chanted were something very meaningful that my Indian friends and I had in common. I am also very grateful to have learned the gesture of placing my hands together at my heart and bowing, because it allows me to express feelings of reverence in a way nothing in my Western upbringing has prepared me to do. It is in any case a lovely gesture. It has echoes in many cultures and religions, but in Buddhism the hands are placed together as though you're holding something between them. This is because, symbolically, you are. Between your hands is the wish-fulfilling jewel, the potential for Enlightenment innate in all human beings. If we bowed to one another in this way, we would be acknowledging our shared potential.

This raises an important point: that faith in the ideals of Buddhism necessarily includes faith in oneself, in one's potential. This can present quite a problem. I need to believe that I, me myself, have the capacity to follow this path. It's not just for other people who don't have the difficulties I have – my friend, for example, who's a natural meditator, while I struggle away and feel like I'm getting nowhere. I need to feel that the path is my path too. What I have been calling faith (the Sanskrit word is *shraddha*) is sometimes translated as 'confidence', and perhaps that's a better description. Many women feel a lack of self-confidence; this is often said to stop us engaging fully with the spiritual life. But lack of self-confidence, it has been said, is really lack of faith. Buddhism is a universal teaching, so we can have no reason to suppose that it won't work in our case.

We may not lack confidence, but our confidence may be based on something that will change. One might feel confident in one's role, or career, or place in the family – but this kind of confidence is bound to falter sooner or later, because it is dependent on something outside one's control. We need to develop the kind of confidence that endures no matter what happens. We need confidence that we can change, and that we can have an effect. In fact, we can't help having an effect. I used to have a feeling – well, I confess I still have it sometimes – that I was invisible, like a little brown mouse, scarcely impinging on the world. I have needed to acknowledge – and this has been painful as well as 'empowering' – that I do have an effect, and that I need to take responsibility for making that effect as positive as possible.

Confidence – faith – is the key to a change which is vital to spiritual progress: the move from devotion to commitment. One can be devoted to the spiritual ideal – think it is wonderful, beautiful, lovely, and very much admire those who live in accordance with it – but miss the point by failing to see it as something one can commit oneself to. In a way this is what has happened in Eastern Buddhist countries, where, apparently, serious spiritual practice tends to be left to monks and nuns. To commit oneself, a leap of faith is required – a leap of faith in oneself.

Doubt, of course, arises – often – especially, perhaps, once the commitment is made. Here, though, a distinction must be made between two kinds of doubt. Rational doubt, questioning, testing, is fundamental to Buddhism as to no other religion. 'Test my words as gold in the fire,' said the Buddha. Unquestioning, blind faith is not required of the Buddhist; there are no creeds, no miracles to assent to, beyond the great miracle of the possibility of spiritual development. Faith is not needed to paper over the cracks of unbelievable doctrines.

But sceptical doubt – unquestioning blind doubt – is another matter. It amounts to deliberate indecision, a refusal to commit oneself. In this sense, doubt – or vagueness – is another of the imprisoning fetters that impede our progress.[23] Fettered by doubt, we sit on the fence, either not trusting ourselves or not trusting the process of the spiritual life, wanting to keep our options open. It's hard to believe in our heart of hearts that the only way to satisfy our desires is to follow the path to Enlightenment. Not for us, anyway. There are still quite a few things we can try: get a new job, find a new lover, have a baby.… Everybody experiences this in some way. And, of course, it pulls in the opposite direction to faith. It has been said that – to put it simply – we won't go and look for something we've lost in the next room if we are convinced that it is in this room.

The antidote to doubt is clarity. We need to be clear about what we really believe, where our life is going, what we are doing. This is, of course, difficult; doubt has emotional roots that go very deep. But it is immensely valuable to make the effort to gain clarity. We need to learn to be uncompromising. Women especially, perhaps, are not well practised at this; our conditioning nudges us towards fitting in, doing a balancing act to keep everybody happy.

It isn't all that easy these days to get a clear idea of what Buddhism teaches. The aura of Buddhism is lending a glow to the general haze of New Age philosophy, its wide-ranging teachings seeming to acquire a stretch-to-fit quality. This is a shame. Buddhists of all times have been careful to point out what makes their beliefs distinctive; Buddhism's history of tolerance towards other religions by no means equates with any idea that all beliefs are the same. Buddhism is not dogmatic – each of us is responsible for applying its principles to our own circumstances – but we can still be clear about what those principles are. Indeed, in these very confused and confusing times, we must be.

At present in the West, many of us have leisure and freedom to practise whatever religion we choose. This is a blessing – one which it is hard for us really to appreciate because we take it for granted. But in Tibet, only their unswerving faith is sustaining Tibetan Buddhists as they suffer great oppression. I have heard Tibetan people say, so strong is their belief in the basic Buddhist teaching that actions have consequences, that they feel compassion for their oppressors, whose actions will have terrible consequences for them sooner or later. In Myanmar (Burma), Aung San Suu Kyi is bravely continuing to hold to her faith in Buddhism despite the persecution she is experiencing.

Those of us in the West who have committed ourselves to Buddhism need to ask ourselves how deep our commitment goes, and what we are doing to help it to go deeper. Although the general impression of Buddhism in the West may be that it is rather languid, gentle, and ineffectual, in fact heroism is a strong feature of the Buddhist tradition; and one day we too may need to demonstrate that we have the courage of our convictions.

Whether or not we need to face external struggle, we are certainly up against a struggle in ourselves. In this, we are on our own. Although the support of other people is very important, when it comes to changing ourselves, no one can do it for us. Perhaps women are particularly prone to feeling that we must all do it together, or not at all. This has its very positive side, in terms of co-operation and mutual encouragement, but sometimes we just have to go it alone.

This is recognized in the ordination ceremony used by the Western Buddhist Order. The ceremony has two parts. The second is a gathering of all those being ordained, together with other members of the spiritual community, all rejoicing at the step being taken. But before this can happen, the first part of the ceremony has to take place. In this, you leave the shrine-room where everyone is meditating, and go on your own to meet the person ordaining you, your preceptor.

In the year I was ordained, the ordination retreat took place in Scotland, in mid-winter. As I left the warm shrine-room and stepped out into the cold, I did feel very much on my own. It was a night of deep frost: ice crystals crunched underfoot; through the silhouettes of trees, only the moon and the stars watched me as I went out into the dark to find the hut by the waterfall where my preceptor was waiting. I had been told the significance of this short journey: that even if I was the only person in the world to do so, I would still go forth in search of truth. And that's how it felt.

Of course, the second ceremony was equally important. The Buddhist tradition has always acknowledged the value of collective practice, 'gathering in large numbers' as the Buddha put it. It was this that I experienced in the puja on my first retreat, and I continue to experience it in Buddhist gatherings in a way I find surprising given my view that I am a shy person who doesn't like crowds. But perhaps I shouldn't be surprised; it isn't really like being in a crowd. It's difficult to pinpoint the difference, but I think it's that each person is there, as much as they can be, as an individual, not as part of a group.

Last year I went to hear a talk by Sangharakshita on 'Great Buddhists of the Twentieth Century'.[24] One of the characteristics that the men and women he chose to talk about had in common, he said, was single-mindedness. Each of them was intent on pursuing their vision, and did so undistractedly, even when it meant being alone, which it often did. It can be useful to ask ourselves what we are really seeking, and how we are going to find it. When I ask myself this question, I find that I am seeking a sense of authenticity and wholeness, so that what I give is a reflection of who I am, and there is no falsehood in me anywhere. My progress towards this seems slow. (Perhaps I need to ask myself how I am going to measure progress. Another thing noticeable about the 'great Buddhists' was that their single-mindedness was reflected in clear and tangible objectives: to restore the Buddhist temple at Bodh Gaya, for example, or to travel to Tibet.) But if I am looking for wholeness, what is getting in the way? Distractedness. I am simply unable to focus the whole of my life on my aims, even though they are important to me. My desire for the truth is not yet strong enough.

I remember once being up at dawn, leaning on a gate watching the pale sun rise over misty fields. I felt that I could watch for ever. But in fact, after ten minutes or so, I turned away from the beauty and walked the other way. I suppose I just couldn't bear it.

The Buddha's insight arose out of his patient daring to look steadily and unwaveringly at the nature of life. The Buddhist life is one dedicated to the attempt to keep looking, to learn to look for longer. As we learn to meditate, our distractedness lessens and we can hold the gaze of the truth for a little longer. And as we become more individual, we are less inclined to flow, amoeba-like, into the shape the world suggests for us, and more intent on being ourselves.

It is now almost ten years since my first retreat. In that time, I've learned quite a lot about the Buddha's teaching, though I know I haven't yet learned sufficiently the ancient truth – that I know nothing – which is the beginning of true wisdom. I think it is true to say that my faith in Buddhism is still based on that relationship between pragmatism and idealism, reasonableness and mystery, which was my experience of it on that first retreat. Of the Buddhist texts I have studied, the ones that have made the deepest impression on me have been the myths and stories. I think this is because Buddhist myths are neither to be taken literally – a classic mistake which leads to a lot of theological contortions – nor to be dismissed as being 'just stories', i.e. untrue. More than anything, in my experience, they give one a feeling for the truth; and perhaps this is as good a description of faith as any.

That's what appeals to the idealist in me. More pragmatically, I have faith in my friends, whose courage, honesty, and kindness encourage me every day of my life. (In being able to say this, I know I must have changed at least in some respects, remembering the lonely, miserable being I was on that first retreat.) And I have faith in my teacher Sangharakshita, whose teachings I have come to trust. The great miracle seems to be working for me too.

The visualization practice I chose when I was ordained was that of Vajrasattva, an archetypal Buddha who represents innate purity. He holds a vajra, a symbol of truth, to his heart, and gazes down at it, seeming to say 'Look for the truth in your own heart.' For me he is a symbol of the authenticity, the transparency, that I seek, of my desire for the truth, and this is what I connect with when I think of him. The more of my heart, the more love, I can give to this image of perfection – personified because we can relate more easily to people than to abstract ideas – the more, I believe, the truth can shine through my own life.

II Buddhism and Womanhood

Varasuri

Varasuri was born and raised in New York City. She has been a student of Buddhism since the mid-1970s and has practised meditation for over twenty years. Since 1987, Varasuri has helped to establish FWBO centres in the San Francisco Bay area and in Missoula, Montana. She was ordained in 1995. Varasuri is married and has two sons, aged 16 and 9. Currently living in Missoula, Montana, she divides her time between Dharma activities, family, and part-time work as a nutritionist.

Varasuri

From Womanhood to Buddhahood

One Woman's Struggle with Buddhist Views of Women

MY FIRST ENCOUNTER with Buddhism was as a teenager, through the strong filter of my beatnik-communist-poet brother who turned me on to the Dharma via Jack Kerouac, Alan Watts, and D.T. Suzuki. I had the impression at that young age that Buddhism was about sitting cross-legged watching your breath through a haze of either pot or Jack Daniel's. In Nepal in the late sixties I got a very different taste of Buddhism in everyday Asian life: pujas in the forest with kids and pigs running around, chanting and incense at local funerals, but most of all the inter-mittent stream of Tibetan refugees coming down from the Himalayas, with brilliantly grinning white teeth beneath tired, worn faces. I was struck by their ability to find joy in the midst of such adversity, and their energetic perseverance in just getting right down to making a new life for themselves. Somewhere between these two extremes I had yet to find out what it would actually mean for me to practice the Dharma.

It wasn't until several years later, encountering the fierce silence and unremitting sitting practice of Zen, that I experienced the power of meditation for myself. And I thought that was what Buddhism was about: individual practice and growth; like psychotherapy, only better. Meeting the FWBO changed all that. I started doing the Metta Bhavana practice,[25] and slowly began to see that spiritual friendship meant much more than meditating together, that it was possible to do serious practice as a non-monastic, that I could study Buddhist texts and books with like-minded folks and talk openly about my questions and concerns. I felt I'd found a context for practice that was far more comprehensive than I'd imagined possible.

Then the inevitable disillusionment hit. I'd always in the past experienced some kind of serious shortcoming or hypocrisy in the avenues of personal growth I'd tried (Christianity, TM, psychotherapy, sexual experimentation, psychedelic drugs). Was Buddhism too, going to let me down? In the FWBO it was the attitudes to women: women being 'disadvantaged' in the spiritual life, having less 'spiritual aptitude' than men,[26] being tied to the 'lower evolution' by their biological drive to be mothers.[27] This smacked too much of the misogynist views that I'd struggled against in my life.

I couldn't just accept the edict that women are automatically at some disadvantage simply because they are women. I wasn't about to sit by and let men – and even some women – tell me, once again, how I couldn't do something because I didn't have a Y-chromosome. And I heard enough other women also questioning this idea or, even worse, discounting the Dharma because of it, that I felt obliged in some way to speak my mind for them as well. So, writing this chapter is a means of working through this issue for myself and hopefully also helping some other women and men find some clarity around it. I don't intend it to be a definitive statement of Buddhist views on women, but rather my own attempt to explore and understand this complex issue.

My focus will be to examine women's conditioning and how it affects the challenge of spiritual development. This is a useful and important exercise for several reasons. Firstly, it's not as if someone in the FWBO invented the idea of 'women's disadvantage'; it is a view that appears repeatedly in Buddhism, especially in early Buddhist texts.[28] We may choose to ignore this, or explain it away as a product of ancient Indian culture, or we may look it in the face and see if there is some underlying meaning to it. I feel it is important to consider what in our conditioning as women may be contributing to our reputed disadvantage, and to evaluate for ourselves whether or not these factors are making it more difficult for us to pursue our spiritual aspirations. The Buddha himself has advised us not just to blindly accept traditional teachings, but to put them to the test: 'Being adopted and put into effect, do they lead to welfare and happiness, or do they not, or how does it appear to you…?'[29] Secondly, although each person's matrix of conditioning will be unique, we as women share some aspects of conditioning, so that we can work together on overcoming what may hold us back in our spiritual practice. And finally, looking at our common conditioning as women can be a springboard for each of us to explore our individual conditioning more closely.

My primary intention here is to examine what may hold us, as women, back from pursuing the spiritual life with more vigor, initiative, and commitment. In concentrating my discussion on women, I am by no means implying that men do not have sexual and gender conditioning of their own that can also present hindrances to the spiritual life. I am focusing on the difficulties women may face because I can speak more accurately from my own experience as a woman.

* * *

I am standing alone on the top of a high mesa, overlooking the vast expanse of desert extending out in all directions below. There are rocks all around me, sheltering a group of vultures. I see that they are mother vultures, caring for their young in nests scattered about between the rocks. One of them is standing at the edge of the mesa, the wind blowing her feathers, waiting. She looks me in the eye, patiently waiting. Finally, I walk over and climb on her huge back. Immediately, she takes off in flight. The sudden swoop of air all around takes my breath away. I hang on to her back, feel the powerful muscles that pump her wings. As we soar high over the desert, my fear slowly melts away and I feel the sheer joy of what it means to fly in the endless expanse of sky. And then, just as I let myself go into the pleasure of flight, I find I am the vulture. I can feel the powerful muscles of my own wings moving rhythmically and then subtly adjusting to the wind currents as I soar through space, over the desert, the quiet emptiness ... until I feel the air turn cool and moist, and look to see an oasis below, beautiful green palm trees and water. Down I fly into the oasis, and land by a pool of the most beautiful, clear, sparkling water I've ever seen. Just gazing at it makes me feel at peace. Slowly, I bend down to drink the refreshing cool water. As I raise my head I am transformed into a Buddha sitting beside the pond, beneath a palm tree.

This was a dream ... a dream from about twenty years ago.

Buddhism is about transformation. It is not simply about becoming a happier, more ethical human being, although that is a big part of our task. The Buddha encourages us to set our sights even higher, to look towards a transformation so profound that it frees us from the bonds of craving, ill-will, and delusion, those negative mental states that perpetuate our experience of life as suffering.[30]

This process of transformation and liberation has been expressed in different ways. We may choose to see it in developmental terms – as eradicating the negative tendencies characteristic of ordinary human consciousness and developing more skillful mental states based in transcendental insight – or we may prefer the language of disclosure, which describes the spiritual life as a process of awakening to our essential Buddha-nature, our potential to be enlightened beings. In either case, the path of Buddhist practice will change us, and we will often experience this change as uncomfortable. Therefore, before we reach the point of liberation, transformation requires some effort on our part. In this respect, Buddhist practice is not for the faint of heart. It demands vigor, energy, perseverance, and fearlessness, particularly in the early stages of the spiritual path when the pull of our past habits most strongly holds us back.

The Buddhist path is rarely a smooth journey of straightforward progress; we do not always proceed in a satisfying, linear sequence of predictable steps, nor do the layers of negativity easily drop away. The dynamic of spiritual growth is that whenever one takes a step forward, whenever one experiences a breakthrough, there seems to arise some resistance to moving forward, to changing the *status quo*. Parts of ourselves hang back, indeed drag back. It is this pattern of resistance coming on the heels of breakthrough that is characteristic of our conditioning working against our efforts at spiritual transformation.

In my early days as a Buddhist practitioner, resistance most often surfaced as doubt in my own ability to practice or in the efficacy of the path. A few years later, although I had developed a stronger faith in the practice, resistance came, ironically, whenever I felt some progress in meditation. I tended to become emotionally volatile, irritable, and angry, which was disheartening until I realized what was going on – that meditation was sensitizing me to my emotions and putting me more in touch with a source of as yet unintegrated energy. It was only when I started to do twice as much Metta Bhavana practice that this began to improve. In more recent times, I have been much more able to sustain a positive mental state and have been amazed at how much energy that leaves at my disposal. Resistance doesn't come up as often, at least not so blatantly. Now, I must be vigilant to notice its more subtle manifestations, for example, my tendency to react to difficulties by withdrawing into defensive isolation rather than seeking the advice of spiritual friends. The more conscious we are of this process of resistance and change the more we can cope with the vicissitudes of personal growth. And part of this process is the struggle to gain a more objective perspective on our conditioning.

What is Conditioning?

Born in 1947, I was on the early edge of the post-World War II baby boom. I grew up in the lower middle-class neighborhoods of Brooklyn and Queens in New York City. My mother was from rural Tennessee, a sensitive, caring woman with an easygoing attitude to child rearing and house cleaning, and a strong but very private spiritual inclination. My father was the product of immigrants from Finland who met on Ellis Island in the 1900s. A typical Finn, he was aloof in his expressions of affection, but nevertheless devoted and hard-working, and he instilled in his children a love of the outdoors. His limited accountant's income didn't go very far in providing luxuries for a family of six kids. But I remember being a happy child with an active imagination, playing the rough and tumble games of the city streets back in a time when simplicity and some innocence could still prevail in our young lives in the concrete jungle. It was this modest setting – one secure in love if lacking in amenities – that molded my early character.

By nature shy and introspective, I came to be painfully intimidated by the intensity of the 'City', and – once I became aware of the larger world, that New York wasn't all there was – I longed for vast open spaces, quiet vistas with no people around, dreamed of living in Arizona and riding a horse across the open deserts. This frustrated ambition found some expression in art, the haunting forms and intense reds of the South-west arousing some as yet untapped passions. At the same time, as I got older, the harsh realities of my parents' struggles to provide for a large family were impressed on me, and I became aware of the need to make my own way in the world. My father had instilled in us – by his example more than anything else – a strong work ethic, which was impressed on the girls as much as the boys. My artistic propensities seemed frivolous and weren't encouraged as a reasonable way to make a living.

At the same time I became intensely aware of a deep spiritual energy that was no longer satisfied by the hypocrisy and platitudes of the church. I was immensely fortunate in that the Christian youth counselor at Queens College, a trusted family friend, encouraged my persistent tendency to question orthodox Lutheranism and guided me along as I left the church. Otherwise I might have cynically lost my spiritual aspirations as well. My older brother, by the age of 18 a confirmed communist and well on his way to becoming an alcoholic, introduced me to the intriguing thought of the Far East, mixed with the heretical ideas of Nietzsche and Trotsky. We had talks long into the night over beer and cigarettes. The backdrop for all this was the tense reality of the Vietnam war which, at the time, looked like it would go on indefinitely. My two oldest brothers and many young men I knew were struggling with the incessant threat and moral dilemma of the draft. It thrust us, as a generation, into an awareness of the US as a hawkish bully and ourselves as participants in a war that had escalated out of control. The idealism spawned by Kennedy's Camelot had given way to an angry cynicism engendered by the deceptive politics of Johnson and, later, Nixon. It was suddenly time to grow up. At 21, I left home to join the Peace Corps in Nepal.

These are just some of the conditions that have shaped who I am now. Conditionality, in Buddhism, is the principle that all things arise solely in dependence on conditions. Each individual is the product of a unique mix of conditions, and this mix is continuously reconfigured by new experiences and inputs. An individual's 'conditioning' arises from their previous experience, from the particular factors, events, and circumstances (i.e. the conditions) to which they have been exposed. But conditioning is more than just the social factors like economic status and home environment that influence us. Buddhism recognizes that the qualities one is born with – one's genetic tendencies and personality traits, indeed one's very physical form (human, animal, etc.) – are also part of one's conditioning. How one has lived in past lives will influence the circumstances into which one is born in this life.

Conditioning does not predetermine our actions but it does have a very strong influence on our behavior, thought patterns, and emotional responses. We are not totally predictable, but the way we tend to act and think is strongly influenced by how we have acted and thought in the past. Thus, conditioning may be understood as the habitual tendencies one has to act, and even to think, in certain ways, based on the conditions that have prevailed in one's life up to the present.

Hand in hand with conditionality is the concept of impermanence. Buddhism also asserts that all conditioned things are subject to change. Nothing is carved in stone. Our conditioning may constrain us, but it does not bind us. We are not just passive recipients of our conditioning; we can influence it through choice. Just as certain conditions have put us where we are, so we can create new conditions to change where we are. Thus, our conditioning is not static, but rather the result of a dynamic, constantly changing, interactive process. We can always influence the course of our lives through conscious choice and applied effort. Therein lies our infinite potential to change, to transform ourselves and our world.

In order to do this, it is essential to understand the events, people, and circumstances that have shaped one's life in the past, particularly one's early life, because those factors that have influenced us at an impressionable age are often the most tenacious. Conditioning often operates at an unconscious level, and sometimes it is difficult to gain the perspective to see it objectively and evaluate its effect on us. Often it is only in retrospect that the powerful effects of our conditioning become apparent.

Thus, one's conditioning is complex and often deeply ingrained. While there are aspects of our conditioning that are positive, that can propel us forward on the spiritual path, and while it is important to acknowledge these and cultivate them, the more difficult task is that of overcoming whatever conditioning holds us back. And there is much in our conditioning that ties us down, holds us back from committing ourselves to a spiritual path. It is only by clarifying for ourselves what these factors are that we can begin the arduous, adventurous, and ultimately joyful task of transforming ourselves.

Human Conditioning

It is 1984. I am in South Carolina at Thanksgiving visiting my mother and youngest brother, Larry. They have a very close relationship, as is often common for the youngest child and a widowed parent. Larry has gone through a difficult time, having married and separated from his wife in the short span of six months. I talk with him about his concerns for his child shortly due to be born and his desire to be a part of the baby's life.

When I leave to go home, I hug him close, tasting the salt on his cheek as I kiss him goodbye. By Christmas, he is back with his wife and new daughter, sounding cheerful and content. I wish him a happy new year. It is a clear, warm afternoon in April when I get a phone call from my aunt saying that Larry has been killed in a car accident. Four months later, my mother too is dead, of a grief that she could express in no other way.

The fragility and brevity of human life hits us hard sometimes because most of the time we try to avoid thinking about just how tenuous our grip on life is. When the reality of it was thrust on me, it became a spur to take my spiritual practice more seriously.

The most basic aspect of our conditioning is that of being in a human form. We are all subject to the condition of having a body. Whatever the reproductive role of one's body, we all share the common distractions of having a body with its sometimes intense physical cravings (hunger, thirst, sex, sleep), and its potential to experience sensual pleasure and pain. Along with having taken a human form and consciousness goes the propensity to think dualistically (in terms of subject and object, good and bad, emotion and reason, etc.) and to act out of self-referential needs based in greed, ill-will, and delusion. Aside from these shared characteristics, each of us has highly variable physical and mental aptitudes and handicaps.

Buddhism has specified the components of a human being variously as the five *skandhas* (form, feeling, perception, volition, and consciousness), the six elements (earth, water, fire, air, space, and consciousness), and the six senses (sight, hearing, smell, taste, touch, and mental functioning). Thus, mind (or consciousness) and body are intimately connected and interdependent. We experience ourselves as a body–mind, and invest our identity in the particular body–mind conjunction we presently experience. We find it hard to acknowledge that this particular body–mind identified as 'I' will someday cease to exist. But in Buddhist thought there is no fixed entity that can be labeled 'I'. One is constantly changing, one's stream of karma[31] is in constant flux, so it is impossible to pin down a static self or soul, an essential 'me'. At the same time, certain deeply habituated and largely unconscious karmic tendencies persist from one embodiment to the next through the process of rebirth, to have an impact on the particular physical manifestation taken in the next life.

Buddhism does not say that our bodies ultimately determine who we are. Biology is not destiny. It is not the body *per se* that gets in the way of Enlightenment, but rather the tendency to cling to the illusion of the permanence of the body and its attendant consciousness. One's attachment to and identification with one's body–mind act as a kind of thick veil obscuring one's ability to gain Insight into the true nature of Reality.[32] This is because it is such a strong tie to the physical, mundane, conditioned world. Having a body is, in itself, a habit. When we die we are suddenly without a body, confronted as it were with the Reality of unbounded consciousness. We can't stand it. Immediately our stream of karmic energy is drawn to manifest in another body. It is only when we are less attached to the idea of ourselves as separate inherent entities, isolated by the physical boundaries of an individual body and mind, that we can begin to experience that which is unconditioned, which goes beyond our delusion of a separate self. Attachment to one's body and mind is so strong that it cannot be transcended by conceptual thought alone. For this reason, there are specific meditation practices to break down the identification with and attachment to the body and its constituent parts or elements.

But all is not bleak. Having a human form is also seen in Buddhism as being very propitious. We are told that each of us has a 'precious human body',[33] that being born as a human is a tremendous opportunity for spiritual development. 'This human body, which presents a unique occasion and effects the right juncture, has the power to reject evil and to accomplish good, to cross the ocean of Samsara, to follow the path towards Enlightenment and to obtain perfect Buddhahood.'[34]

Buddhism recognizes that, as humans, we all have the potential for Enlightenment. Indeed, Buddhism says this potential is shared by all sentient beings, whether presently in a human form or not.[35] This potential for Enlightenment can also be seen as part of our conditioning. It's not that we work at 'getting' Enlightened; Enlightenment is not something to be gotten. What we work at is setting up the right conditions for Enlightenment to arise in us.

The advantage we have as humans is seen to lie in our particular combination of both reflexive self-awareness and the ability to experience suffering in the sense of *duhkha*.[36] We may not think of experiencing suffering as an advantage, but it is this which most often gives us our initial motivation for seeking a spiritual alternative. It is only when we can acknowledge, even provisionally, that conditioned existence is inherently unsatisfactory, insubstantial, and impermanent that we can begin to tread the path.[37]

But, just as it is not inevitable that our past conditioning will determine what we do, so it is not inevitable that we will become Enlightened without some effort on our part. It is up to us. It is only we who can deny ourselves Enlightenment. Although we all have the potential for Enlightenment, we do not all have the same aptitude or capacity to move towards it in a given lifetime. Our differences lie in our individual conditioning. While each of us brings certain strengths and assets to the spiritual life, we each also face certain handicaps in pursuing Enlightenment. These individual proclivities have a tremendous impact on how well one is able to take on the challenge of the Dharma. This is not to say that one has a fixed quantum of spiritual aptitude, but rather that one's aptitude is a product of many factors, that it varies from one person to another, and that it can even change from one stage of life to another.

It is this combination of negative propensities and positive potential associated with having a human body and mind that constitutes our human psycho-physiological conditioning. We have an obligation, therefore, to take care of our bodies, to cultivate our minds, to respect them as the vehicles through which we act in the world. Our responsibility as Buddhists lies in making the best use of the advantage we have in being human. Only then will we be able to work towards realizing our full potential, which is to transcend the delusion of being a separate self and thereby become an agent for compassion in the world.

> *May I become an inexhaustible treasure*
> *For those who are poor and destitute;*
> *May I turn into all things they could need*
> *And may these be placed close beside them…*
>
> *Just like space*
> *And the great elements such as earth,*
> *May I always support the life*
> *Of all the boundless creatures.*
>
> *And until they pass away from pain*
> *May I also be the source of life*
> *For all the realms of varied beings*
> *That reach unto the ends of space.*[38]

Sexual and Gender Conditioning

I live with a man who is a paragon of rational thought. There is no way I can 'win' in a debate with him. As a result, I have developed a strong tendency to defer to him in making decisions or even forming many of my opinions, which has whittled away at my confidence. I have only gradually come to realize how I have projected that ability to think and reason on to him and thus failed to develop it in myself. It has taken me many years to discover and cultivate my own competence in this area, and begin to feel that I can hold my own with him.

Sexual conditioning can be seen as a subset of psycho-physiological conditioning. Given that each of us is born with a body–mind, we need to recognize that one of the manifestations of our psycho-physiological conditioning is the sex we take on, which carries with it a certain weight. We need to be aware of both sexual and gender conditioning, and we especially need to make them more conscious so that, to whatever extent they may hinder spiritual development, we can work with them.

I will make the following distinction between sex and gender. The two are commonly equated in the dictionary and in scientific usage, but in feminist discussions the following distinctions are often made, and they are useful here.

Sex: the fact of being either female or male; the biologically determined reproductive function of a person.

Gender: The social identification of a person as woman or man, girl or boy; one's inner sense of being female or male, feminine or masculine.

Sexual conditioning consists of the psychological as well as physiological tendencies that arise as a result of having either a female or a male body, particularly those factors that are specific to the reproductive functioning of the body. Buddhism sees the body and mind as manifestations of the same karmic energy; our sexual conditioning therefore also encompasses those psychological and emotional states that are influenced by our reproductive form and sex hormones. Whereas the physiological aspects are relatively obvious, the psychological component of our sexual conditioning is often a more subtle and variable factor. Examples of sexual conditioning are, in women, the hormonal fluctuations of the menstrual cycle, and their effect on emotions and mental functioning; and in men, the ability to have erections and ejaculate, which can cause them actively to seek out and initiate sexual intercourse. Some examples of the more subtle psychological manifestations of sexual conditioning are women's tendency to be protective of themselves and their children, and men's tendency to be competitive with other men.

Gender conditioning consists of the behavioral and psychological tendencies that result from having been exposed to the particular cultural and social influences and expectations that are specific to one's sex. This varies, of course, depending on the culture and circumstances in which one is born and raised.

The sex we are born with cannot be altered in a given lifetime (with the possible exception of transsexuals, although they don't become biologically functioning members of the opposite sex), and our sexual conditioning is very deeply ingrained because it has a powerful physiological component (i.e. hormonal and instinctual factors) over which we have little conscious control. Gender conditioning, on the other hand, is more variable and, relatively speaking, easier to alter, although it too can be quite resistant to change. But sexual and gender conditioning are intertwined; it is very difficult to isolate and separate out their relative influences, to say which is the dominant factor in a given situation. It is simplistic to say that only one aspect of our conditioning is at work, or even that one aspect overrides the other in all cases.

From a Buddhist perspective, the whole question of nature versus nurture, while it may be useful for understanding the complexities of human sexuality, is something of a red herring. Making the distinction between sexual and gender conditioning is important, but only to the extent that it helps us to clarify what these different aspects of our conditioning are and to understand how tenacious they can be. It is not important to decide – even if we could – which is the dominant influence. The crucial point is not to deny any of it or get stuck in any of it, but to free ourselves from any conditioning that limits the scope of our potential to grow. Only by acknowledging the power both sexual and gender conditioning have in shaping our sense of identity and our role in the world, in polarizing us into female and male domains of influence, can we begin to transcend their influence. Overcoming one's sexual polarization is an essential aspect of spiritual growth. Buddhist practice will have the effect of loosening one's tendency to over-identify with being female or male.

What do we mean by sexual polarization? Our cultural conditioning has prompted us to label certain qualities as 'feminine' or 'masculine', usually because ordinary women and men, respectively, tend to exhibit those traits. Thus, we come to identify certain characteristics as being representative of 'femininity' and 'masculinity', and we are socialized into cultivating the traits specific to our gender, and looking to members of the opposite sex to manifest the others. But for those aspiring to Enlightenment, both the 'feminine' and 'masculine' qualities are essential and must be cultivated. It is only when an individual has begun to integrate all of these aspects that they can make an effective commitment to the spiritual life. So, just as any person needs to foster the so-called 'masculine' qualities of initiative, energy, and risk-taking, likewise the so-called 'feminine' qualities of receptivity, sensitivity, and caring must be valued and cultivated. Regardless of the labels we apply to these attributes, the ideal is to integrate them all. Until we reach that point we must be alert to the tendency to project those unintegrated aspects of ourselves on to others, particularly those of the opposite sex.

Buddhism goes even further, saying that we need not only to integrate all of these attributes, but also to 'perfect' them, i.e. transform them from qualities that are based in ego and self-referential need to ones that enable the individual to transcend self-concern. It is the integration and perfection of the usually polarized feminine and masculine aspects in an individual that bring about the liberation of energy necessary for transformation and insight.

Thus, not only must we guard against projection, but we must also be careful not to make the related error of inflation. This can happen in two ways. One is by confusing the mundane manifestation of these traits – prone as they are to human failing – with the transcendental perfection of qualities like wisdom and compassion. Thus, it would be a misconception to equate the masculine quality of unintegrated energy with the spiritual virtue of *virya* (energy in pursuit of the good). Likewise, the feminine attribute of nurturing should not be elevated to the status of compassion, which has its basis in equanimity.

The other error is to compare the ordinary, conditioned characteristics of human beings with an inflated archetypal notion of either the masculine or the feminine. This particular tendency can be seen in some of today's attempts to undo sexism by demonizing men (as in 'all men are rapists') while inflating the feminine (as in 'the sacred feminine'). This is an unfortunate reaction to what was a common trend in the past, that is, to demean women (as in the view that women should not be in positions of power because they are ruled by their hormones) and reify the masculine (as in sanctioning violence by spiritualizing masculine aggression, as was done in the Crusades). Either exaggeration exacerbates the tendency to see the 'feminine' and 'masculine' as polarized opposites rather than complementary aspects of the integrated individual.

The major challenge in all of this is to deal with the resistances that arise when we attempt to contact and integrate those untapped, polarized opposites in ourselves. As women, a large part of our psychological and spiritual work is to discover and reclaim those aspects of ourselves which we have projected on to men, which we have essentially 'given away' to men. In particular, we need to cultivate those 'masculine' attributes which may lie dormant, obscured by our female conditioning. Clearly, men will have a complementary task.

Women's Conditioning

The arrival of my first period hit me like a ton of bricks, at the age of 11. My mom had explained it all to me before, but when I saw that first bloodstain, I was convinced it was divine retribution for all the masturbation I'd done in secret. It was only when my mother responded with pleased surprise that I relaxed. Immediately, I went out and told every girl in the neighborhood, which caused quite an unpleasant ruckus and quickly ended my career as a sex educator.

As puberty struck, I was suddenly confronted with having to protect myself because I was a girl, having to hold my purse tight to my side, avoid looking people, especially men, in the eye and, on a more subtle level, to be suspicious of strangers. Sex was something hidden, not to be talked about; so why did men insist on feeling me up on the subway? This shattering of innocence was difficult to take. I was a serious student, immersed myself in studies and relished the achievement of being at the top of my class in math and physics, even if it meant that the cute boys with cars were too intimidated to ask me out. My high school guidance counselor, when I asked her earnestly about pre-med programs, insisted that I apply instead to nursing school, because once I had babies I would lose interest in medicine and have wasted my time aspiring to be a doctor. Fortunately I had the sense to ignore her.

The sexual and gender conditioning we have as women is different from that of men. This should be obvious, if in no other way than our capacity to bear children, which is certainly not inconsequential, especially if we do indeed become mothers. And we cannot ignore the fact – as much as we might like it not to be the case – that girls and boys are socialized differently. Even if we try to minimize sexist conditioning in our children, they still get a certain amount of it from the ambient culture.

So, what is distinctive about our sexual and gender conditioning as females? This is not exactly the same for all women and will obviously vary with the stage of life. Recognizing that it is difficult to truly separate the effects of the biological (sexual) and social (gender) aspects of conditioning, we can nevertheless enumerate those aspects. First, the sexual aspects, which include but may not be restricted to the following:

Sexual Aspects of Women's Conditioning:

1. Sexual drive or libido, which arises in both sexes at puberty; women's sexual drive may be expressed quite differently from men's.

2. The ability to bear children – and the urge to do so. Under this general heading, we can include monthly hormonal fluctuations and associated menstrual cycles, the capacity for pregnancy and breast-feeding, the instinctive urge to care for infants, and menopause.

3. Relatively smaller size and physical strength of most women compared to most men. This is largely a result of sex hormones. One's size and strength can have a powerful impact on one's self-image and conception of what one is capable of both physically and psychologically.

4. Relatively longer lifespan of most women compared to most men, which is also influenced by sex hormones.

Whereas sex drive, physical size, and lifespan are variables which are present in both sexes – albeit manifested differently in each sex – the ability (and the urge) to bear children is a significant aspect of sexuality that is unique to women, and therefore requires special consideration as a factor in our sexual conditioning.

Many (though not all) women intermittently experience very powerful urges to have a baby. This makes sense from a strictly procreative point of view, because a desire to have children will help to perpetuate the species. In addition, the psychological and emotional bond between mother and child is usually extremely powerful. I would venture to say it is the strongest bond that can be experienced between two ordinary human beings. This is not to minimize the power of the father–child bond nor that of very deep friendship, but the mother does seem to have a more visceral attachment to her child, especially as an infant. It is an aspect of motherhood that is not often emphasized, and when I encountered it immediately after the birth of my first son it was quite sobering; it almost felt as if I no longer had an entirely separate consciousness, but now shared it with this other human being.

Even if we do not become mothers, we still experience monthly hormonal cycles and menopause. Some women experience very distracting and painful PMS symptoms, mood swings, painful menstruation, or major menopausal changes. These may also contribute to tendencies, reinforced by some gender conditioning, to be too preoccupied with our bodies, or restrict our viewpoint to self-centered concerns. Whether or not these factors affect our engagement in work or other activities depends on how we deal with them.

As humans, we are not purely instinctual animals; we are not at the complete mercy of our reproductive function. But we do need to be conscious of the power of its influence – otherwise the biological imperative can just take over. The sexual and procreative drives (in both sexes) are extremely potent and have a strong momentum. Like many other aspects of our conditioning, they can compel us to act at an unconscious level. So if we want to modify or minimize their influence, we will need to make great conscious effort.

Gender or Social Aspects of Women's Conditioning:
Gender conditioning encompasses the often complex socialization we undergo based on our reproductive role; this is highly variable, being dependent on one's country of birth, family configuration, economics, educational opportunity, and numerous other factors. Attitudes towards what it is appropriate for women to do and what we are capable of may influence a woman's self-image and confidence, not to mention her critical life decisions.

Women's social conditioning has undergone enormous changes in the last century, particularly in the West in the last fifty years under the positive influence of the women's liberation movement. Changing social values and the availability of reliable birth control mean that many women are no longer so tied to inevitable and numerous pregnancies or relegated to taking on the exclusive role of child rearing. Yet, despite contemporary trends to share the tasks of parenting, mothers still tend to do most of child care and housework.[39] Without minimizing the genuine joys of motherhood, the demands on a mother's time and energy, particularly in the first few years of a child's life, are considerable. The upshot is that, both biologically and socially, women have a disproportionate share of the procreative responsibility, even in the modern West.

Even if they choose not to become wives or mothers, women can still be frustrated in pursuing their individual development because of gender conditioning. Throughout human history women have had – and often continue to have – restrictions placed on them because of fixed views about women's capabilities, views which may be held as tightly by women as by men. It is when these views become fixed that they especially present a problem. It may be the case that certain aspects of women's conditioning are disadvantageous, but as I have said, biology is not destiny; each of us has the potential to transcend all limitations. When views about women's capabilities ossify into culturally sanctioned restrictions, we may be, for example, shut out of educational, work, or other opportunities. When these views are internalized and taken on as part of our identity, we may experience a lack of confidence in our ability to do certain things or a tendency to defer too much to men's opinions. Women in many parts of the world still struggle to gain political, economic, and legal equality with men. While women in the contemporary West have made significant gains on this front, it is important to continue working to overcome any internalized self-limiting attitudes.

I am not saying that women have been or are universally oppressed by all men, or that men have not also experienced social restraints or role expectations because of their sex; but where women do experience social restrictions because of their sexual role, these can present them with a relatively greater handicap in pursuing their individual development and having an influence on the larger world.

The women's movement attempted to redress the errors of past generations which limited women to their reproductive function. However, in doing so, the result – as is common in any revolution – was that some women went to the other extreme, blaming all of women's woes on their gender conditioning and oppression by men. As with any revolutionary trend, this reactivity itself needs eventually to be corrected. We cannot assume that the decline in gender bias means that our sexual conditioning is erased.

Women often have stronger sexual and gender conditioning than men because of our greater reproductive role and our socialization to identify with that role. This can, in turn, limit our vision of what we can do. Even if we stretch ourselves beyond those limitations, our perceived ability to change may still be circumscribed by our conditioning. Thus, both sexual and gender conditioning present significant challenges to women. In a sense we have to dig even deeper into ourselves than most men do to find the strength and determination to pursue the spiritual life or, indeed, any creative endeavor. But, in acknowledging this, let us not fall prey to self-righteous victimization, a trap that can in itself hold us back. Rather let us move on from where we find ourselves. That is, after all, the point of the Dharma as a practice.

Women's Conditioning and the Spiritual Life

Many years ago I was on a women's retreat. Someone suggested thinking about what your response would be if you could walk through the door of the room you were in and become instantly enlightened. Would you do it? If not, what would hold you back? My immediate and almost visceral response was that I couldn't do it because I was a mother with small children. I was quite taken aback by the strength of my reply. What is it about being a mother that holds me back? I have reflected on this question repeatedly over the years, and have come to see that my primary concern arises out of the realization that Enlightenment would mean a complete change – indeed, a 'turning about in the deepest seat of consciousness'.[40] I have so little conception of what that really means, of who 'I' would be on the other side of that door, that I couldn't be sure that I would be there in the same way for my kids. Although I know I have made some significant progress in my spiritual development since then, I still feel at some basic level that I will not be able to completely throw myself into the spiritual life until my boys are off on their own. But, then, if that wasn't there as an excuse, would I just find another one?

Buddhism, as we have seen, considers women to be, comparatively speaking, at a disadvantage in undertaking the spiritual life. Both our sexual and gender conditioning can be seen as factors in determining this disadvantage. Sangharakshita, founder of the FWBO, has expanded on this traditional view based on his experience of his female disciples. 'Sangharakshita … follows Buddhist tradition in regarding women generally as at somewhat of a disadvantage, at least at the commencement of spiritual life. He has however also said that, once men and women have actually committed themselves to the path, differences in this respect become less and less,' and he emphasizes that 'One must take each individual, woman or man, as one finds them, acknowledging and encouraging whatever spiritual aspiration they may have.'[41]

So, while we cannot just ignore what Buddhism has to say about women, we can see it in a more encouraging light than it is often seen. The crucial element, according to Sangharakshita, is reaching the point where one's Going for Refuge to the Buddha, Dharma, and Sangha is effectively the center of one's life. It is getting ourselves to that point that presents the challenge: it requires a heroic effort for most of us to resist the gravitational pull of our negative tendencies and old habits.

As with any conditioning, the strength of women's conditioning lies primarily in the degree to which we invest our identity in it. If we are too attached to being female in the sense of identifying too rigidly with our sexual conditioning, with the sex-specific roles of woman as sexual mate and mother, it will be harder to move beyond that exclusive identification and integrate our 'masculine' side. In order to become a fully integrated individual, one needs to evolve beyond fixed self-views, to experience oneself in a broader plane that encompasses one's full potential. Buddhism holds that being a man is a relative spiritual advantage primarily because men tend to manifest more of the so-called 'masculine' qualities of initiative and risk-taking that are especially critical in the early stages of the spiritual path, when we need to break through the inertia of our conditioning.

This does not mean that women are inferior to men, spiritually or otherwise, and should not be taken this way. Being male is not, in itself, a guarantee of greater spiritual aptitude, nor does it assure spiritual progress. At least in the context of this life, the point is not for a woman to become a man, but for her to become an integrated human being. Individual conditioning, based as it is in individual karmic propensities, goes well beyond sex and gender. Even the most favorable conditions may be squandered. And often seemingly unsupportive conditions can be the spur that propels one on to the path. It depends on what we do with the conditions we have.

This is borne out by Buddhist texts. Despite the frequent messages about women's disadvantage, there is also the pervasive view that women have the same potential for Enlightenment as men, and that the path toward Enlightenment is the same for women and men.

> *And be it woman or be it man for whom*
> *Such chariot doth wait, by that same car*
> *Into Nirvana's presence shall they come.*[42]

It is important not to underestimate the significance of this view, or its radical, politically incorrect perspective at the time of the Buddha. In essence it means that, no matter what difficulties an individual woman or man faces, they can be overcome. It is a view that presents us not just with encouragement but with a challenge. If we are serious Buddhist practitioners, *all* of our conditioning must be examined from a critical perspective and put to the test: does it reinforce our human tendency to get caught in craving, ill-will, and delusion, or does it conduce to progress towards Enlightenment?

So, what is the challenge we, as women, face? It is important to be clear on this. We do not have to deny our womanhood in order to practice Buddhism. Nor do we need to become celibate or renounce motherhood, although many individuals have found these to be powerfully creative choices. But we should carefully consider alternatives to what we have been expected to do, or expect ourselves to do. We need critically to examine our expectations, assumptions, and conditioning. This is not a simple task, and it can be easy to delude ourselves; it is often helpful to undertake this examination in the company of spiritual friends.

We may possess many positive attributes arising out of our female conditioning – qualities such as patience, perseverance, receptivity, and sensitivity – that can help us along the spiritual path. By cultivating these qualities in ourselves within a spiritual context, we enhance our confidence that we can develop qualities that are less typically female, and may present more of a challenge. Although we may indeed bring many strengths to bear on our spiritual practice, it is more important to put our efforts into working with those elements of our conditioning that present obstacles to our progress. While some of our conditioning as women can hold us back, none of it has to.

Motherhood has a big impact on one's life, including one's spiritual practice. That is covered elsewhere in this book, so I won't discuss it further here. But apart from the consideration of child-bearing, there are many aspects of our sexual and gender conditioning that have a potential impact on our spiritual progress. I will look at a few of these, choosing ones that I have experienced in my life or observed in the lives of women

I have known. There may well be different factors that are more important for other women.

It is common for women to experience monthly pain or mood changes that get in the way of, for example, maintaining a daily meditation practice. If this is a problem one should be careful to avoid over-indulging oneself unnecessarily, or inflating these problems in a neurotic way. It is also possible to use physical discomfort as a point of practice in itself, for example, as an opportunity to reflect on the fragility and impermanence of the body. I am not suggesting this as an abstract ideal, but I have struggled with and been able successfully to work with physical pain this way myself.

Many of us have been socially conditioned (although this has begun to change in my lifetime) to think that a woman is not fulfilled unless she has children and a husband, that we are defined by and identified with our bodies, that the socially sanctioned body image is the only one that is acceptable and determines our self-acceptance, self-esteem, and overall value. And there are more subtle things, like being afraid to walk alone in the world out of fear of sexual assault (which often isn't an unfounded fear), and being afraid to take on tasks that require being critical of others, dealing with situations of conflict, or being in a position of power over men. Many younger women raised in the modern West are not as socially conditioned in these ways – which could make it easier for younger women to underestimate the potent and often unconscious pull of their sexual conditioning.

After much reflection, I have come to identify three main areas of conditioning that can hold women back from undertaking a more committed spiritual life. One is the tendency to limit our view of the world, to see our potential influence on the world as limited to a narrow range, usually the home. This is often a strong element in our gender conditioning, but women's sexual programming to create a protective environment for their children can also play a part here. Even if one is not living in a family situation, this conditioning may still cramp one's vision. We may find ourselves trying to recreate a sense of 'family' – in the negative sense of an ingrown, exclusive, and co-dependent group – within our circle of friends, trying to make things cozy and nice, trying to avoid conflict and smooth things over when interpersonal difficulties do arise, and avoiding those bigger responsibilities that the men so readily take on.

Another aspect of our conditioning as women – which is related to the tendency to keep our focus too narrow – is that we may tend to view the world too much through our subjective, feeling aspect, and give our feelings too much weight in our decisions. We need to be able to acknow-ledge our emotions and make decisions using all of our awareness (conceptual, rational, and emotional), but in order to be skillful our actions need to be based on more than just self-referential needs. Acting from metta means moving beyond personal likes and dislikes. To do this effectively, one has to work at transcending one's subjective feelings, especially when they get in the way of one's ability to see the objective needs of a situation and act accordingly. If, for example, one consistently avoids taking on a certain activity because one 'doesn't feel like it' or 'doesn't feel capable of it' one will never stretch oneself to the point of being able to take it on in an effective way.

A third area around which women frequently have some strong con-ditioning is that of conflict resolution. In this respect women and men are often acculturated in opposing ways. When faced with a conflict of interest or opinion, men will often take a position of confrontation and competitiveness, whereas women more frequently err in the direction of avoidance and denial. Along with this may be the inclination to defer to men, to be afraid to put forward or even value our own ideas. Women are usually strongly conditioned to see disagreement as disharmony. We tend to get quite anxious whenever there is any friction between people, and all too often this means that we find ourselves trying to placate and pacify in situations where a disparity of views is inevitable and even appropriate. Controversy can exist without ill-will. Two people can be in disagreement over some issue and still relate to each other from a position of metta. But being able to engage in vigorous debate over differing views while maintaining an attitude of loving-kindness is not easy; it is a skill that needs cultivation. We can only learn it by doing it.

These three factors may present a handicap in the spiritual life in several ways. They may make us hesitant to take on roles of leadership and mentorship or even in-depth friendship that challenges our fixed views. They may thwart our attempts at creativity which take us beyond what is comfortable and familiar. And they may limit our ability to develop the vision and imagination to think beyond our personal situ-ation and immediate concerns.

Breaking Through our Conditioning

I have worked off and on for a couple of years on writing about this topic. Daring to put some of my thinking on paper has brought a mix of responses, both appreciation and criticism. My initial reaction to criticism was to withdraw. But when I did start to pull back, it struck me that this was an old habit, my old, conditioned response to attack or fear of attack. It felt constricted; so I experimented. I began to go in deeper, to take on the criticisms and try to be more objective about them. I found that some were valid and helped me to clarify my thinking, while others I could just put aside as being unclear. This was immensely liberating. I was able to tap into an energy and confidence I didn't know were there. Since then, I have gone back and forth, struggling with the sense of fear that comes with putting myself on the front lines of controversy, and finding new depths of positivity and creativity when pushing through that fear.

In struggling with my own conditioning, I have come to see that successful change comes only to the extent that I take responsibility for my own growth and development. A talk I heard recently identified three aspects of responsibility in the spiritual life: care, ability, and commitment.[43] We could see these as conditions we can cultivate in ourselves which help to liberate us from the bonds of our more negative tendencies.

Care: Women tend to be conditioned as the primary care-givers of children, family, the sick, and the elderly. This is, of course, not a bad capacity to develop, and has the potential to develop into a more broadly-based compassion. But if the focus of one's caring is too narrow, centered on just a few people, one is in danger of over-investing in those relationships. And if one's caring is not reciprocated in some way, this can lead to feelings of martyrdom or resentfulness. The best way to avoid this is to broaden the scope of our caring and extend the circle of one's intimacy, taking the intensity of love we may feel for children or sexual partner and moving it out beyond those narrow focuses. Of course, one of the best ways to practice doing this is through the Metta Bhavana meditation, which enables us to transform our dependence on exclusive erotic love into the freedom of boundless metta, to expand our motherly love for our children into a more inclusive compassion and love for all sentient beings. At the same time, it is important to do whatever psychological work is necessary to break down any tendency to neurotic dependence in relationships.

Ability: Here we have to strive for a balance between taking on what we are able to do and stretching ourselves to enter new fields of action. I think we tend to err in the direction of not challenging ourselves, sticking to the familiar, even discouraging each other from taking on new endeavors. Of course we need to use our energy carefully and not overtax ourselves. But creativity means taking risks. It means being willing to bear criticism. It means sometimes diving in at the deep end. Then we may find we have more ability, more skill, more energy than we'd thought.

Very closely connected with ability is confidence. We need both to value our strong qualities and to develop those that we find more difficult to access and express. Living and working with other women can enhance this process, allowing us to experience ourselves in a context that is hopefully not so bound by gender roles, one in which we can find our own pace and style in exploring creativity and leadership in conditions that are not determined by men. We can see – through the good example of more spiritually developed and psychologically mature women – how to express spiritual commitment as integrated individuals. I think that the lack of sufficient female role models has been a crucial and much overlooked factor in why women have not, until recently, taken a very active role in the spiritual life. Fortunately this is changing, and more and more women are now finding they can pursue the spiritual life in depth. If we see only men as spiritual teachers, it is difficult for us to believe that we can ever do the same. So it is imperative that more women take a lead in teaching and supporting Buddhist groups. Otherwise, we fall back on the conditioning we have as females to let men take the reins. We need to be willing to take the risks and the criticism that inevitably come with positions of responsibility, not back away from these challenges. As each of us moves forward on the spiritual path, we must take the hand of a woman behind us and light the steps ahead. We must not doubt the value of stepping up to the podium, writing our thoughts, leading classes, starting Right Livelihood businesses (or ventures) and Buddhist centers, creating works of art, or simply reaching out in friendship. Other women are waiting to see our example.

Commitment: Sangharakshita has said that 'Commitment to the spiritual life is commitment to the unknown.'[44] I find this provocative and a bit mysterious. I've tended to view commitment as a dedication of oneself to some cause or ideal that one espouses as true, which implies a kind of certainty; or a pledge of loyalty to another person, which implies that one has some knowledge of that person on which to base one's trust. So it is very interesting to me that Sangharakshita has emphasized commitment to what one doesn't know. What is it that we don't know? It is Reality. It is our own potential to be Stream Entrants, Bodhisattvas, Enlightened beings. We cannot know what any of these are as long as we have fixed, conditioned views of ourselves and others. The way I've come to relate this understanding of commitment to my own experience is that it corresponds to how I view the spiritual life at its best: as a commitment to live with insecurity, as a pledge to myself to seek out and stay with the edge of what feels uncomfortable, for it's only there that I have found even a modicum of liberty. This is quite a different view from the one many of us have been conditioned to hold, that is, to seek security in home, family, sexual relationships, work, possessions, to build a 'nest' where we can retreat from the vicissitudes of the world and protect our children from its dangers. The challenge is this: can we commit ourselves to the unknown?

Conclusion

> *What should the woman's nature signify*
> *When consciousness is taut and firmly set,*
> *When knowledge rolleth ever on, when she*
> *By insight rightly comprehends the Dharma?*
>
> *To one for whom the question doth arise:*
> *Am I a woman, or*
> *Am I a man, or what not am I then?*
> *To such a one is Mara fit to talk.*[45]

All of us, women and men alike, have conditioning that can get in the way of spiritual development. The Buddhist path demands energy, effort, and perseverance, a willingness to break out of the boundaries prescribed by our conditioning and take on those challenges of life that make us feel insecure. That is uncomfortable for most of us. We tend to want to make harmony, and this is often at the cost of making discovery. In our efforts to avoid controversy, we also avoid creativity. That said, none of this is anything that we cannot overcome. But it is new territory for a lot of us.

We cannot expect to change spontaneously. Nor can we sit around and wait for inspiration to descend. We have to throw ourselves into the 'crucial situation'[46] and the energy, the confidence, will develop from there.

Until the Dharma has permeated all aspects of one's life, one needs to be vigilant and mindful, unrelenting in one's efforts to overcome the tendency to fall back into comfortable and static old habits, to be seduced back into fixed views and conditioned impulses. But once the tenacious grasp of those negative tendencies has been broken, one's momentum takes a new direction. Freed from the compulsion to grasp at false security, one finds confidence, faith in one's potential. On the basis of that faith arises joy.[47] New conditions have been created. Transformation can now occur. One has taken the first step toward the great unknown of Enlightenment.

Maitreyi

*Idealistic and inspired by collective living and working,
Maitreyi has been involved intensively with team-based Right
Livelihood businesses and residential communities ever since
she first got involved with the FWBO. Initially she worked in a
vegetarian restaurant attached to the London Buddhist
Centre; then a strong interest in body work led her to set up
a massage practice and subsequently to train as an
Alexander Technique teacher. She was a founder member of
Bodywise, a centre for complementary therapies run by a
team of women Buddhists with whom she lived for many
years. Recently she has taken on a new role helping women
prepare for ordination.*

Maitreyi

Feminism and Buddhism

WHEN I FIRST LEARNED to meditate at the London Buddhist Centre in the early eighties my life was in considerable upheaval. I had just turned 30 and had been working for a year at the Women's Aid refuge in Leeds in the north of England. For the six years before that I was actively involved in the women's liberation movement in London. I identified quite strongly as a feminist though I was somewhat confused as to what kind of feminist; it was hard to keep up with the development of the new groupings which so rapidly emerged during the seventies and early eighties. Feminism had given my life a meaning and focus which had been lacking, a structure through which to understand the world and my life up to this point, and many new and creative outlets for action.

I was drawn to working in a Women's Aid refuge because I wanted to make a real contribution to changing women's lives, and to put into practice some of the theory I had learned in years of discussion in consciousness-raising groups and numerous women's conferences and events. However, working in the refuge brought me sharply up against the limitations of some of those theories. It was clear that refuges were much needed. Many women were subject to violence at the hands of their husbands or partners, some severely so. The refuge provided an oasis in which they could find companionship and support, re-evaluate their lives, and eventually be rehoused and begin a new life with their children. For some women this was a lifeline, and they were able to make a fresh start. Others, within weeks of being rehoused, had taken in their partners again and were once more living in an atmosphere of fear and violence.

Faced with these facts, I was forced to question my ideas. Giving women the opportunity to live an independent life was not enough.

There were deeper emotional and psychological issues which a new home and welfare benefits did not address. The lack of real friendship was one, as was the lack of real community. Feminist theories, to the extent that I understood them, did not tackle these deeper emotional issues. Neither did they address the increasingly angry debates taking place within the women's movement, which led to more and more exclusive groupings. In some circles it seemed no longer possible to communicate with another woman unless she shared the same race, class, and sexual orientation.

Much as I still related to what I saw as the positive aspects of feminism, I could not erase from my consciousness the graffito I had glimpsed from the top deck of a bus, close to an area in which I had lived for many years: 'Kill Men.' I can still feel the recoil in my guts. How could I identify with a movement, an extreme faction of which spawned such hatred? My heart and mind cried out for something much more all-embracing than what I had found so far, something that could give meaning to the lives of both women and men, and that could overcome hatred. What I longed for, did I but know it, was compassion, and the wisdom of the Enlightened mind.

In my early days of involvement with the London Buddhist Centre and the FWBO, I experienced a sense of homecoming, but it was not without ambivalence. My response to learning meditation and hearing the Buddha's teaching was wholehearted, but I had mixed responses and reactions to the public face of the FWBO. I was attracted by the emphasis on separate women's and men's activities and institutions; there were women's retreats, women's residential communities, and women's co-operative businesses. It was encouraging to see that the idealism of such collective practices had not been undermined by cynicism. At the same time I missed a certain dynamism and excitement that had fuelled the feminist projects I had been part of, a sense that anything could happen, could come into being, if one only had the will and energy to make it so. I felt concerned that activities at the Buddhist centre were almost entirely run by men. There were fewer ordained women than men and far fewer women involved in public teaching of meditation and Buddhism.

My feminist antennae were on the alert. Although actively engaged in working in one of the women's businesses, a vegetarian restaurant, and regularly attending classes at the Centre, I reserved judgement on the members of the Sangha and the workings of the movement. Was

Buddhism compatible with feminism or was it inherently patriarchal? Did this new Buddhist movement break new ground in teaching and practising Buddhism in a way that was as relevant to women as it was to men?

The fact that I am now a Dharmacharini, a member of the Western Buddhist Order, makes it evident that I came to a satisfactory resolution of these questions. But I would like to investigate both feminism and Buddhism more closely in order to clarify the points of overlap and divergence between them, and to attempt to provide some ideas that may be of use to others who are grappling with the same issues. In making this investigation I will be asking to what extent feminism, and Buddhism, enable women to change both themselves and the world, to overcome a limited view of what they are capable of, and to be effective in the world so that they can realize their full potential.

First, what is feminism? I have found it almost impossible to arrive at a satisfactory definition. There seem to be almost as many versions of feminism as there are women (or men) who call themselves feminists. The best general description I have come up with is that feminism is both an ideology and a reform movement based on the belief that women have been, and are, discriminated against because of their sex.

It may be more helpful to begin by looking at the 'why' of feminism rather than the 'what'. This involves examining our recent history. I am restricting my account to a short period of the history of women in Britain, as it is in this country that I have had most experience of feminism.

It is important to know our history as women. For Mary Wollstonecraft, writing in the eighteenth century, the position of women in society was plain: they were a subspecies of humanity. 'It is time to restore women to their lost dignity and to make them … part of the human species,'[48] she wrote in impassioned vein in 1791. Fifty years later, following the legal abolition of slavery, John Stuart Mill was of the opinion that 'There remain no legal slaves anywhere in the British Empire except for the woman in every man's home.'[49]

Until the end of the nineteenth century women had no civil rights, could not own property, vote, make wills, testify in court, or serve on juries. They could not obtain divorces, and their children belonged, according to the law, exclusively to the father. If married, a woman was the property of her husband; if unmarried, the property of her father.

Until 1885, scarcely more than a hundred years ago, a man could still sell his wife or daughter for the purposes of prostitution. (The law passed in 1885 made it illegal to sell or kidnap a girl for the purposes of prostitution until she was 16 years old.) In 1889 a test case prompted the passing of a further law which forbade men to keep their wives imprisoned under lock and key.

But it was not until 1918, more than a century after Wollstonecraft's *Vindication of the Rights of Women* was published, that the first organized women's political movement, commonly known as the Suffragettes, brought about women's suffrage, the right of women to vote. The following year saw the Sex Disqualification (Removal) Act which allowed women to enter the professions.

A contemporary account by Ida Alexa Wylie gives a flavour of the excitement and emotional liberation experienced by these women: 'For two years of wild and sometimes dangerous adventure I worked and fought alongside vigorous, happy, well-adjusted women. I slept on hard floors between elderly duchesses, stout cooks and young schoolgirls. We were often tired, hurt and frightened. But we were content as we had never been. We shared a joy of life that we had never known.'[50]

Twentieth-century women owe a great deal to these early feminists. Without their efforts we might still be regarded as the property of father or husband without the freedom to choose our way of life. These women thought the unthinkable and dared to express it. Whatever we may think of their methods, we do stand on their shoulders.

Changes in law, however crucial, do not immediately or necessarily create changes in behaviour and consciousness. The whole weight of women's cultural and gender conditioning, as well as the entrenched attitudes of society, were stacked against them in their efforts towards individual emancipation. The next wave of feminism sought to explore gender conditioning: to what extent were women and men formed by their biology and to what extent by their cultural conditioning? It also sought to propound an ideology of a dialectic of sex. Taking Karl Marx's perspective one step further, sex war replaced class war as the 'truth' of history. In this war man has the role of the oppressor, woman the role of the oppressed. This ideology led to visions of a future in which women would be completely freed from their reproductive function, thus striking at the root of their oppression. Other branches of feminism imagined a utopia in which, conversely, women's biology was celebrated, in which 'female' values of nurture and creativity would be supreme – a naïve vision of a matriarchy free from war and aggression.

Feminists continued to protest, demonstrate, agitate. They protested against the sex discrimination that persisted in many places of work and education; against the presence of nuclear weapons in Britain; against the way women were depicted in the media; against pornography. They agitated for better provision of child care so that more women could participate in the wider world. All over Britain women's centres sprang up, women's bookshops, women's refuges, women's health centres and self-help groups. The late sixties and seventies was a time of unprecedented activity and enthusiasm among thousands of women of diverse age, race, sexual orientation, and class background. The slogan 'Sisterhood is Powerful' resounded throughout the country.

It is in describing this period that the terms feminism and feminist cease to have coherent meaning. What has been retrospectively referred to as feminism was at the time called 'the women's movement' or 'the women's liberation movement', a description which gave a better idea of the diverse range of views, lifestyles, and interests of the many women who were involved. It is, however, possible to discern two broad theoretical trends in the response to discrimination against women. The first of these is 'liberal feminism'. This approach sees woman as no better or worse than man, intellectually or morally, but as simply human. As such she is entitled to equal opportunities in work and self-development. Liberal feminists are generally concerned with campaigning for changes in legislation to redress inequalities, especially in the area of work and financial independence, focusing on such things as equal pay, removal of discrimination in employment, provision of child care for working women, maternity leave, and so on.

The second approach is that of 'radical feminism'. Radical feminists see the inequalities of a woman's situation as the result of patriarchy, a deliberate attempt by men to conserve power in their own hands and thereby to oppress women by depriving them of this power. They place a high value on women's concerns and achievements and view women as both sexually pure and mystically nurturing, whereas men are seen as aggressive and violent. Radical feminists are generally more concerned with issues to do with sex and violence; for example, demonstrating and campaigning against rape and pornography and initiating the 'Reclaim the Night' marches of the seventies.

In describing these two trends within feminism I want to emphasize that they are broad generalizations and cannot do justice to the activities and experiences of many individual women who call themselves feminists. But making this distinction does give a starting point for a more in-depth discussion as to the relative merits for women's development of feminism and Buddhism.

What is Buddhism? This term covers many schools of thought and methods of practice and is difficult to define in a few words. The word 'Buddhism' is a modern Western term; in the East, Buddhists speak of the 'Buddha-Dharma' or simply 'Dharma'. The Buddha was a human being who by diligent effort and practice attained the state of consciousness that has since been called Enlightenment. He then communicated this experience through words and images to his followers to help them also to become Enlightened. This teaching of the Buddha is the Dharma. It is both the truth itself and any teaching which helps us to realize this truth for ourselves. Buddhism is essentially a path of development by which we can grow beyond our particular conditioning and realize our full human potential.

We can now begin to see the link between Buddhism and feminism. Both are concerned with emancipation, with overcoming the limitations of our conditioning and restricted self-view. Both recognize that to achieve this there have to be changes in consciousness, and not merely changes in the external world; and by this recognition both go beyond the sphere of political activity in which external change is of paramount importance.

In this respect it is worth mentioning two phenomena which arose out of the women's movement of the sixties and seventies: the consciousness-raising group and the idea that the personal is political. Both were means for focusing on the importance of inner change and of putting one's ideals into practice on an everyday level. My own experience of being in a consciousness-raising group was crucial to my development. It is hard to believe now that it was a radical thing then for women simply to meet together to discuss issues concerning women. We looked at our conditioning as women: the effect that our upbringing and society at large had had in shaping us – mostly encouraging the development of receptive, nurturing qualities and discouraging more robust, outgoing qualities. These explorations were a revelation to me. They helped me to make a shift from 'This is how things are' to 'Why should things be this way?' This shift raised the possibility of change.

But change in what way or in what direction? In order to be beneficial change needs to be progressive, not just a swinging between action and reaction. Changing my fixed patterns of behaviour and methods of relating through feminism was definitely beneficial to me. But the changes and consciousness-raising brought about by my practice of Buddhism were far more radical and far-reaching. Buddhism is concerned with spiritual development, the development of skilful mental states and the eradication of unskilful mental states. Unskilful mental states are those consisting of or associated with craving, hatred, and delusion, the three poisons which are the causes of suffering in the world. Skilful mental states are those consisting of or associated with the absence of these three poisons – states associated with peace of mind, friendliness, and wisdom.

This opens up an ethical dimension which is absent in both liberal and radical feminism. This is not to say that feminists do not express strong views about what is right (morally and politically speaking) and what is wrong. But there is no consensus among feminists about the criteria that distinguish ethical from unethical actions. According to Buddhism the practice of ethics is the necessary basis upon which higher states of consciousness can arise. These states, combined with reflection on the Dharma, can lead in turn to insight into reality, an understanding of human life that goes far beyond the intellectual and brings about a fundamental change in our being and our relationship with others. Feminism does bring about change, but it is change on a psychological and social level. Though this level of change can help us to overcome some of our restrictive conditioning as women it does not begin to give us access to our full potential as human beings. Indeed, some aspects of feminism are inimical to this process.

In an interview in *Dakini*,[51] a magazine for women Buddhists, Sangharakshita talks about the aspects of feminism he considers to be a hindrance to spiritual development. He makes a distinction between feminism and Feminism which I think largely corresponds to the one I have made between liberal and radical feminism. The first, he says, 'is the attitude that a woman, no less than a man, should be free to develop whatever capacities and interests she has'. My experience of feminism in this sense causes me to think that it has had much to offer women who wish to grow and develop. It helps us to look at our conditioning as women and therefore to see that we can change. It widens our horizons and shows us that we have options other than to be a wife, mother, or 'single woman'. It creates a culture that values the communication of women's experience. It encourages the development of skills and abilities that allow us to create things in the world and to participate in public life. Without these skills women are confined to the domestic sphere or dwell in the inner world of the psyche. Every human being needs a degree of autonomy, both material and emotional, in order to become an individual. Feminism has, I think, been a strong force in creating the conditions for women's autonomy.

Of Feminism (with a capital F) Sangharakshita says that it 'covers many other attitudes. One of these … is the tendency to see woman as victim.' To identify oneself as a victim is not helpful to one's development. It undermines one's capacity to take the initiative and act creatively, however difficult the situation. In this shift from feminism to Feminism the idea that women have been discriminated against becomes the basis for an ideology, a dogma that does not allow for the individuality either of the woman who upholds it or of the man she casts in the role of oppressor. Such an ideology, as Sangharakshita points out, also encourages hatred, and hatred is utterly incompatible with the Dharma. Moreover, it creates oppression within its own sphere: certain views become taboo and politically incorrect and are not allowed expression. A group mentality prevails. Bonding with other women against the 'enemy' is not the same as true friendship. One of the fundamental practices of Buddhism is the development of loving-kindness or metta; and metta does not distinguish between male and female. Within this ideology there is also the confusion of power with freedom. Feminists demand the transference of power from the oppressor to themselves, the oppressed – but there is no guarantee at all that women would use that power, once gained, in a better way. Men and women are equally afflicted by greed, hatred, and delusion.

From a Buddhist perspective feminism is clearly not enough. It is only a possible starting point in our efforts to develop true individuality. For while feminism asks us to look at our gender conditioning, Buddhism asks us to look at our conditioning as human beings, at how the poisons of greed, hatred, and delusion underpin everything we do and limit us to habitual reactive patterns. While feminism investigates the dichotomy between men and women, male and female, Buddhism urges us to strive to overcome the dichotomy of self and other, the view of ourselves as the centre of the universe, a fixed self separate from other beings. In overcoming this dichotomy we eventually transcend identification with being either male or female.

No branch of the women's movement, whether feminist or Feminist, addresses the fundamental facts of the human condition. The investigations do not go deep enough, the goal is too limited, the scope does not take in the full range of human experience. Buddhism offers us a far greater challenge; it demands much more of us – and has much more of value to give in return. It was the gradual understanding of this bigger picture that caused me to ask for ordination into the Western Buddhist Order in 1987, to come off the fence and commit myself to the task of realizing my potential both as a woman and as a human being.

But it still remains to answer my question: 'Is Buddhism inherently patriarchal?' Am I deluded in thinking I can make real progress as a woman in a spiritual movement founded by a man – even if he was a Buddha, an Enlightened man – and perpetuated on the whole by men?

When the Buddha's attendant Ananda asked him whether women were capable of gaining Enlightenment, the Buddha was unequivocal in his response. He said that they were. So saying, he admitted women into his community of spiritual renunciants. They left behind their homes, families, and possessions, begged for almsfood, and lived a life of meditation and contemplation in the forests of India.

For women to take this step in the society of his time was revolutionary. By agreeing to it, the Buddha could in fact be regarded as one of the earliest feminists, in that he made his decision not on the basis of women's traditional role and society's norms but on the basis of their potential for development. The *Therigatha* ('Psalms of the Sisters'), which documents the experiences of these first women renunciants, attests to their achievements. Many became Enlightened; some were renowned as Dharma teachers and had many disciples.

In the centuries following the Buddha's death the organization of his followers became more institutionalized and centred on monasteries. Within this structure the achievements of women practitioners were no longer recorded or recognized to the same extent, and gradually the full ordination of women died out in most of the Buddhist world. This lack of full participation by women in the spiritual life is clearly not in accord with the Buddha's own teaching.

Returning to the original spirit of the Buddha's teaching, Sangharakshita has established an order which is neither lay nor monastic and in which women and men receive equal ordination. Both are free to take up any position of responsibility within the movement. As well as giving this equality of opportunity, the structure of the movement enables both women and men to develop on a broader basis and gain access to both 'masculine' and 'feminine' aspects of themselves. Beyond introductory level and outside public centres, most activities are organized on the basis of same gender, so that the movement has a women's wing and a men's wing. The women's wing runs its own retreats, has its own retreat centres, and conducts an ordination process for women. Many women live together in residential communities and run a variety of businesses.

In the early days of my involvement with the FWBO the process of establishing these two wings was just beginning. With hindsight I can see that my experience of entering the movement was coloured by this development. From my feminist perspective the women I met, though friendly and having a certain depth, seemed to lack the dynamism and exuberance I associated with my friends in the women's movement; the men, while welcoming me to the Centre, seemed reluctant to form any personal relationship with me. Of course in retrospect I can see that it was a very daunting prospect at that time for the women to begin the process of establishing their own facilities, and the men were wary of looking to women for emotional support.

Today the outlook is very different and the fruits of practising within a same-gender environment are apparent. I was among the first group of women ordained by the women preceptors to whom Sangharakshita passed on this responsibility in 1989. At the London Buddhist Centre there are now 29 women Order members, many of them involved in teaching public classes, giving talks, and leading Dharma study. A further fifty women involved with this one centre alone have asked for ordination. This is just a small proportion of the women around the world who are increasingly discovering that the practice of Buddhism can provide a context and a method for change and growth, a context which can take them beyond the limitations caused by the conditioning of gender, race, and class. I remain grateful to feminism for providing me with the doorway through which I have been able to enter the realm of the Dharma.

Vajrapushpa

*Born in Helsinki, Finland, in 1952, Vajrapushpa was the elder
of two sisters. In 1976 she finished her studies at the
University of Helsinki, where she read comparative literature,
history of art, and comparative religion, and then worked as a
translator and editor for a publishing company. After years of
practising yoga and being interested in Eastern religions, she
learned to meditate, attending classes at the FWBO centre in
Helsinki. She moved to London early in 1979, and became
part of the administrative team at the London Buddhist
Centre for a few years. She was ordained in 1981. She now
lives in Cambridge, England, with her husband and two
daughters and works part-time as a counsellor. She leads
Dharma study groups for women; for several years she has
also been co-editor of the FWBO magazine for women,* Lotus
Realm *(formerly* Dakini*).*

Vajrapushpa

Motherhood

From Myth to Reality

STILL SUFFERING FROM the pain and from the effects of the general anaesthetic, my whole body feeling battered and bruised, I looked at the tiny round face of my new-born baby daughter, and I fell in love.

The waiting was over. I had spent the night before her birth wide awake. I had been told of the doctor's decision to perform a caesarean section at nine o'clock the following morning. During that sleepless night I still couldn't comprehend what was about to happen. Who was going to be born? During the four weeks I had had to spend in the maternity hospital in the East End of London, I had heard the cries of so many new-born babies. I had seen Pakistani and Indian families, orthodox Jewish and British working-class and middle-class families, take their babies home. And now my own baby was going to be born. Someone I didn't know at all, someone who was going to be intimately and irreversibly connected with me for the rest of my life.

Since those first moments of gazing into her eyes, I have continued to love her. I have also felt utterly frustrated with her, I have missed her, and I have yearned for a break from her never-ending demands. The closeness between us, woven into the fabric of everyday routine, has allowed us to become familiar with each other's bodies, thoughts, and moods.

Four years later I gave birth – this time naturally – to my second daughter. The experience was again powerful, although to some extent familiar. I went along with the tide of events, more content, less afraid, and less surprised. But the feelings of strength and resilience, of vulnerability and rawness, which had begun to emerge during pregnancy, stayed with me once again for several months.

I had reached my early thirties before even considering whether to have children. Life had in many ways been interesting and satisfying. I had studied and worked, I had travelled and made friends. I had moved to Britain from Finland and learned to use a new language. I had learned to meditate and I had studied the Dharma; I had been ordained within the Western Buddhist Order. I had moved forward; I had gone forth. Having a baby might have seemed, might still seem, like retreating into the safety of a nest, going backwards, settling down. Perhaps I didn't know how to move forward and wanted to slow down; perhaps it has been useful to take this particular detour. Perhaps the detour is now part of the main road.

It wasn't difficult to see the many reasons against having a baby: the time and money involved in bringing up a child; having to give up interests and responsibilities that had been such a large and enjoyable part of my life; having fewer opportunities to go on retreats and deepen my spiritual practice and friendships. I knew I couldn't express my commitment to Buddhism in the way I had done before. Soon after having my first child I started leading study groups again, and I have maintained and developed many friendships with other women, but my contribution to the FWBO has inevitably been limited by the demands of looking after two young children.

Even though I consciously chose to become a mother, I can't say that I was, or that I am even now, fully aware of all the reasons that led to the decision. I had a strong feeling at the time for the kind of physical and emotional wholeness that having a child would give me. Another reason was wanting to be more rooted in and connected with life and society in a country that was not my own. I was attracted by the contrast and fulfilment that being a mother and an Order member and a working woman out in the world would bring to my life. I could be many things. I was also drawn towards my own childhood, its light and dark passages, its freedom, its fantasies and discoveries. As a mother, I could perhaps recapture some of my own imagination and creativity.

Having a baby can be a way of having a break, a break from work, from a busy lifestyle, from having to face dilemmas and choices about what to do next. It is also often an expression of yearning for an intimate and satisfying relationship.

And yet, although the question 'Why children?' can have so many answers, nothing seems to answer it completely. Are there simply blind forces that pull us towards child-bearing, towards unknown areas of deep craving, the place of forgetting and not knowing, where we succumb totally to the demands of our unenlightened being, the demands of our biological and psychological conditioning? I think that if we are practising as Buddhists, our increasing self-awareness and the opportunity of talking things through with our friends can help us become aware of at least some of the reasons why we seek motherhood. Each reason tells us something about ourselves as women and as individuals. We can examine our thoughts and feelings as openly as possible, and whether or not we choose to become mothers we can make use of these as we continue to pursue our psychological and spiritual development.

In spite of my confidence, becoming a mother felt like a risk. Now that I was creating such a deep bond between myself and another human being, and a nest around it, would I really be able to practise in a way that would help me overcome tendencies that made me cling on to what was safe and known, tendencies that made me want to protect myself as I was? In creating a bond with my child, was I only making it more difficult for myself to overcome my separateness from other people?

During a discussion among women Order members shortly before my pregnancy was confirmed, someone brought up the question whether we needed Stream Entrants (that is, spiritual aspirants who have broken through their conditioning enough to make their progress on the spiritual path irreversible) or babies. Not that the two need be mutually exclusive, I thought. But behind the slightly provocative (provocative for the purposes of the discussion, at least) equation of no family responsibilities with spiritual progress lay the reality of the situation in which we found ourselves in the early 1980s in the women's wing of our order in Britain. There were only about twenty of us and we were all aware that everybody's effort was needed to provide the facilities – communities, right livelihood businesses, meditation, and study retreats – that were going to benefit so many other women. I couldn't help feeling uncomfortable in my decision to have a child, and wondered how people would receive the news of my pregnancy. They might think that I was setting a bad example (now *every* woman would start having babies…). The responses ranged from envy to delight, from disapproval to indifference. Perhaps some did think I was setting a bad example. In the end, as it happened, there was a mini 'baby boom' around the London Buddhist Centre that year. Not many committed women have chosen to become mothers in the last few years but the fact that some of us have has perhaps helped other women to explore the issues from more angles – and more realistically.

Fantasies about motherhood often centre either on the Good Great Mother, the ever-loving, nurturing, pure Mother; or on the Terrible Mother, the witch, the monster who is capable of devouring her children, if not physically, then at least emotionally. Motherhood continues to exist as a myth. In her essay 'Motherhood in the Imagination', the psychotherapist Julia Vellacott points out that what many definitions of motherhood have in common is 'a way of presenting what it means to be a mother as something pre-given and innate – mothers may vary over time and place, but there is something inescapably "eternal" about mothering.'[52]

In her book *The Myth of Motherhood*, which caused quite an uproar when it was first published in 1980, the French academic Elisabeth Badinter examines motherhood from a historical and a sociological point of view. She argues that the 'maternal instinct', let alone maternal love, has been very fickle and changeable over the centuries, dependent on the economic, social, and ideological circumstances of the day. For instance, urban women in seventeenth- and eighteenth-century Europe who could afford to do so farmed out their babies to peasant wet-nurses to be brought up in the country for at least the first few years of their lives. No woman of even moderate wealth breast-fed her own child. According to Badinter, 'the eighteenth century launched the idea of parental responsibility for the child's happiness, the nineteenth confirmed it, emphasizing the mother's role, while the twentieth century transformed it from maternal responsibility to maternal guilt.'[53]

In the earlier part of the twentieth century, at least till the post-war years, women were still encouraged to produce large families, to find satisfaction and pride in motherhood. What has ensued has been a curious mixture of idealizing and, at the same time, denigrating motherhood. Women could devote themselves to a necessary and noble task that men could not take on, and they were praised and respected for doing so; but somehow the role of a full-time mother was still regarded as inferior to male pursuits.

Badinter sums up the message to women over the last two centuries: 'Be good mothers, and be happy and respected. Make yourself indispensable to the family, and you will gain acceptance.'[54] For a woman today, living in a society which no longer wants large families and which takes for granted the many options – including motherhood – open to women, the message is immensely more complex and perhaps difficult to decipher. If she becomes a Buddhist, the situation may be more complex still. The voice promising happiness and fulfilment is still heard. The voice telling us that women can now lead financially and emotionally independent lives may also be believed. We may also hear another message: 'Be a mother and retreat into the sidelines of the Buddhist movement; become enmeshed with the mundane and jeopardize your spiritual development.' We would also like to listen to the voice which says, 'Be true to yourself, do what is right for you' – but that really means listening to and examining all the other messages.

Much religious imagery, particularly Christian, sentimentalizes and idealizes motherhood. As a continuation of that quasi-religious sentiment, there is a movement among some women today towards finding a spiritual path in motherhood. It is probably true that the failure of institutionalized religions to give women a visible and valid role has made women seek dignity and self-respect through motherhood, looking for salvation through a path unique to them. Carol Wallas LaChance talks of the way of the mother as 'a profound journey' which in our times 'is becoming the lost journey of the feminine'.[55] She claims that 'woman is essentially mother' not only in a physical sense, but also in the sense of participating 'in birthing and nurturing new life, physically, psychically, and spiritually'.[56] However, I don't think it wise to equate the 'feminine' with the maternal, and it is even less wise to equate the two with 'feminine spirituality'.

I agree with Tsultrim Allione when she talks about 'the duty of the women who are spiritually awake' to make connections between their everyday lives and the Buddhist teaching. But she goes on to make a confusing statement, asserting that 'the path of a mother should be given its deserved value as a sacred and powerful spiritual path.'[57] Of course those of us who have children have to continue to practise the Dharma in the family situation. We have no choice. Spiritual development is not something we can put off till some future time when the children have left home. But to identify with the maternal to give a sense of purpose and spiritual direction would be limiting and ultimately unsatisfying.

For the woman herself, there is almost always a gap between a fantasy of motherhood and the experience of it. Women do look to motherhood for things which it either cannot provide, or can only provide temporarily, or to a limited extent: emotional closeness and security, self-esteem, a career, a spiritual path, a new source of creativity.

As perhaps in other Buddhist movements, during the early years of the FWBO some of the women who had children (not that many of them did) had unrealistic expectations of the amount of support they could get from the spiritual community. Perhaps some men, in particular, were unnecessarily judgemental in their attitude towards women and children. Many people feared that motherhood was a threat to a woman's spiritual development and what was perceived to be the spiritual integrity of the movement. As a number of women committed to the FWBO have had children in the last few years, some of the myths and fantasies surrounding motherhood have lost their power. There is now a growing sense of realism about what it means to be a mother and a practising Buddhist, and to bring up children within the ambience of the Buddhist spiritual community; about what kind of support is needed by mothers (and fathers, for that matter) and what kind of conditions are conducive to the healthy development of a child.

The feeling and the knowledge of carrying a new being within my own body made me aware of the strength and the fragility of the relationship that was being formed. The bond between two people can be so strong. It can be severed so easily. Life and death are so close to each other. When I was pregnant, I had a sense, too, of being involved in one particular climax in the cycle of life and death; there was no escape, no turning back, no other way than to experience the pain, the relief, and the joy of giving birth. I enjoyed meditating while I was pregnant; it was as if the added closeness with another consciousness, the pulsating of another lifestream in my body, helped me melt some boundaries in myself.

After the birth of the baby, the rhythm of life suddenly slowed down. Everyday tasks, and getting from one place to another, took so long. I became much more aware of old people – how slowly they walked and how difficult it was for them too, to get on and off buses, and how they too, just like mothers of young children, were often happy to have someone to chat to. I had time to think, reflect, and experience myself without the roles that had previously been part of my self-view. I did experience the bliss and happiness of looking after a new-born baby, and yet confusion and turmoil were there too. It was impossible to understand and respond to all the needs of the baby, and my own needs alternated between being unimportant, almost non-existent, and unexpectedly pressing and urgent. Not being able to rely on getting enough sleep and having regular meals, not having many choices, had the effect of focusing my mind on what was essential, although my thoughts also wandered into a distant future when life would be ordered again. Within the chaos there was a delightful and liberating simplicity.

As mothers we inhabit, for a time at least, a very small world, and we can make that world smaller still by identifying with it completely, by seeing ourselves and the rest of the world reflected in that particular mirror. Mothers can become masochistic and exaggerate the sacrifice they are making for the sake of their children, which means they are not making a real sacrifice anyway; or they can demand a sacrifice of some sort from their children. Both tendencies speak of lack of individuality in the mother, and stultify the growth of individuality in her children.

The small world of the mother and child needs support and input from outside. If they are lacking, the situation becomes psychologically unhealthy and spiritually disadvantageous for the mother – and unhealthy for the child too. 'The emotional ambience of merged attachment', as Susie Orbach calls the mother–child relationship,[58] has its function while the child is young, but we may try to maintain it for too long, or create it inappropriately in other relationships. If spiritual development is understood as consisting of a cultivation of progressively more positive mental states and a continuous process of letting go of self-view, it follows that over-identifying with a particular role or function in life – and a way of relating to other people which stems from this function – is going to be a hindrance. A person without a clear sense of identity and personal authenticity cannot begin to free herself from a fixed and dependent way of being.

It is very valuable for mothers of young children to be able to maintain a regular meditation practice and to have the support and stimulation of their spiritual friends. Without the active participation of the other parent, or another parental figure, motherhood can put a woman under a lot of strain and undermine her both physically and psychologically. Shared parenting, either within a single family or within a communal living situation, benefits the child and enables the mother (and the father) to enjoy periods of solitude and participation in shared spiritual practice with other Buddhists.

The time in a woman's life when her children are young is often very busy and absorbing; but for many women it is also a period of change in their lives, a period when they could be receptive to the Dharma. Meditation classes and retreats with crèches can give a woman a chance to experience herself more fully as a whole person and to put her experience of motherhood in the wider context of spiritual development. What many mothers also value, however, particularly when they have learned to meditate, is being in a child-free zone, attending retreats and meditation classes without their children.

A mother of young children spends a great deal of time performing routine mundane tasks: feeding, cleaning, washing, cooking, pushing the pram. Although it can be mentally and physically exhausting, it is also possible to create some inner space within the boredom and relentlessness of this particular lifestyle. Mental and spiritual nourishment in the form of meditation, study, reflection, and conversation can be assimilated and absorbed while she is doing other things.

It is usually clear that the baby's needs come first. Beyond that, we have a choice between 'having' and 'being'. We often give up positions and lose some of our identity when we become mothers; and yet within that loss of identity is also potentially a freedom to re-evaluate our personal priorities, to concentrate on what is essential, and to let go of habitual perceptions of ourselves. Our deep and initially symbiotic involvement with another human being can sometimes itself become a source of expansion and change. It carries within it the potential for closeness with other people – a closeness that overcomes fears and barriers but doesn't seek to merge with another person. Bringing up children has made me much more aware of the tremendous changes we all go through in the course of our childhood, and it has helped me see other people as less fixed, less defined by their conscious adult selves.

Reading and discussing stories, conversations, going on trips and excursions, sharing everyday experiences with our children – all these things add a new dimension to motherhood. The child becomes aware of our interests and values, our lifestyle, and our attitudes towards the outside world. The mother and child become two separate people, still in love, still secure in the intimacy of their relationship, but also exposed to each other. The child can be uncannily aware of the mother's weaknesses and vulnerable spots, and deeply influenced by her emotional states, positive as well as negative. As mothers of growing children we have to rely more and more on our own integrity, our emotional truthfulness, and our ability to be both separate from and emotionally close to our children.

The relationship between her body and her mind is regularly highlighted throughout a woman's life, and in a particularly powerful way while she is pregnant and breast-feeding. The connection between body and mind becomes close and fluid – sometimes painfully, sometimes blissfully so. There seems to be something in a woman's biological and psychological conditioning that makes her want to withdraw at times from an active outward-going life, to nurture and to serve, to be aware of and sensitive to the link between her body and mind, to create, and to make it possible for something new to emerge out of combining and connecting things rather than discriminating and dividing. Many ancient myths describe a descent into darkness which a female figure undertakes in order to find what is missing. In her book on the mother–daughter relationship, Nini Herman talks about the ability of the feminine psyche – by extension, I would say, the 'feminine' in both women and men – to hold together and to create harmony out of opposites.[59]

Motherhood can quite clearly be used as a practice by somebody who has embarked on a spiritual path. Every day presents numerous opportunities to practise patience and awareness, to generate love and compassion, to use energy wisely and mindfully, to work with the irritation and frustration that come from constant demands and interruptions. Moreover, we can try to develop what Rita Gross calls a more 'egoless' and 'detached' style of mothering:[60] to lessen, with the help of meditation and reflection, the identification with our children that causes the bonds of attachment between ourselves and our children to grow deeper and deeper. The fear and anxiety we feel for our children, as well as the pride we take in their achievements, go into the heart of motherhood; they bind us to what we have and what we are. The practice of letting go of our children as extensions of our ego becomes an essential part of good mothering.

Motherhood in a more symbolic sense is an attitude or a function, an aspect of the female psyche – with which we may or may not identify – which we can use to help ourselves and to help others. It is the ability to listen, to be present, to support that which is still unformed, not to discriminate prematurely, to give the right kind of emotional and spiritual nourishment.

Whether relating to motherhood as a practice – as actually bringing up children – or as an attitude, we need to give it respect and validity. We also need to give it an overall context. That context is, first of all, our own individuality, our self-confidence as women who can and want to be more than mothers. A still more meaningful context is provided by the path of a practising Buddhist, the path which can truly help us find our freedom as individuals and overcome the fear and unhappiness that accompany our ego-centred way of being.

Buddhism doesn't give motherhood any spiritual status or significance as such. Maternal imagery and symbolism is, however, something that Buddhism, particularly the Vajrayana, like so many other spiritual traditions, has made use of. Some of the archetypal female Bodhisattvas are seen as supreme mothers: Tara is compared to a mother and she has 'a mother's compassion and instant response to suffering.' 'She cares for all beings as though each were her only child. Like a mother she is very accepting.'[61] Prajnaparamita, 'the mother of all Buddhas', is 'mature in having given birth to countless Buddhas' and she regards the Buddhas 'like a mother fondly watching her children at play'.[62] But the Bodhisattvas, the transcendental ideal mothers, are also essentially androgynous. We can become perfect, ideal mothers only when we become Bodhisattvas, when we no longer identify with our gender or feed our sense of ego.

For most of us, motherhood is a mixed experience. In becoming mothers we enter the realm of impossible passions. Our child demands total love from us – and is bound to be disappointed. Motherhood is, for the child and the mother, 'the greatest possible illusion of a possibility for total love';[63] and yet it offers us an opportunity to deepen our love for our child, and for other people, in a situation that sometimes pushes us right against our personal limitations.

Nini Herman singles out two main threads that run through a woman's experience of motherhood: one is the theme of separation; the other, the woman's authenticity as a human being.[64] As mothers we need our self-confidence, as well as the help of other people and supportive structures, to be able to pursue our multifaceted lives, find psychological maturity, and deepen our experience and understanding of the Dharma. We can be free to express the many aspects of our lives and aspirations, and remain free and confident in being mothers: in nurturing and supporting; in trusting the emerging independence and confidence of our children.

When I became a mother I felt connected with what generations of women had done and experienced before me; I also felt more connected with, and concerned about, society at large and the culture around me. I found out some basic facts about customs and institutions in British society that, as a foreigner, I had never discovered before. I also became, to some extent, immersed in my own private world. I experienced both rootedness and isolation. Yet I also felt strongly connected with my spiritual aspirations.

Over the years, I have met many new people and made many new friends; I have worked; I have studied and practised the Dharma, on my own and with other people. Motherhood is always part of it all, a constant point of reference, sometimes visible, sometimes invisible; a reminder of the bond that will always connect me to my children; a bond that will perhaps, in its unique way, help me towards a deeper understanding of human existence with its pain and delight – and potential.

Samata

Samata grew up on the south coast of England. At 19 she worked for a year in India, before studying modern history at the University of East Anglia. In 1976, whilst still living in Norfolk, she came across Buddhism. Since then she has helped to establish two FWBO restaurants and trained as a yoga teacher and as a psychosynthesis counsellor. Samata lived in East London for eleven years in women's communities associated with the London Buddhist Centre, and helped to found Bodywise, a health centre run by local Buddhists. From June 1991 she spearheaded the fund-raising and then the property search for a new retreat centre – Tiratanaloka – where she now lives and works as part of the women's ordination team. Samata was ordained in 1985 and her name means 'the Wisdom of Equality' or 'the heart and mind that is free of prejudice'.

Samata

Buddhism or Motherhood?

I WAS BROUGHT UP a Roman Catholic, the youngest of five. By the time I was 17 I no longer rationally believed in God and had rejected the Catholic church. But it was many years before I freed myself from the feeling of guilt associated with sex as well as the fear of an unwanted pregnancy. When I was 18 the idea of freedom was uppermost in my mind. Sexual freedom, travel, and a passionate response to social injustice all formed a part of my emerging views on life. While still at school I hitch-hiked in Europe during the summer holidays, and later, when I was 19, I spent a year in India working with Voluntary Service Overseas, returning home overland. I wanted to do something useful to alleviate the suffering in the world around me. But it was becoming all too clear that it was not going to be easy to find a way of doing this which would meet my ideals. By the time I was 25, having completed a university degree and a business diploma, and having worked for a while in London, I knew what I did not want to do and what I was disillusioned with, but I still had no idea what I did want to do. I was recovering from a serious car accident and my life felt utterly empty and meaningless. It was at this crossroads that I came across the Dharma.

One aspect of the dilemma I was in was a conflict I have had to face many times and in various forms over the years: whether or not to have a child. With hindsight I can see that I was torn between wanting to step out into the world away from my family and to make something of my life (motherhood represented settling down and a loss of freedom) and a deep-seated though largely unconscious need for security.

Eventually I came to the decision not to become a mother. I reached it gradually, through an accumulation of countless smaller decisions which began with my first sexual relationship at the age of 17, and which have been inextricably linked with other questions about the meaning and direction of my life. External factors and the attitudes of others have played their part over the years. No one single factor determined my decision, although looking back I can see that certain guiding ideas have informed my choices. It has not always been a straightforward route and at various times I have felt myself going against the current of social conditioning. Sometimes I have experienced tension arising from my conflicting wants and needs; sometimes the tension has come from outside, in particular from the views of my parents.

Some years ago I met a friend whose first child was then just one year old. He told me that his partner felt that becoming a mother had brought her fulfilment as a woman, and asked whether I thought this would be the case for all women, and whether I wanted this experience myself. During our conversation I experienced again the largely forgotten, but not unfamiliar, sense of social pressure arising from such questions. Was it true that as a woman I could find fulfilment only by becoming a mother? Was I missing out on something by choosing not to have children? At the time I was not sure – but somehow I felt that I was not missing out on anything. Realizing afresh how entrenched is the ideal of woman as mother made me see just how radical a decision it still is not to have children. It is interesting that there is no adequate word in the English language to describe a woman who positively chooses not to have a child. The words we use – 'childless', 'single', 'spinster' – all imply some kind of lack.

Among the women Buddhists I know, some became mothers as a result of a conscious choice arrived at after consideration and discussion of the implications of having a child. Others say that they never considered not having children. Sometimes these same women go on to say that had they come across the Dharma earlier in their lives they might never have become mothers. Some see motherhood as a proper and fulfilling path, or experience pressure from their family to believe that this is so. I have found myself at times believing, or wanting to believe, that becoming a mother would make me more whole as a woman. Alongside this belief I invested motherhood with the power to provide me with a sense of security, to make me a useful member of society with a clearly defined role. But whenever I had an urge to become a mother, the impulse seemed to come from an underlying sense of a lack of fulfilment and meaning in my life, often allied with an inability to imagine sufficiently strongly what I could do if I had enough determination and courage.

Over the years my practice of Buddhism has had its part to play in the decision-making process. When I first learned to meditate, I had already begun to consider whether or not to have a child and there seemed no reason why it should not remain an open question. Buddhism is a path of individual spiritual development that addresses itself to all individuals. Whatever one's circumstances, no one who wishes to practise the teaching of the Buddha is excluded.

One of the first committed Buddhists I met lived in Norfolk with her husband (also a Buddhist) and their two young daughters, the youngest just a few months old. It was clear to me, therefore, that being a mother did not rule one out as capable of taking up the spiritual life. Taking up a spiritual practice such as meditation involves the intensive development of skilful mental states, and had I chosen to have a child, this could only have enhanced my ability and effectiveness as a parent. On the other hand, I could see that it was also possible to live a fulfilling life in the spiritual community without having a child. It was not long before I met other women Buddhists who were not married and did not have children. Many of the latter lived in newly-established residential communities associated with a Buddhist centre in north London and were involved in the search for new premises, which later became the London Buddhist Centre.

I was already veering towards not having a child. While I could see that motherhood was not incompatible with living the spiritual life I soon realized there was a range of activities I wanted to experience first-hand, learn from, and be involved with on a full-time basis, in a way which would not be possible if I had a child. One example was helping to set up and establish a Right Livelihood business. It was a great relief to be able at last to engage my energy in a context which included all aspects of my life, and in which my contact with others was based on shared values. As my meditation began to go deeper it also became clearer to me just how much work I needed to do on myself to grow into a more integrated and aware individual. Right from the start, my progress on the spiritual path has been neither easy nor smooth. Despite this, the positive changes I have experienced over the years have given me tremendous faith in the practices and teachings of Buddhism.

At various times the urge to have a child has forced itself to the forefront of my consciousness. This urge has had a tumultuous effect, and at times I have felt strongly tempted to respond to it as it has tugged and seduced, sometimes gently, sometimes fiercely. From the early years of my involvement with Buddhism there have always been women whom I have been able to trust and talk to freely about personal or spiritual matters. Whenever I felt in conflict over the question of whether or not to have a child, I would always seek out one or more of these friends. The friend I turned to most was happily single and childless, and lived a full life. But I also spoke to others, one of whom had two children. These spiritual friends took a balanced approach, neither explicitly encouraging me to give in to my desire, nor discouraging me from doing so. Just by listening to me, they helped me to explore my thoughts and feelings, encouraging me to take my time and think through all the factors involved. Before coming to such a crucial and irreversible decision, I needed to find out how strong my desire was. Was it just the nurturing instinct coming out very strongly? Or was it a powerful desire to have a baby of my own? And was it so strong that it was actually stopping me progressing on the spiritual path?

Between 1979 and 1991 I had a sexual relationship with a man, also an Order member, who did not want to become a father. At one point in this twelve-year relationship I experienced a very strong desire to have a child with him. It seemed impossible to reconcile our needs and we ended the relationship. I then met someone else who was happy to have a child with me, but I discovered that having a child was not the most important thing; what I really wanted was to resume the relationship with my ex-partner. We got back together two years later, and I continued to feel content not to have a child.

In 1984 I was present at the birth of a friend's second child. I saw for myself that giving birth is both a deeply personal experience and a universal drama, for we are all born from a womb. Witnessing this for myself released me from the mystique of childbirth. This, coupled with the experience of living with children some years previously, added to a growing conviction that at best motherhood would probably be a rewarding experience but not one to which I wanted to devote many years of my life. Although I like children, I began to think that they did not interest me sufficiently to make me want my own. Strong as my desire for a baby has been at times, the urge to remain free of domestic ties has been stronger.

If the baby question presents one with a real conflict, it seems to me crucial that one feels free either to have or not to have a child, allowing oneself to engage imaginatively with either course of action and think through the consequences, noting any thoughts, feelings, and prejudices one may have. If we do not feel free to make our own decision, we run the risk of further conflict arising later. It was important for me to know that I could choose to have a child, that I was able to take responsibility for my actions, and that I felt confident of my capacity to be a mother. I then felt freer to make a positive choice not to have a child.

If one's craving for a child of one's own is so overwhelming that it begins to block further spiritual progress, then the best course of action may be to go ahead and have a child. Of course it is not always necessary to act on strong feelings – we can overvalue our feelings and impulses – but such feelings do need to be taken into account. My contact with other Buddhists suggests that when a strong feeling or attachment is involved, as is often the case with the desire to have a child, a woman may feel that 'Buddhism', or even a particular person, is telling her what she should or shouldn't do. She may even experience this as a pressure to conform to a set idea of what is right and wrong. This is a sensitive and difficult area. If a woman is not very sure of herself in this area in relation to spiritual practice she can sometimes think others are putting pressure on her to take a particular course of action, to toe the line: anything else is not really acceptable or will be seen as second best. If you find yourself becoming defensive about this or any other aspect of Buddhist life, the important thing is to retain as open a mind as possible and talk over your views with others.

Buddhists sometimes talk of 'Going Forth'. This term originates with the story of the Buddha, who, as Siddhartha Gautama, left his father's home and went forth as a wanderer in search of Truth. To go forth in a family situation can mean working against over-identifying with the role of motherhood as an end in itself. Through reflecting upon and letting go of the view that a child is a part of herself and belongs to her, the mother comes to understand something about attachment and the truth of impermanence. This does not mean she then ceases to provide the emotional sustenance required by her child – but her positive emotions flow more freely towards others and she has less need to cling to the false idea that she owns someone or something. As her children grow older she has to let go of them as they prepare to leave home. In some cases, Mum is the first to go, leaving the house to her grown-up children.

Going Forth has two aspects: a moving away from, and a moving towards. For example, we go forth from limited ideals, which gives us the freedom to move towards a more expansive ideal. My decision not to have a child could be seen as a going forth from the ideal of mother-hood as being in itself fulfilling. What I have gone forth to, as I see it, is the opportunity for a more intensive involvement with, and greater expression of, the altruistic dimension of spiritual life.

The vision of Buddhism is of total transformation: the overcoming of greed, hatred, and spiritual ignorance in all their forms within ourselves and the world around us. What has inspired and motivated me more than anything else over the years has been the desire to help create facilities so that the conditions necessary for Buddhist practice to flourish are available to more and more people. My work has benefited me as much as others. At times I have felt less than adequate for the tasks I have taken on, but if I had decided to have a child I could not have put myself so wholeheartedly into helping others to contact the Dharma. The opportunity to work and live with other like-minded people has enriched my life far more than I could have imagined, and I have seen many people benefiting from the situations I have helped to create.

Of course, such opportunities are not closed to women with children. But my experience of women practising Buddhism who are also mothers suggests that, while motherhood is not incompatible with a spiritual life, it imposes restrictions that would have prevented me from developing in the way I have. Initially a great deal of time and energy is taken up with child-care. It is difficult to do anything that requires concentration; periods of withdrawal such as meditation, study, or going on retreat may be almost impossible. When women who are committed Buddhists decide to have children and to raise them in separate, small families, their opportunities to give and receive intensive Sangha contact are, for the time being, greatly reduced. Generally speaking it seems to be difficult for mothers to live in a residential community or work in team-based Right Livelihood, and thereby to have intensive experience of the benefits of a continuity of communication with others in the Sangha.

In 1993 I became an *anagarika*, which literally means 'cityless' or 'home-less one'. One aspect of this commitment is the practice of celibacy.

Becoming an anagarika is not a higher ordination but an intensification of the practice of the third ethical precept (abstention from sexual misconduct). Taking this step has brought me far more joy than I could have imagined. It arose out of several years of reflection and the ending of the twelve-year sexual relationship I mentioned earlier. This relationship ended well, with mutual consent, and I felt no need to embark on another. I had at last transcended the need for the kind of security a sexual relationship provided, and I felt freer on all levels of my being to live my own life. Being an anagarika is not just about being celibate; it expresses a deepening of my commitment to the spiritual life. In the ceremony itself I felt I was giving myself more wholeheartedly than ever before to the Sangha, the spiritual community.

Shortly before I decided to take this step, the need had become obvious for a number of Dharmacharinis to commit themselves full-time to forming an ordination team. I was very inspired by this project, and I have had the good fortune to become a member of the team, whose purpose is to help women to prepare for ordination. We needed a centre where our team could live as a community, and where we could hold retreats. It took three years to raise funds and search for a suitable property, all the while continuing to run retreats for women. More than anything I have yet done, this project has helped me to grow spiritually, but my ability to contribute as much as I have has been due to all that went before. It has been, and is, tremendously fulfilling to see what we are creating and the benefit so many others are deriving from our efforts. I feel more joyful, more content, and more energetic than at any other time in my life. I experience a deep confidence that all my previous decisions, the choices I have made and the conflicts I have overcome, are now bearing fruit. I can indeed say they have led me to where I wish to be; and they continue to lead me in the direction of liberation and the realization of truth.

Navachitta

Navachitta has been a practising Buddhist for sixteen years, and ordained for six. A homoeopath and massage therapist by occupation, she is also a mother, and has been active in various social and environmental agencies, including a national project to make New Zealand nuclear-free. She was expelled for life from French Polynesia in 1986 for addressing an anti-nuclear and pro-independence rally in Papeete, Tahiti.

Navachitta

Abortion

A Buddhist View

MY FIRST AND UNREMEMBERED experience of abortion took place in the womb. My mother tried to abort me. Even though her attempt was of the 'gin-and-hot-bath-wishful-thinking' variety, I still speculate about the effect it may have had on the unborn child that was me. I often find myself thinking, 'I shouldn't be here, I'm not wanted,' which creates such anxiety that I find myself suddenly extricating myself from situations, and later wondering why.

As a hippie living in Darwin, Australia, in the seventies, I had to seek medical assistance for a uterine haemorrhage not caused by pregnancy. I went to Darwin Hospital where the staff, it seemed, judged that I had tried to abort a pregnancy. I was treated with hostility, and made to wait. For a long time I sat in the public waiting-room, haemorrhaging, with blood all over my clothes. Eventually the doctors examined me and realized I had not tried to terminate a pregnancy. They thawed a little. I found the experience humiliating, and for the first time began to reflect on abortion.

In 1974 I became pregnant. During the first three months I had a serious viral illness requiring hospital treatment. I had heard that the effects of this virus on a pregnant woman in her first trimester were similar to those of rubella. However, I gave birth to a healthy daughter, neither deaf nor deformed.

In 1976 I became pregnant again. I was in a volatile state of mind and was not coping with motherhood. My husband was set on abortion and I meekly agreed, delighted to hand the decision over to him and unaware of the long-term effect on me. On 16 May 1976, at an abortion clinic in Auckland, I underwent, fully conscious, a vacuum aspiration and heard the nurse say 'It's a boy.' Back home I developed septicaemia which fortunately antibiotics cured. In my mind I filed the matter under 'forget quickly', but it was then that, for no apparent reason, I began to resent my husband. Not long afterwards, our marriage collapsed.

In 1981 I gave birth to a baby girl with trisomy 13, a rare chromosome disorder which prevents formation of the septum in the nose and the heart and gives rise to other deformities. She lived for three hours. About six months into the pregnancy I experienced in-depth communication with this little being. For an hour or so one night in bed I felt as though we were both enfolded in a wonderful golden web of communication. As a result I felt that I knew her so deeply that if she died it would be all right. My consciousness was lucid and expansive for days afterwards. This was the highlight of my pregnancy. Had I known she was deformed, I am fairly sure I would not have opted for an abortion.

In 1993, seventeen years after my abortion, the whole experience emerged again in the middle of a three-month solitary meditation retreat. Feelings of grief surfaced in my meditation practice. I realized I needed to re-enact the events somehow, and decided to perform a ritual. Oddly, I had with me much of what I needed to perform it. It was enormously freeing and helpful, and I include it at the end of this chapter for those who may find it useful.

My painful reproductive history is just one among many. Happily, along with my own pain has come greater understanding, and I am reluctant to judge what may appear to be callous behaviour in other women. Abortion is an issue that involves so many factors – socio-economic, ethical, legal, psychological, genetic, political, and spiritual – that it almost defies discussion. Yet years of Buddhist training and my own experience have enabled me to begin to approach the subject in the light of some universal principles.

As I listen to the two main factions in the abortion debate, I am repeatedly struck by the way each party over-identifies with its view. In all areas of life, the more one fixes a view as being absolute, the more polarized one becomes; the middle ground crumbles into the abyss and communication becomes very difficult. In the abortion debate the phrase 'I don't know' is seldom heard, and dogmatism prevails.

It is not surprising, of course, that feelings run high on both sides of the debate: 'pro-life' and 'pro-choice'. The view held by pro-choice people – stated at its simplest – is that a woman has the right to make her own decision about whether to continue with a pregnancy, as she would about any other kind of medical intervention (the implication being that a foetus does not become a person until birth, and so need not be taken into account). History shows the origin of the pro-choice movement. Although in the modern West it is now relatively safe to bear children, in the past child-bearing was dangerous, and in some countries it still is. Women have always needed to consider the future of the rest of their family in the event of their death in childbirth. Out of such considerations, along with the misery of poverty, fear of bringing shame on their families, fear of being beaten up by their husbands when they learned of the impending mouth to feed, women have resorted to abortion, sometimes turning to natural medicine, to such herbs as pennyroyal, tansy, rue, juniper, and parsley, and to oils and massage, to terminate an unwanted pregnancy.

Many women have committed suicide as a result of unwanted pregnancy. Others have resorted to back-street abortions, risking arrest and imprisonment, accidental sterility, infections such as gangrene, perforated uteri, and death. Thousands of women have bled to death or died of septicaemia or tetanus. These horrors cannot be dismissed as belonging to the remote past; women in many countries are still subject to such dangers. The pro-choice movement has arisen partly out of fear and suffering.

In this era of technology and legalized abortion, thousands of frightened women are getting relief, but we have also begun to normalize the unthinkable. Abortion is becoming an easy option. Women are now having abortions not just because they are frightened or at medical risk but as part of choosing between motherhood and career, relationship, travel, delayed parenthood, and so on. In a nihilistic, materialistic society abortion has gradually come to be regarded as a contraceptive. 'There is convincing evidence that it is to a large extent an entirely new clientèle that is now granted legal abortions [in Sweden], that is, women who would not have had an illegal abortion if they had been refused the legal one.'[65]

It is estimated that there are around 1,000,000 abortions in the world each year. In the United Kingdom 150,000 abortions are performed annually, 87% taking place before the foetus is 12 weeks old.[66] Over 90% of all abortions use vacuum aspiration. The mother's cervix is locally anaesthetized and then dilators or rods are inserted to stretch it. A small tube called a cannula is inserted into the uterus, and connected to the vacuum aspirator, a machine that sucks out the contents of the uterus. Once the cervix has been dilated, the aspiration takes five to eight minutes. In later stages of pregnancy abortions require surgical measures. The doctor is obliged to dismember the foetus inside the mother and extract it in bits. The foetus's skull needs to be crushed to facilitate extraction. Most operations of this kind are performed only when the mother's life is at risk.

Legally, there are anomalies here. A woman can procure a legal abortion when the foetus is 24 weeks old. But if the mother had given birth at 24 weeks and then killed the baby outside the womb, she would be tried for manslaughter. Does medical intervention somehow sanctify the procedure? One horrifying account is given by nurses in a New York hospital who were expected to alternate between caring for premature infants and disposing of viable foetuses, aborted at 24 weeks.

In the context of these distressing stories, the pro-life lobby has become both vociferous and active. Again put simply, the pro-life argument is that human life begins at conception and that therefore abortion is wrong because it is taking life – human life – a form of violence of the most extreme kind. I should say straight away that this is the traditional Buddhist point of view. This is made clear in the Vinaya (the monastic code of conduct), where any monk procuring an abortion for a woman, or assisting in one, is regarded as having committed one of the most serious offences, the taking of human life.[67] Any committed Buddhist who follows tradition would never have, or advise someone else to have, an abortion.

However, while the Buddhist ethical position is clear, it is also clear from Buddhist doctrine that acts of violence cannot be remedied by violent means. It is horrifying to hear of the tactics employed by the most extreme crusaders for the pro-life lobby, which have including pouring glue into the keyholes of clinic doors, murdering doctors who perform abortions, and placing foetal remains in a children's playhouse in an abortion clinic. A pregnant clinic worker miscarried after being punched in the stomach by a crusader. Apart from such cruel activism, one finds a strange inconsistency in the view of many upholders of the 'pro-life' stance; it is inconsistent, for example, to be 'pro-life' while advocating forms of violence such as capital punishment, as some fundamentalist Christians, for example, do.

To be very clear about the ethical position, one needs to address a simple question: at what point should a foetus be considered to be a human being? The implication of the traditional guideline is that, according to Buddhism, a foetus should be regarded as a human being from the very moment of conception. But when is a foetus 'ensouled', as Aristotle and Augustine put it? Both philosopher and theologian believed that a male foetus was 'ensouled' at 40 days, and a female at 80–90 days, and saw no problem with abortion before that point – but there are many other views on the crucial question of when a foetus should be regarded as human. Most theologians agree that a human being is created at the point when sperm fuses with ovum; medical science, though – together with Islamic tradition – dates conception from fourteen days later, when the united ovum and sperm settle on the wall of the uterus.

Exactly when the living collection of cells from which the foetus develops can be thought of as a person is impossible to determine. New embryological data suggest that conception is a process over time rather than an event, and this is supported by experiments in past life regression which indicate that some consciousnesses enter and leave the foetus several times before birth, some spend most of the pregnancy in the womb, while others enter the baby's body just before birth and some even just after.[68]

This of course brings in the backdrop to a Buddhist consideration of abortion: rebirth. Stated simply, according to the Buddhist doctrine of rebirth, when we die our consciousness leaves the body to enter an 'intermediate state' (*bardo*). In this *bardo* we have the opportunity to leave the cycle of birth and death altogether, and, recognizing the blinding light of Reality as our own nature, become Enlightened. If one is very spiritually advanced, this is a real possibility. Most of us, though, frightened and bewildered by this strange 'disembodied' state, seek the reassuring familiarity of rebirth in another human form. It is said that we are attracted to the man and woman who will become our parents in our next life through the momentum of our past karma. 'Conception', then, is the meeting of three things: the sperm of the father, the ovum of the mother, and the consciousness of the being seeking rebirth.

As we have seen, it is difficult to determine exactly when the consciousness enters the embryonic form of the body. But even if consciousness has not taken full control of the embryo, it may still be disoriented or affected by the embryo's destruction, because its process of identification with that particular organism will have begun. 'People who have an abortion, or want to have an abortion, usually do not know if the foetus is already inhabited and so do not know if, by killing the foetus, they cause a person to go through an awful experience.'[69] Although the exact time of 'ensoulment' may be uncertain, the ethical position is clear: to use a homely phrase, better safe than sorry. If we do not know whether or not we are doing violence to a fellow human being, it is clearly better not to take the risk, just as, if we do not know whether or not anyone is in a building, it is better not to set it alight.

In Buddhism much emphasis is placed on the preciousness of human birth as a tremendous opportunity. Life is to be cherished in all circumstances. Of course, in many circumstances, it is difficult to choose not to resort to abortion. There can be nothing more difficult than having to make a decision involving a pregnancy resulting from rape. The prospective mother has been subjected to a deeply traumatic ordeal, and in pregnancy and motherhood she would often be reminded of that trauma. The action perpetrated against her has come out of an extremely unskilful state of mind. But committing another unskilful action, abortion, cannot but bring more suffering. Counselling, adoption, spiritual practice, and the support of kind friends and family are all possible aids in such a difficult situation. Other options for care either within or outside the family group can also be explored. In the same way, much care and concern need to be given to a woman pregnant with a child who is malformed in some way. As far as unwanted pregnancies are concerned, the focus needs to be on avoiding them in the first place, with the provision of sex education programmes and free contraception.

The Buddhist contribution to the abortion debate is a consideration of the inevitable suffering that the breaking of the First Precept brings both to the woman having the abortion and to the being awaiting rebirth. It is very difficult to have a sense of the intangible future effects of this action when faced with the very real and tangible effects of continuing with a problematic pregnancy. This is, of course, true more generally; many of our actions have consequences that aren't immediately discernible. But one consequence that many women experience, as I have, is a deep feeling of regret and sorrow that can surface many years after the event. Having an abortion is something that we can never really forget; although if we have had one, meditating, performing rituals, and talking with friends can help us come to terms with what we have done.

But although the traditional Buddhist position can be said to be 'pro-life', it would be un-Buddhistic to enforce this in an authoritarian way. Buddhists try to develop empathy and sensitivity towards all that lives, aligning themselves with universal principles such as non-violence and interconnectedness, and trying to uphold these principles consistently. If non-violence is one of your guiding stars, it needs to govern all facets of your life. The person who abhors abortion would naturally also abhor war and armament manufacture, the exploitation and killing of animals for food, and coercion of any kind – including the coercion that forces someone to have, or not to have, an abortion.

The question whether or not abortion should be illegal presents the biggest dilemma of all. Woman have always had abortions. If abortion was made illegal, and our society remained as it is today, a return to back-street abortions could lead to the deaths of thousands of women. However, the legalization of abortion can lead to its being viewed as a method of contraception. Living in a chaotic, violent, and unhappy world, I see legislating against abortion as a disaster, and yet if I am truly to practise and advocate Buddhist ethics I cannot support legalization. There is no easy answer. All I can do, I feel, is to continue to work on transforming myself and the society in which I live.

I dedicate this chapter to my son Sam, who would have been 18 at the time of writing.

A Buddhist Ritual to Mark Abortion

I performed the ritual on the evening of a full moon. Within a length of my great-grandmother's bridal train, which I'd been using as a shrine cloth, I placed a crystal, symbolizing for me Vajrasattva, the Buddha who connects us with our primordial purity. I also placed in the bridal train rose-quartz, for healing old hurts and forgiveness; a bead Philippe and I were given when we were married; and three little stars, each the colour of one of the Three Jewels. I then performed the Metta Bhavana meditation and set out in the rain, with candles and other ritual objects, on to the wide empty beach. I made two circles, one of shells, the second of pampas grass. My ritual went like this:

Purification
I stepped into the circle of shells with a tin whistle blowing my guilt and other unskilful mental states away to the wind.

Enactment
Chanting *sabbe sattha sukhi hontu* ('May all beings be happy'), I looked at the bundle of things, recognized and named my baby Sam. I acknowledged him in the presence of each of the five Buddhas. I left the first circle and walked to the second, where I put him in the prepared grave on the reeds that lay at the bottom. I chanted the Vajrasattva mantra three times and covered the grave with sand and flowers.

Acknowledgement of Learning
I put incense and flowers on the grave and reflected in silence.

Closing
I stepped out of the circle and blew out the candle.

Absorption
Back in my retreat hut I performed a special confessional puja from the *Sutra of Golden Light*.

III Skilful Relationships

Dhammadinna

After growing up in Somerset, Dhammadinna studied biology at London University. In 1970 she attended her first Buddhist retreat; she was ordained in 1973. She was secretary of the FWBO's main London centre for two years and then, at Sangharakshita's request, spent several years involved specifically with the increasing number of women in the movement: she arranged retreats and study groups, and travelled around various FWBO centres, including those in Finland, Holland, and New Zealand. During this time she helped to found several women's residential communities. From 1982 to 1992 she lived and worked at the London Buddhist Centre, as well as reading for a degree in religious studies. In 1990 she joined the Women's Ordination Team, and now lives with other members of the team at Tiratanaloka Retreat Centre. She now spends most of her time attending retreats, helping other women to deepen their commitment to the Buddhist way of life and to become members of the Order.

Dhammadinna

A Noble Relationship

Women and Friendship

What a woman thinks of other women is a test of her nature.[70]

NOT MUCH HAS BEEN written on women and friendship. In *A Room of One's Own* Virginia Woolf describes her search for a tradition of female friendship in literature: 'those unsaid or half-unsaid words which form themselves no more palpably than the shadow of moths on the ceiling, when women are alone, unlit by the capricious and coloured light of the opposite sex.' However, what she found in her search is that 'Chloe liked Olivia.' So she concludes 'Do not blush. Women do like other women. Chloe liked Olivia.'[71]

According to Vera Brittain, the idea of female friendship is mistrusted. In her record of her seventeen-year friendship with the novelist Winifred Holtby, *Testament of Friendship*, she says: 'From the days of Homer the friendships of men have enjoyed glory and acclamation, but the friendships of women, in spite of Ruth and Naomi, have usually been not merely unsung, but mocked, belittled, and falsely interpreted. I hope that Winifred's story may do something to destroy these tarnished interpretations, and show its readers that loyalty and affection between women is a noble relationship.'[72]

I have never doubted this; and I have always wanted friendships with other women. As a child, with an older brother who both protected and bossed me, I longed for a sister. I also had fantasies of belonging to a group of like-minded and free-spirited girl friends. It wasn't, however, until I left my mixed-sex and fairly rough primary school to go to a girls' secondary school that I began to make real friends, who sustained me through some difficult times at home during my teens, and with some of whom I am still in contact.

Because I was good at science at school, I applied for and was awarded a place in the biology department of a large, conservative, science-based college of London University where the ratio of men to women students was 30:1. Not that before I went to college men were absent from my life. I first fell in love (or rather, developed a crush) when I was 5, and this feeling, unfortunately unrequited, continued throughout my primary school days. I remember early stirrings of envy for my desk-mate, who was pretty and received declarations of love from the boys in the class.

Perhaps going to a girls' school throughout my teens meant that I valued my friendships with other girls as a base from which to explore. After school we hung around the town and its coffee bars making contact with boys, discussing our experiences fully with friends at school the next day. Around the age of 14 or 15 I began to fall in love rather dramatically. I found this very painful as it seemed to render communication between myself and the object of my love totally impossible. Although the feelings were intense, I could also fall out of love, and fall in love with someone else, rather quickly.

At university, for the first time in my life I felt uneasy about being a woman. I was shy and self-conscious and felt uncomfortable being outnumbered by so many men. At home I had had a great deal of freedom and though my background was working-class I had mixed with all kinds of people. The men at university came mainly from public schools and they had had little contact with women, or the world. The few women came mostly from middle-class homes. The social scene was dominated by the rugby club and the only bar in the students' union was exclusively for men. It seemed that women were accepted if they were quiet and well-behaved.

I adopted various strategies to deal with this, from trying to be one of the boys to being outrageously flamboyant and unacceptable. Despite these strategies, I did make friendships with both men and women, but I was relieved to leave university and become part of the sixties counter-culture, where men and women mixed together much more naturally and easily.

During this phase in my life I formed a long-term sexual relationship and lived with my partner, eventually marrying him. This was the central emotional relationship in my life. However, it was not a conventional marriage. Our small flat was always full of people passing through for the evening or staying with us. We had other lovers and affairs and were always open about this. Although my husband and I were emotionally close and had lots of friends and acquaintances of both sexes, I always valued spending time alone with women friends.

It was in this hippie 'underground' milieu that I became interested in Buddhism and got involved with the FWBO. The people at meditation classes and retreats were of all ages and both sexes, and I made friends with both men and women. I also met Sangharakshita.

The Idea of Spiritual Friendship

During my early years of involvement with the Dharma, I was confronted with a number of experiences and ideas that began to change my views on friendship. I heard, for example, the famous remark made by Ananda, the Buddha's companion. One day he exclaimed, 'Lord, I think that friendship is half of the spiritual life!' 'Say not so, Ananda, say not so. Friendship is the whole of the spiritual life,' came the even more famous reply.[73]

What could this mean? Clearly it did not mean that the other spiritual practices I was hearing about, such as meditation, ethical awareness, and creative work, were unimportant. The point was that they all had to take place within a context of spiritual friendship.

But what was 'spiritual friendship'? And how could you develop it? My previous experience of friendship was of being attracted to certain people simply because they were fun to be with, or of becoming friends with people I happened to find myself with in a particular situation. Friendship, I thought, was something that just happened.

But Sangharakshita spoke about a kind of spiritual friendship that you could consciously develop. He called it *kalyana mitrata*. *Mitrata* means friendship; *kalyana* is a word with many connotations, including lovely, whole, beautiful, morally or ethically good. Essentially, *kalyana* is a state of mind more ethically sensitive, aesthetic, and refined than our normal consciousness. This state or level can be approached through meditation practice, through aesthetic awareness, and through friendship.

Kalyana mitrata, then, is 'friendship associated with the beautiful'. Within the Western tradition this is similar to Aristotle's 'love of the Good' (*kalos*), which includes the True and the Beautiful, and which he sees as true friendship, as opposed to the two other levels he enumerates: friendship based on use, and friendship based on pleasure. These definitions point to a distinction between spiritual friendship and 'ordinary' friendship, although perhaps this is a difference of degree rather than kind.

I also discovered that Buddhist teaching emphasizes non-exclusive loving-kindness or *metta* rather than exclusive attachment or *pema*. In his teachings Sangharakshita placed a special emphasis on spiritual friendship: friendship based on common commitment to the Three Jewels of Buddhism. The Buddhist tradition teaches that friendship and friendliness can be cultivated by the practice of the Metta Bhavana meditation, the 'development of loving-kindness'. Metta is a strong feeling of well-wishing for all beings. In the meditation you begin by cultivating feelings of loving-kindness towards yourself, then a close friend, then a 'neutral' person, then a person you find difficult, and then towards all life. So love for all does not exclude strong feelings towards our friends, or mean that we shouldn't have close friends. Friendship is based on mutual loving-kindness and provides the basis of our spiritual growth and development.

Spiritual growth involves moving away from, and eventually transcending, egoistic concerns, selfishness, and self-involvement, as well as the delusion, aversion, and greed that these are based on. True friendship, while being enjoyable for its own sake, also provides us with constant opportunities to respond to the needs of our friends rather than automatically to our own.

Spiritual friendship based on metta, as well as being mutual, can involve what is sometimes called a 'vertical' element. We may realize through our communication with someone that they are more spiritually developed than we are, and can help us in our growth. Our feelings of loving-kindness towards them will naturally find expression as receptivity, even as faith and devotion. And if we are in communication with someone who is in some ways less experienced than us, or troubled and in pain, our feeling of metta will naturally become compassion.

Metta is the antidote to hatred, but also to pema, or sentimental attachment, which includes over-idealizing someone, falling in love, and feeling strong sexual desire. Although in our culture it is commonly assumed that it is within romantic love that the strongest feelings can be expressed, in fact metta is stronger than pema. Sangharakshita once said that metta, in contrast to pema, is 'hot but not sticky, warm but not clammy'.[74]

Another phrase current at the time was 'fierce friendship'. Friendship is not necessarily about being 'nice'. But although fierce friendship has sometimes been misunderstood to mean being critical, it is not fierce in this sense. 'In essence it involves the willingness to open up within the communication issues and areas which are deeper and more far-reaching than the other person supposed, perhaps pointing out the implications of the other's actions in such a way that they feel a sort of abyss opening up beneath their feet.'[75]

All these ideas struck me with some force. Having been involved in both the counter-culture and left-wing politics, I was inspired by the ideas of co-operation and collective action. This was the first time, however, that I had come across a well-developed idea of spiritual friendship.

The Single-Sex Idea

At around the time I was discovering these traditional ideas, a new one began to emerge among the men and women involved in the FWBO – new, at least, to us. This was the idea that single-sex activities provided the best situations in which to develop individuality and friendship. I found myself confronted and challenged by this, having been brought up in a society which seemed to believe that the more mixing together of the sexes there was, the better. The single-sex idea says just the opposite – and to begin with, like many other people, I found it difficult to accept. But my experience on retreats and in communities showed me that mixed situations involve a degree of the tension of opposition and attraction.

I also began to see that, as part of our development, we need to identify with our own gender. We need to be, and to be happy with, who we are. In single-sex situations we experience ourselves simply as women among other women, rather than feeling we have to adopt strategies to attract or repel men. With sustained experience of same-sex situations comes a further change: a move from a fixed identification with our gender to a healthy provisional identification with it, and from this to no identification with it at all. Psychologically and spiritually, if not physically, we become both 'masculine' and 'feminine'.

Sangharakshita discusses this issue in his book, *The Ten Pillars of Buddhism* (in which he explores ten ethical principles), in the chapter on the

Third Precept: abstention from sexual misconduct, or contentment. 'For those who wish to develop as individuals, and to progress on the path to Enlightenment, meditation and all kinds of single-sex situations are, in the absence of transcendental insight, absolutely indispensable.' This is to 'give both men and women some respite from the tensions of sexual polarization and to provide them with an opportunity of transcending, for a few moments, the state of sexual polarization and being simply a human being and – to some extent – a true individual'.[76] Single-sex activities foster friendships with one's own sex, help us to develop contentment, and eventually enable us to have straightforward relations and friendships with the opposite sex.

One of the dangers for women of being mainly in mixed-sex situations and not having strong friendships with other women is that we may project certain capacities on to men. For example, we may see men as more 'spiritual' than women, or more pioneering, and this may mean that we do not try to develop those qualities in ourselves. Of course, the absence of men does not automatically mean that we immediately develop deep and meaningful friendships with other women. Certain projections may be absent but other obstacles can get in the way. For example, if we have tended to let men take the lead in mixed situations, we may expect another woman to take initiative in women-only situations. On the other hand, although women often say they want to see women taking a lead, when this happens they may feel resentful or envious.

The same thing can sometimes lead us to be over-cautious about another woman's desire to take initiative. Recently a friend of mine wanted to put herself forward for a position of responsibility. She felt that, rather than encouraging her, her colleagues – she was working with a team of women Buddhists – advised her to be careful, wondering if it would be too much for her and whether she could cope. Of course it was important to be realistic, but my friend felt that she could have been given more encouragement.

I have heard women over the years express a fear of women-only situations because they think women together will become over-involved with emotional states, focus on trivia, and become too subjective, indulging in too much self-disclosure. This has been described as 'the swamp'. Women together can intuit one another's emotional states and feel impelled to respond. Someone else's pain is hard for us to bear and we want to 'make it better'. But these are not reasons for avoiding women's situations. We need, rather, to learn to develop the objectivity and emotional distance that enable us to be really helpful to one another.

A Passionate Exchange

In the FWBO we have developed a tradition of 'reporting-in'. We have many different kinds of collective activities: retreats, study groups, Order meetings, community evenings, where it can be helpful to 'tune in' to one another, either because we are coming together for the first time, or, if working in a team, because we need to know how everyone is so that the working day can be harmonious. While this is a useful practice, we need to be aware that its purpose is to communicate something of value. Reporting-in can turn into a sort of therapy session, in which people feel they have to reveal their worst traits to others they hardly know.

Perhaps this happens because of our society's increasing focus on therapeutic methods and its tendency to become a 'confessing society'. We see this trend taking up a lot of space on television, where people seem happy to 'tell all'. In *A Passion for Friends*, having quoted Michel Foucault on the confessing society, Janice Raymond says that psychology has created a new type of person: the human confessing animal.[77] She also says that this kind of self-disclosure blurs the boundaries between the intimate and the public. She calls this sort of emotional over-indulgence 'therapism', by which she means an exchange where communication is debased into a perpetual 'show and tell', where a manifestation of feelings without due discernment becomes a substitute for friendship. She calls it 'gossip about oneself'.

We need to be aware of this when we report-in. On retreats at Tiratanaloka, we have noticed a tendency for participants, when reporting-in before a study group, to mention all the uncomfortable feelings they have had since the group last met. The mood of the group then becomes more subjective. In recent times we have reported in much less, just saying a quick hello before the group. Reporting-in can be spiritually helpful if it is a considered communication. But it need not always focus on feelings; it might be about ideas, books you have read, or something you would like to do. And it can become more of a discussion than a one-sided communication. True confession involves a genuine understanding that we have done, or said, something we regret in relation to the ethical precepts we follow. It is not a merely psychological venting of all our mental states without reflection or discrimination.

Raymond contrasts 'therapism' with a genuine passionate exchange or self-revelation which comes out of an intensity of inner experience. And she asks if we are sharing a profound inner life, self-centred (in a positive sense), work-centred, and thoughtful; a creative existence with people whom we have freely chosen to be our friends through due judgement and discernment.

A True Friend

In my early days in the FWBO, having an ideal of spiritual friendship sometimes seemed to get in the way of actually making friends with other women Buddhists. Sometimes I was so busy thinking about what friendship *should* be like that I overlooked quite ordinary human communication. I mistakenly thought we ought always to be talking 'deeply and meaningfully' rather than relaxing and enjoying simple pleasures together.

Another factor which hindered my friendships with other women, ironically, was that I became a member of the Western Buddhist Order, and took on responsibility for encouraging women coming along to the FWBO in their spiritual lives. I sincerely wanted more women to enter the Order, and did what I could to help them, leading retreats and study groups. But I was inexperienced in handling the projections that came my way. Women sometimes fell in love with me, or projected authority on to me, or found it difficult having another woman leading retreats or teaching. I tended to take the idea of vertical friendship as an aspect of *kalyana mitrata* too literally, thinking that meant I should not show my own weaknesses or imperfections or pain; this, of course, opened me up to more projection.

I was trying to take stock of all this when I met a woman at the Buddhist centre who had the open-heartedness to meet me as I was, to see me as a human being and not get involved in the projections I had previously brought upon myself. My developing friendship with her brought about a real change in my attitude, and it has sustained me through my spiritual life and enabled me to integrate my ideal and vision of friendship with a genuine expression of it.

When we first met, I had just returned to London after three months in India. I was living in a large, rather intense, women's community. We didn't have much money, so we didn't go out much, and spent most of our time working on the house, meditating, studying, and talking about our inner lives. My new friend (Anne, now Parami) burst into this rather enclosed atmosphere and took me off to see *Star Wars*, the first film I had seen for ages.

She has an enormous amount of energy and is very extrovert, always managing to be involved with several different activities at the same time and to have a large circle of friends. When we met I had been an Order member for a few years while she had only recently got involved in the Glasgow Buddhist Centre. I was always impressed by her energy and enthusiasm. After this first meeting she kept in touch by letter. Twenty-page letters would drop through our letter-box, full of her activities, thoughts, enthusiasms, ideas, and idealism. She would attend women's days at our community, hitching down from Scotland on Friday night after work, spending Saturday with friends and going to an all-night party, then turning up fresh and full of energy for the day retreat on Sunday.

She has always had an ability to connect deeply with all sorts of people. She always knows all the local shopkeepers and has a talent for getting people to talk and tell their stories. This interest and concern for others has led her, apart from working within the FWBO, to work with those suffering from HIV and AIDS.

I have learned many things from her. By watching how she engages with strangers, I learned not to be so shy myself. I think she is completely unshockable and this enables people to confide in her. This open-hearted woman helped me to explore and acknowledge many difficult aspects of my own character, so that I was able to overcome them. Living with her in various communities was always stimulating and challenging. She could never bear 'atmospheres' and was always brave enough to ask what was going on.

Our friendship exists on many different levels. We have always enjoyed each other's company, finding one another stimulating and interesting. We can have fun together. We come from similar backgrounds, which may help, although temperamentally she is much more extrovert than me. We have never fallen out, but we can challenge each other, and have helped each other to explore the shadow aspects of our natures, to bring them into the light and transform them. We both love the Dharma and can get very excited and inspired exploring the teachings and finding ways to communicate them and put them into practice. Our friendship has now spanned sixteen years and endured long geographical separations. There have been times when my tendencies to nihilism and self-doubt might have defeated me if I had not had her for my friend. It seems crucial to me to have at least one friend with whom I can be completely myself, in my heights and depths.

Friendship cannot remain static; it has to be a dynamic communication between two changing people. Having been very close, there was a point, some years ago, when Parami and I were in danger of drifting apart. She had decided to come out as a lesbian, to identify with and spend time with other lesbians. As a heterosexual woman, I realized that this was an area of life and experience we did not share. We had a long, deep, honest, and intimate conversation in which we both had to accept the other for what she was, but in which we also realized that our history and what we had in common was greater than our differences. One of the joys of this friendship is that although it is very close, it is not exclusive. We both have many other friends, and share friends in common.

A Sense of Identity

My experience of, and reflections on, women and friendship have shed light on both the benefits and the difficulties of such friendships. The benefits of female friendship for our development seem to me to be enormous. One of these benefits is that friendship helps us to see ourselves clearly. In 'The Pillow and the Key' Robert Bly tells the story of a young male friend of his who had mainly female friends, whom he appreciated very much, at school, college, and work. However, he has a dream that he is living in the forest with a clan of she-wolves. One day they all run to a river bank. When they look into the river all the she-wolves are reflected, but the young man is not. Bly suggests that male companionship produces a 'face' for men.[78] I would say that this is true for women also. Our friendships with one another give us a face, a sense of identity; we are reflected back to ourselves, as women amongst women. Same-sex friendships help us to bring our true selves into being.

From a spiritual point of view this provides a basis for us to know ourselves deeply, free from the 'capricious and coloured light of the opposite sex' described by Virginia Woolf. Among other women, we have the opportunity to be free from the tensions that can arise in mixed situations, and to experience ourselves simply as human beings.

The Romantic Myth

In our society, friendships between women are not valued much, though this has changed over the last thirty years or so, due mainly to the women's movement. In my experience women are now much happier to spend time together without men than they used to be. But it is still pretty obvious that our society exalts the romantic myth, valuing the sexual relationship, preferably between a man and a woman, more than any friendship or other relationship. The romantic myth involves the idea that there is one person out there who will complete us. I think most of us in the West grow up with the idea that we will fall in love with Mr or Ms Right, find our soul-mate, and live happily ever after. This myth is backed up by songs, Hollywood films, fairy tales, advertisements, and all kinds of novels, from Jane Austen to popular romantic fiction. If we hold this view, we will tend to see our friendships as second best, to be jettisoned when Mr or Ms Right comes along. You may remember that old song by the Beverley Sisters, 'Lord help the Mister that comes between me and my sister', which unfortunately ends, 'but Lord help the sister who comes between me and my man.'

A few years ago I was on holiday with Parami, something we try to do once a year now that we live in different countries. We took a risk and a last-minute flight to Ibiza, and stayed in a Spanish-style hotel. We were more than happy with each other's company, the pool, a pile of books, and the various friends we made, but were both amused and saddened to see several women left by themselves, because the female friend they were on holiday with had met Mr Right Holiday Romance. Perhaps they had agreed that this would be all right, but it was obvious that romance was considered more important than friendship.

How is it that the myth of romantic love is so strong in our culture? In *The Art of Loving*, Erich Fromm says that a great change took place in the twentieth century. 'In the Victorian Age, as in many traditional cultures, love was mostly not a spontaneous personal experience which then might lead to marriage. On the contrary, marriage was contracted by convention – either by the respective families, or by a marriage broker.

In contrast especially in the last few generations the concept of romantic love has become almost universal in the Western World.'[79] Conditioned by our culture, we have an idealized image of Mr or Ms Right with whom we will fall in love. We do not really fall in love with a person, but with our own projected idealized image which they may provide a hook for. Fromm also says that the increasing materialism of our society encourages us to see the other as an object to possess among other objects. Our society is also increasingly fragmented, with greater mobility and the breakdown of the extended family. Cut off from our relations and our old friends, we expect the romantic relationship to meet all our emotional needs.

When we fall in love we suddenly let down barriers – we might even describe it as experiencing 'oneness' – but this is destined not to last once we become better acquainted with our lover. In fact the intensity of the infatuation may only prove the degree of the preceding loneliness. Given that it is impossible to sustain such projections if we spend time with a person, and that the corresponding sexual attraction begins to wear off, it is no surprise that so many marriages end in divorce.

The romantic myth leads us to believe that we will find that perfect mate, that we will then feel whole and fulfilled, and that we will live happily ever after. Thinking that one person can fulfil our lives leads us to depend on that person emotionally, to make them the centre of our lives. Stanton Peel and Archie Brodsky explore this kind of dependency in their book *Love and Addiction*,[80] in which they explain that falling in love, being in love, and the resulting emotional dependency, are not merely analogous to drug addiction, but actually are an addiction.

Falling in love is not necessarily a bad thing in itself, since we feel a heightened emotionality when we are in love. I remember an artist friend once saying 'The artist is either in love or creating.' However, it does usually involve an element, even a strong element, of projection. We imagine that the other person possesses certain qualities which are really aspects of our own deeper self. Sangharakshita's advice is to keep away from the person we have fallen in love with.[81] Then we can dwell on the feelings and try to develop them so that we experience that part of ourselves previously not known to us, reclaiming and integrating these qualities into our conscious awareness. This is not unlike the ritualization of medieval courtly love, where the object of such love was deliberately kept at a distance so that the feelings could be intensified. This distancing is also part of the Platonic tradition, especially as expressed in the *Symposium*, and practised by Persian Sufi mystics. Upon falling in love, a Sufi poet would apparently go into the desert for several years and contemplate the loved one. The point of doing this kind of thing is that it heightens and refines the feelings which can then be directed into love not just for one person, but for all people.

We usually think of the romantic myth happening between a man and a woman; this is the way it is reflected in our culture. However, men also fall in love with men and women with women, and the attachment which often results is as inimical to friendship and spiritual development as the heterosexual relationship. From a Buddhist perspective this kind of homosexual relationship is an aspect of sentimental attachment just as much as heterosexual relationships are.

The tendency in our society to see the romantic relationship as central to life obviously affects how we view friendship, perhaps especially same-sex friendship. In contrast to falling in love, which we expect just to happen to us and which we hope will be immediately fulfilling, friendship involves developing our capacity to love and respond to the other as a person in their own right. It is usually less dramatic than falling in love, and takes longer to develop, although its rewards are infinitely more long-lasting, sustaining, and fulfilling.

Looking at the effect of the romantic myth on my own life and friendships, I find that although I have tended to fall in love, my most important sexual relationships have begun on the basis of friendship and grown into loving relationships. This did not, however, prevent me from becoming dependent and attached, losing my individuality, and being devastated when the relationships ended. In my favour, I can say that I now have friendships with most of my ex-partners. This has involved a lot of hard work, letting go of jealousy, pain, and resentment, and if I had not been a practising Buddhist I might not have been able to do that work. I have sometimes chosen long periods of celibacy in order to work against my tendency to be over-dependent. This has given me time to get to know myself better and also to develop my friendships with other women.

I do think that it is possible for a woman to have friendships with men. But it seems to me that my ability to be straightforward in such friendships has developed in direct proportion to my development of female friendships, and time spent living and practising with women. The less I have depended upon men for approval, and the more I have managed to untangle my ambivalent feelings towards them, the more individual and the more able to have friendships with them I have become.

I have several long-standing and very enjoyable friendships with men. Sometimes in the past this has been important to prevent me from projecting the 'enemy' on to men collectively. I have one long-standing platonic friendship in particular which has been very important to me. This friend probably knows me as well as my closest women friends. I think that because he is a man he has been able on occasions to reflect me back to myself in a way that a woman could not have done, and this has been very helpful.

Working Together

Friendship does not just exist in a private realm. Ideally it should be a stimulus to action and activity. It needs to contain a third, higher factor, something transcendental, a shared ideal which both friends are working towards bringing into reality. We are not friends just to *be* together, but in order to *do* something together. A common cause or task can reveal deep affinities which go beyond mere attraction.

This has certainly been my experience of developing friendships with other women. Yes, I want to share my deepest thoughts and feelings, and get feedback, both critical and encouraging, on my actions and habits. But more than this, I want to live and work with other women, to create something of lasting value with and for other women. This does not mean that I want to be part of a separatist project. I am part of an extended mixed community of Buddhist practitioners. My work is mainly with women, but I have an interest in the overall work of the FWBO and am more than happy to be involved in mixed-sex activities when appropriate.

At the moment I am fortunate to be involved in a project with other women to create resources for women involved with the FWBO. When we formed the ordination team our idea was to buy a building as a retreat centre where we could run ordination courses for women. Four of us moved to a rented house in the country and started a fund-raising drive and property search. We had no finances to begin with and none of us had been involved in buying property before. It took us three years to raise the money and buy the property, during which time we also ran several weeks of retreats a year as part of the ordination process.

Although we had known one another for a long time, and some of us had lived together in women's communities many years previously, we had not lived and worked together for some time. The work was demanding and new to us. Under pressure we got to know one another, our strengths and weaknesses, much better than if we had merely been hanging out together. Given that we are committed to living and working together for the foreseeable future, I think those three years were invaluable in forming us into a team and community who now know one another very well and can rely on one another. As well as being intimate and warm, our friendships take place within an objective situation which includes a strong spiritual vision.

I would add that, in order for our communication with other women to be a genuine passionate exchange, rather than 'gossip about oneself', we need to have an intense inner life, and a sense and experience of aloneness. Although I practise Buddhism within the context of spiritual friendship, I also need time on my own, time to meditate, to reflect, to pursue my creative impulses. It might seem paradoxical, but I know that my capacity for friendship has deepened as my capacity to be alone has developed. After I have been on retreat, especially on solitary retreat, experiencing my own aloneness and uniqueness, I can bring more of myself to my friendships.

Looking back over my life and experience, I have more than realized my childhood dreams and visions. I have many 'sisters' with whom I can share my life. I cannot and do not live with all of them, but we share a vision, whatever our circumstances; many of my friends are mothers with children at home. My experience is that our meetings with one another, one to one, on retreat or in study groups, stimulate us to be more deeply ourselves. Each time we meet we are working against all the obstacles, internal and external, to being truly open with one another, and creating bonds of friendship that transcend all our diversities and differences. It is within this context, and on this basis, that I believe that I and other women can realize the freedom of transcendental vision in this life.

Varabhadri

Varabhadri writes: I was fortunate in spending my childhood in Dorset, a beautiful hill county where I could wander freely, becoming familiar with Nature and the changing seasons. I was also inspired and comforted by long involvement with the parish church, where I was introduced to art and music. Less fortunately my artistic aspirations were thwarted by a biased education; also I was raped aged 8, besides undergoing ten years of sexual abuse from my father. Running away at 16, I tried for A and S levels at a local college. No money was available, however, and everything went downhill — into promiscuity, stealing food, taking drugs. From there I went hitch-hiking in North Africa, the Middle East, and India for a few years. Eventually settling in London, I worked happily for a while in a kindergarten, leaving to have a child of my own in 1970. I became mildly involved with political activism — squatting, women's liberation, gay liberation. Discovering the Dharma in 1978, I soon realized that Buddhism could give my life the meaning I longed for. To my surprise I got more involved, and was ordained in 1984. Since 1988 I've been Mitra Convenor for women at the London Buddhist Centre. My life has been transformed. I'm happiest taking study groups, leading retreats, giving talks, and meeting other Dharma explorers. I write poetry, like to live in fields in summer, and still enjoy going abroad. At present I'm 50 years old.

Varabhadri

Sexuality and a Buddhist Way of Life

*Monks, I know of no other single [form ... sound ...] scent ... savour ...
touch by which a man's heart is so enslaved as it is by the [form, sound,]
scent, savour, and touch of a woman. Monks, the [form, sound,] scent,
savour, and touch of a woman obsess a man's heart.*

*Monks, I know of no other single form, sound, scent, savour, and touch
by which a woman's heart is so enslaved as it is by the form, sound,
scent, savour, and touch of a man. Monks, a woman's heart is obsessed
by these things.*

This is what we find the Buddha saying to some of his disciples in a
scripture from the Pali Canon, the oldest surviving written account of the
Buddha's teaching. The implication here and in other teachings is that
the Buddha considered sexual activity to be a major drawback to spiritual
growth. It is also true, though, that in no scripture do we find the Buddha
discriminating against anyone on the basis of their sexual orientation, or
implying that sex is 'unclean', or insisting that sexual activity should take
place only in the context of marriage.

What were your thoughts on reading the quotation, on reading that sex
is regarded as a drawback to spiritual progress? Did it seem to suggest
notions of repression or guilt? Perhaps you thought, 'If I enjoy something,
religion will tell me it's bad for me.' Such responses are not surprising.
Our culture gives out very mixed messages about sex, and we are subject
to many influences, from the past as well as the present. These influences
are often contradictory, but tend overall to persuade us that sex is good
for us, from our teens right into our old age, and that *not* to be sexual is
the modern version of deviance.

Sex is in the thick of the materialistic pursuit of instant gratification, treated as a commodity which everyone is supposed to feel entitled to. In Britain at the moment, the Christian church is in disarray because of revelations of homosexuality within its clergy; there is controversy about blessing gay relationships; non-celibacy among Catholic priests is making headline news; and the sexual misdemeanours of Members of Parliament, usually male, are reported salaciously. Religions more recently established, such as Islam, struggle to propagate their moral codes in a context which the younger generation finds to be at variance with inherited traditions.

Buddhism expresses fundamental truths about life, and so rises above habit, convention, and current fashionable views. Its teachings, deriving from these truths, are universally applicable. How sexuality is seen in the light of Buddhist understanding I shall attempt to convey in this chapter. Does sex occupy a healthy, appropriate place in our lives? And how does it relate to our spirituality? I hope these pages will open up the subject to some extent.

Looking Back: In the Beginning was Sex

The sexual instinct, of course, has its origins in biology. Sexual desire is an innate and crucial part of our make-up, something which, alongside our overall evolution as a distinct species, we have in common with the animal kingdom. Without this instinctive desire, life simply wouldn't continue past the next generation. This primary function of sexuality is a basic fact of life, carrying no moral overtones. Most animals have a mating season, which highlights the fundamental purpose of sex. Our mating season, though we don't usually call it that, lasts all year round! We have woven into sex all sorts of emotions and needs and attitudes. Our sexuality is shaped by a combination of biology, social influences, family conditioning, and some mysterious element in our personality. Sexuality is a point of intersection between biology and culture, the result of what each man or woman makes of these influences. So sexuality for us is far more complex than reproduction: it involves all the attitudes, values, beliefs, and behaviour patterns that have come to have sexual connotations in our society.

Sexuality is not a fixed state of being. It is subject to prevailing views and fashions and to the different phases in one's life; it can be suppressed by religion or political ideology, or given undirected licence, as we have seen in the West since the 'swinging sixties'. Socially sanctioned patterns of sexual expression include – in different cultures – polygamy, polyandry, monogamy, betrothal from childhood, marriage for life, unions dissolvable by common assent. For a traditional Catholic, sex is about having children; for an orthodox Jew it can only happen at prescribed times. Female virginity has been almost universally idealized, yet prostitution is described as the oldest profession. Besides our biological predispositions, how we express our sexuality depends on where and when we were born. For women in the Victorian age sex inevitably resulted in motherhood many times over. To be married was the norm: an unmarried woman was a socially disadvantaged rarity. In all social classes, sexual experimentation was kept in check by the conventions of the time. Long and chaste engagements were standard and many a same-sex attraction was left to smoulder in the intense furnace of romanticized friendship.

In the twentieth century the social impact of the World Wars and, later, the advent of the contraceptive pill, brought a new perspective to childbearing and attitudes to sex; then the gay liberation movement initiated public awareness of homosexuality and strove to remove the shroud of prejudice and suspicion that darkened the lives of gay men and women, and forced the majority to lead double lives, colleagues and family seeing one facet while their secret selves were confined to furtive bars and clubs and a few close friends. Today we live in an atmosphere of sexual freedom unthinkable to previous generations. Things were very different even fifty years ago; sex was not discussed openly, and certainly not analysed by the popular press as it is in today's magazines, with their liberal advice on all aspects of sexual matters. Earlier generations' attitudes to sexuality were restrained and understated. That people had extra-marital affairs we cannot doubt, for we know the terrible stigma attached to illegitimacy. In past times a woman could even be incarcerated in a mental asylum for having had an illegitimate child; her respectable family had her 'put away'. A lapse in the accepted moral standards of the times brought shame and confusion, often made worse by denial and secrecy.

It is scarcely more than a generation since the Pill became available, enabling women to separate sex from child-bearing more safely and successfully than ever before. The implications of this for future generations of women in terms of their view of themselves, their individuality, and their sexuality, have yet to be seen, but it is already obvious that our identity no longer needs to be so bound up with our potential for motherhood.

Greater sexual freedom has brought its own problems, however. Sex has been elevated to a high place in the happiness stakes, but does it really fulfil the promises made on its behalf by popular psychologists and the media alike? People do not seem noticeably happier. It became apparent fairly soon after reliable contraception became freely available that women, especially younger women, felt a greater pressure to be actively sexual. Their boyfriends could argue there was far less risk of pregnancy – a woman's major defence against unwanted sex – and other girls could create peer pressure by claiming that they'd 'done it'. In 1986 Liz Hodgkinson wrote a best-selling book called *Sex is Not Compulsory*, which highlighted some of the less beneficial consequences of the new ways of behaving and relating, private and public. AIDS, revelations of childhood sexual abuse, paedophilia, and questions relating to sex education, are brought to our attention every day, not to forget the misuse of sex in advertising, reminding us that all is far from happy and straightforward in our modern sexual sphere. Have we in fact, collectively at any rate, made significant progress towards an integrated and healthy sexuality?

What is Sexuality?

How do we define 'sexuality'? Is it simply being aware of ourselves as sexual beings, or do we use the term to refer to the expression our sexual instincts take? What does it mean to each of us individually? How does society influence our sexuality? Sexuality is one way of defining ourselves; others include our occupation, our leisure habits, our family relationships. We attach a lot of labels to ourselves, some very temporary indeed, like 'customer', and we can have several labels simultaneously. At any given moment we can categorize ourselves in several ways, some more obviously fluid than others. We might say we're married, or living with someone, or gay, or bisexual, or single, or unattached. Our statements about our sexuality imply views about ourselves and others. 'Marriage', for example, presupposes a more stable arrangement than 'living together', while 'single' could be understood as 'free and available'.

In the decade or so before I contacted the FWBO in the late 1970s I came to the conclusion that I was predominantly sexually attracted to other women. I had had sexual relationships with both women and men since I was about 17, was married briefly at 19, and later, at 24, had my daughter and was a single parent throughout her childhood. I found my relationships with women more emotionally and physically engaging than those with men and eventually stopped having sexual contact with men.

In the early 1970s, following the partial decriminalization of male homosexual acts in 1967, British society saw the rise of the gay liberation movement, with large numbers of people coming out for the first time. In the climate of those now distant times I found I had to defend my preferred sexual orientation, often in hostile circumstances. More than once I was physically attacked, by heterosexual men and women alike. Once I was spat on merely because I 'looked like a lesbian'. Taunts and insults were not unusual: sometimes it was enough simply to walk down the street or sit in a café with a female friend to incite the 'anti-anything-different' sentiments of the local Londoners.

These days I tend not to call myself a lesbian. My sexuality is important to me, but I no longer need to identify myself in that way. I'm committed to Buddhism and call myself a Buddhist. I'm not committed to being lesbian, even though I think it unlikely that my sexual orientation will change drastically. My sexuality is always under review, as are my thoughts, emotions, and ideas. Buddhism encourages natural ethical behaviour based on metta, loving-kindness, and non-exploitation of others; it is concerned with developing human relationships from a basis of unselfishness. Attachment and desire result in unhappiness: in this respect, whether we are straight or gay doesn't matter. Whatever our sexual inclinations, it is the meaning sex holds for us that we need to examine.

I started meditating and taking part in FWBO activities some time in 1978. Although I had had a few brief encounters with Buddhism in the sixteen years before that, this was the first time I'd come across a situation in which I felt I could begin to develop my interest in it. It was with a deep sense of relief that I began to realize that here at last was the gateway to spirituality for me.

Having come from a milieu where sexual relationships were central in people's lives, I soon began to appreciate the different atmosphere at the Buddhist centre. Before, sexual relationships had had a controlling effect on group dynamics. They determined who you sat with in the pub, and created undercurrents at feminist meetings and in the network of friend-ships in the housing co-op. On Buddhist retreats and at meditation classes I noticed that sexual relationships didn't have this effect. I didn't know, and couldn't easily tell, if there were any such relationships between those I met; people didn't behave in a provocative or possessive fashion towards one another. Something else seemed to be at the centre of their lives. This something, I gradually discovered, was 'Going for Refuge', the gradual orientation and transformation of one's life and values towards the ideals embodied in the Three Jewels – the Buddha, Dharma, and Sangha. These 'Jewels' become Refuges for us as we open to their inner meaning.

This was what I picked up on, this Going for Refuge. And it began to change my life. However, I had landed among women who, as far as I could tell, did not have similar life experiences to me. None were openly lesbian, or knew much about the women's liberation movement or gay liberation. Nor had any of the women I met at that time brought up a child without help from a man as I had. They had not sold themselves to men for sex as I had done. They were not consciously coming to terms with the effects of years of childhood sexual abuse. Indeed, I found few women who were willing to believe or really listen to me about this abuse. In those days the subject was taboo – but I'd left home because of what had happened there.

This apparent lack of common background, together with the new values, ideals, and lifestyles I was learning about, resulted in my putting my sexual persona to one side, as it were, for quite a while. Although I think I went a bit too far in ignoring it, I now had room to learn more about myself in other ways, and this proved very beneficial. I had a lot to discover about myself. Eventually – after having chosen to be celibate for about eight years – I learned that I wasn't yet ready for life-long celibacy. I had the feeling that I would understand and integrate more of myself in close relation to someone else, and that this would include sexual expression and communication.

Stillness, Simplicity, and Contentment

To sustain life, we need just a few things: food, shelter, warmth, and safety. These are essentials. Sex is not on that list. Sex is not essential to the individual. To the continuation of society, yes (so far there has been no shortage of volunteers), but not to the individual. No one ever died from not having sex, despite what your first boyfriend might have tried to tell you. Providing we have these basic requirements for survival, we can start to consider what makes life more meaningful. We might add things such as: play, friendship, health, sense of purpose, not too many worries, satisfying work, having children perhaps, and culture – art, music, literature, sports, and recreational activities. The list could go on. And what about sex? At some point in their lives most people would include sexual relationships somewhere in the list, for sex is very much part of worldly existence.

So that we may live our lives in harmony with one another, and further our own spiritual development, Buddhism offers us a guiding principle: metta, the principle of non-exploitation, or loving-kindness, non-selfishness. This principle is made explicit in the Five Precepts, which you will come across elsewhere in this book. It is the Third Precept which interests us here. It says: 'I undertake to refrain from sexual misconduct,' expressed positively as 'With stillness, simplicity, and contentment, I purify my body.' In Buddhism, sex is not seen as sinful or shameful. On the other hand, it is not sanctified by marriage, or considered a spiritual activity. The Third Precept is simply about bringing sex under the influence of metta, loving-kindness, so that we act more and more from genuine love and care and less and less from self-centredness. Not that practising this precept is simple. As we have seen, the Buddha recognized the deep intensity of sexual attraction. The downside is that in sexual relationships we can find ourselves susceptible to over-attachment, over-dependency, jealousy, emotional manipulation, insecurity, possessiveness, and exclusivity, as anyone who has had a bad relationship knows.

Applying the Third Precept to our lives means becoming more aware of our motivations for being sexual, and more conscious of what's going on in our relationships. It means looking at the nature and result of our desires. It is not about who we are sexual with. There is no prejudice about whether one is gay, straight, or bisexual, whether one is 'legally married', no puritanical stance – but neither is there the idea that selfish indulgence is somehow good for us, a view that has been fashionable in recent years.

Given the pitfalls that sexual relationships can entail, some people choose to give them up altogether. I will consider the Buddhist attitude to celibacy later in the chapter. But for many if not most people a sexual relationship is important, at least for some time, maybe for many years of their lives. The positive aspect of the Third Precept, 'With stillness, simplicity, and contentment, I purify my body,' means that we need to be very aware in such a relationship. We have wants and needs, but our wants and needs may be very different from those of our partner. How well can we take each other into account? We need metta to counteract the tendency to pema (selfish attachment). Sexual relationships work well when there is delight in one another's individuality, and badly when undercurrents of control, sometimes due to infantile reflexes, rise to the surface. It is natural to act to fulfil our needs for intimacy, relaxation, and physical contact. When we seek to have these needs met within a relationship, we have to be extra careful to see ourself and our partner as growing and changing individuals, whose existence goes much further than what we get from one another. The old idea of oneself being half of a couple does not usually lead to a creative, vibrant dynamic.

If we are to cultivate the positive side of the Third Precept we must avoid what is termed sexual misconduct. This of course means not using sex for wrong purposes, in a way that harms others or ourselves. The grossest form of sexual misconduct is rape. Rape is almost too obviously wrong to need comment: sex is used violently, destructively, and forcibly in an extreme gesture of selfishness, lust, and aggression, an act committed through coercion, deception, and a disregard for another's wishes and feelings. Besides rape, the sexual abuse of children should obviously be included as sexual misconduct. We cannot know whether this happened in the Buddha's time or culture, but it is not unreasonable to suppose that it did, given what we now know about the secrecy and taboos surrounding the subject. It is a very serious and potentially far-reaching kind of exploitation.

People who have been the victims of such cruelty as rape and abuse will not inevitably go on to perpetrate or be party to such actions themselves, but their attitudes to sex and sexual relationships are often adversely affected. This means that some healing work will be needed to overcome the consequences of having been the victim of sexual misconduct by another person. Buddhism teaches us that we can gain a clearer direction to our future actions and find a way to become free from the detrimental influences of the past.

Adultery is also regarded as misconduct. Though not at first glance in the same league as the previous examples, adultery can nonetheless cause a lot of upset, which may even result in violence, even extreme violence, through jealousy or fear of abandonment. Here the term applies to any committed relationship, legalized or not. It is misconduct because, if monogamy has been agreed on, a breach of trust and fidelity is involved, and someone gets hurt. It is important to get clear at the start of a relationship whether you are going to be monogamous or have an 'open' relationship. When a relationship is new and everything is going well, it is easy to overlook issues that may cause major upset or disagreement later on. It might not seem very romantic, but if we voice our ideas and expectations early on we can avoid a lot of painful misunderstandings. For instance, since from a Buddhist point of view abortion is taking life, the possibility of an unplanned pregnancy needs to be fully taken on board. The most elaborate contraceptive methods have been known to fail.

So, monogamy or non-monogamy? Suppose you agree that you want an open relationship: it is difficult to know just how relaxed you are within it until it is tested by one of you having an affair. Can you really know how you'll feel? Beware rationalizations! What if all sorts of uncomfortable emotions are set loose? Yes, it will tell you something about dependency and attachment, but don't wait for an affair to expose your vulnerability. We need to be super-aware in relationships if we are to remain self-confident and avoid either vindictiveness or helplessness at testing times.

Good sexual relationships, monogamous or non-monogamous, don't just 'happen'. They need to be worked at. That's an important thing to realize. Making them work, once the first rushes of passion and fascination subside, means we have to start going deeper in our communication with each other. Will attraction to someone else bring anxiety, restlessness, and discontent? Are we using attraction to someone else as a way out of an unsatisfactory existing relationship? Sexual misconduct has diverse forms, and relationships are therefore quite a challenge to our skilfulness. 'Contentment' as a positive quality may sound a bit placid or cosy, but real contentment comes from being able to appreciate what we've got with someone, from openness of heart and mind to one another. It means learning to receive and give so that the relationship stands a chance of becoming richer and more meaningful; delighting, not binding, each other, for those who feel bound will surely one day want to break free.

Many of the above considerations apply if we have no primary relationship but are happy with casual uncommitted encounters. Promiscuity does of course carry health risks. (Promiscuity here simply means having sex with lots of people.) It therefore also carries responsibility: get an infection yourself and you could then pass it on to someone else. But even if you are undeterred by the risks, and determined to take all possible care, there is still the question of expectations; you might not want an ongoing relationship, but the other person might be hoping for just that.

Rape, abuse, adultery; these are the major areas of sexual misconduct. But there is one more aspect, more subtle, that I want to mention. I want to mention it here because I think it may affect women more than men. It has to do with the lack of self-esteem, of self-worth, which many women seem to suffer from, below the surface at any rate; and it shows up as passivity. No one, woman or man, should ever assent to sex that they don't want, but even when that is not the case, motives can be somewhat mixed. We like to think sex can be a happy experience, but it won't feel good in the long run if it's used to disguise an underlying dishonesty or neurosis.

These subtler forms of misconduct, against ourselves primarily, include: using sex in an attempt to keep a relationship alive; hoping it will cure loneliness; seeing it as evidence that we are loved/loving; mistaking it for true intimacy; confirming poor self-views ('I'm only valued for my body', 'As long as she/he wants me I know I'm OK'), finding ourselves repeatedly co-dependent or addicted; using sex to reinforce other psychological bad habits related to insecurity; interweaving sex with projections, unreal expectations, and fixed role-playing. Here sex is not an emotionally free, loving, and energizing means of being together, but an alienated clasping of bodies longing for something not yet evolved or integrated within either person.

Having sex is a healthy human activity when two people have sufficient positive regard for themselves and each other, so that sex then becomes yet another dimension of communication between them. Freeing ourselves from such hidden agendas gives us a chance to enter upon a relationship honest and self-possessed, able to be both intimate and free, relating from our inner strengths and richness, passionate, tender, respectful, playful, truly adult, delighting in, but not hanging on to, the other person.

All this having been said, I'll close this section by recalling what Sangharakshita has said; namely, that we shouldn't let sexual relationships become central in our lives. They cannot be an ultimate Refuge, and we shouldn't mistake them for one.

Celibacy

Some Buddhists choose to give up sexual activity altogether and become celibate. They feel that this option will be more supportive to the development of stillness, simplicity, and contentment. This is very much in accordance with tradition. The best conditions for spiritual growth, according to the Buddha, are to have few possessions, to meditate, to spend your time talking about the Dharma and teaching others, and to practise celibacy. Some of the order of monks and nuns he established followed a more or less settled monastic lifestyle, living in single-sex communities some of the year and travelling on foot from town to village the rest of the time, spreading the Buddha's teachings. Others lived alone in dense forests, spending most of their time in deep meditation.

All these people took up celibacy by making a vow of *brahmacharya*. Any Buddhist who takes a vow of celibacy, whatever their lifestyle, is said to practise brahmacharya. The word is difficult to explain briefly, but it means something like 'dwelling in a god-like (i.e. blissful) state'. We shouldn't imagine, though, that brahmacharya is some sort of elevated and refined hedonism. The purpose of dhyana, concentrated meditation, is to loosen the pull of the world of sense desire; we begin to hang looser to life. Freedom from sexual polarization and tension is also a result, together with becoming less strongly identified with our particular gender. (Some people, however, may first need to feel more positive about being a man or a woman. This is one reason not to take on brahmacharya prematurely – you can give up sex for the wrong reasons, just as you can engage with it for the wrong reasons.)

For the practice of brahmacharya to be most effective, it probably has to be long-term, combined with ample opportunity to meditate and spend time alone. In the Buddha's day a monk or nun vowed to be celibate for as long as they were a member of the order; if they engaged in any form of sexual activity, they had to return to lay life. If they found that they couldn't sustain celibacy, this was taken simply to show that

that particular lifestyle was not suitable for them at that time. It didn't mean they were a hopeless case, spiritually speaking.

The Buddha saw celibacy as one of the conditions most helpful to spiritual practice. It's not hard to imagine why. For one thing, if the wandering mendicants of the Sangha (calling them 'monks and nuns' perhaps gives the wrong idea) had started having sexual relationships, the desire to settle down and make a home would probably have re-emerged. There would certainly have been children, and it would follow that work would need to be found to support the family. In short, these seekers after truth would inevitably recreate the world from which they had gone forth. The Buddha didn't say you couldn't gain Enlightenment if you had a home and family, but he did say that it would probably be more difficult; progress would probably be slower. He knew the strength of worldly ambitions, the desire for children, and the attractions of sexual relationships.

Today our materialistic society offers multiple distractions on top of these pulls. The monks and nuns of the Buddha's time, and through the successive centuries, 'went forth' from household life to the homeless life by gaining admittance to the order. They gave up all worldly affairs so that they could devote themselves completely to their spiritual practice. This still happens in the more orthodox schools of Buddhism today. In the Western Buddhist Order we do not make such a sharp distinction. It is not necessary to be celibate in order to be ordained. But going forth applies to us all. Like a butterfly, we only change by shedding what we no longer need.

In the Western Buddhist Order an increasing number of women and men are taking a form of the Third Precept that commits them to celibacy, as part of the process of becoming anagarikas. *Anagarika* means 'homeless one'. They are not usually literally homeless; what is important is having an attitude of homelessness. One is not attached to any specific place or situation; if you like, everywhere is 'home' to an anagarika. Thus, being an anagarika implies a different lifestyle, an extension of brahmacharya into a life committed to practising and teaching the Dharma. Some anagarikas choose to remind themselves of the lineage of Buddhist celibate practitioners by wearing robes on retreats or festive occasions. (In our movement, only Order members can become anagarikas.)

But not all of us are ready to take such a step. Our sexuality can't be separated from our overall experience. Repression or over-indulgence in any part of our lives leads to one-sidedness and lack of integration. The Buddhist precepts give a model of human behaviour that encourages balance and clarity. The implication of the Buddha's teaching may well be 'Give sex up, it will only end in tears,' but we each need to find out for ourselves what to do when, what's best for us. The Buddha is simply a 'shower of the Way'; there is no insistence on any particular course of action.

The Buddha did not expect people suddenly to stop being sexual, or leave their homes and responsibilities to take up a monastic or wandering life; he recommended it, but recognized that not everyone would be able to do it. Most of us can't give something up solely on the strength of being told it's not good for us. Only when our personal experience bears out the truth of what's being said are we able to act with conviction to change things. If our relationships bring more pain than pleasure, we may feel like stopping them; but often we stop only to brighten up with the hope of another relationship, which will be 'better next time'. Or we settle down with someone and get into a routine pattern that little by little erodes our personal horizons.

Suppose we decide not to be in a sexual relationship or sleep with anyone for a while. At first this may be difficult; we may feel lonely or start fantasizing about people. But after a while we may enjoy being single and not want to look for someone else. We may experience a little of the contentment of celibacy. At the very least a spell of celibacy helps us re-evaluate our thoughts and feelings about our sexuality, and understand our motivations. Even from a mundane point of view, celibacy has advantages: more time to yourself, no fears of contraception failing, fewer arguments, more energy available for meditation and friendships.

To grow spiritually may mean that we give up sex altogether. If we do, it will be because we feel that there is something better to be experienced, something that lasts longer than even the best relationship. Meditation and Dharma study, consistently practised, can result in our reaching a state of inner completeness, no longer needing anything from anyone else. I don't mean that we can be entirely self-sufficient in all respects. If we just take a look at our homes, or think about our food, clothes, and transport, it is clear that we are dependent. In fact we are all interdependent, our human condition being such that without interaction, cooperation, and mutual helpfulness we would not survive.

But psychologically and emotionally we can become self-reliant, building up resources of friendliness, compassion, energy, clarity, and generosity, until giving becomes our nature, we do not have any hidden needs, and even the 'need' to give disappears. People like this radiate a steady stream of contentment, an aliveness both deep and joyful. Theirs is a higher level of attractiveness: contact with them inspires and opens up new possibilities of personal growth. They are the *kalyana mitras* – true spiritual friends. Would such people still have sexual relationships?

Before we can know the answer to that question, there's a lot we can do to make the sexual side of our lives more conscious and more positive, so that we are in a better position to know the significance of our sexuality, and to know what place sex has in our growth and development – if indeed it has any place at all.

IV At Work in the World

Dhiranandi

Born in Lancashire, England, in 1959, Dhiranandi was a pioneer of Right Livelihood in the FWBO, setting up a window-cleaning business as well as helping to establish the Lancashire Buddhist Centre. (Before this she worked for seven years in the caring professions, had police training as a high-speed motorcycle rider and instructor, and regularly worked out at a karate club.) In 1991 she moved to Cambridge to work for a growing Buddhist business: Windhorse Trading. She is currently a member of the management team and is responsible for the development of the chain of 'Evolution' shops, which are run by teams of Buddhists. She lives in a women's Buddhist community in Cambridge.

Dhiranandi

Right Livelihood the Windhorse Way

IF I WERE to carry a begging-bowl around the quaint streets of terraced houses in Cambridge, I might raise a few eyebrows, but I doubt that I would have hit on an effective way for me and my fellow community members to fill our stomachs, never mind pay the bills. The way in which Buddhist monks traditionally beg for food in the East is not generally appropriate for twentieth-century Western Buddhists; we need to earn a living like everyone else. Most of us spend at least half our waking life at work – even more than that if you count worrying about it, talking about it, and recovering from it. It is therefore vital that our work becomes a creative and integral part of our practice as Buddhists. We can't view work merely as treading water, spiritually speaking, until we can go away on retreat, or spend more time meditating. We would waste so much valuable time.

When I first came across Buddhism, I was feeling increasingly disillusioned about the world of work. I had done a number of jobs, several of them in a 'caring profession', but I felt dissatisfied. I wanted work which would engage much more of me, not just the part that was relevant to the work I was doing. The work I did was not enough in itself: it was important to me who I worked with and to what purpose I was working at all. I wanted work that was worthy of my wholehearted commitment, work into which I could release all my energy, to which I could dedicate myself without holding anything back.

I have heard enough people expressing similar dissatisfaction with work in the usual sense to convince me that my experience is not uncommon. Some people are lucky enough to have a vocation and to be paid for doing what they consider to be of greatest value in life, whether that be working in one of the caring professions or in the arts. But such ideal jobs are rare. Even work which seems to offer conditions conducive to creativity is sometimes plagued with difficulties. One may find oneself working within an established institution in an atmosphere of competitiveness, backbiting, and frustrating bureaucracy. It is not uncommon even to dread going to work, to feel undervalued and cramped.

Right Livelihood is one of the stages of that most fundamental of the Buddha's teachings, the Noble Eightfold Path. But the Buddha gives very few guidelines on how to go about transforming our working lives, perhaps because most of his recorded teachings were given to monks and nuns; so the working out in practice of this key teaching may turn out to be one of the special contributions to Buddhist tradition made by Westerners. To the best of my knowledge, members of the Western Buddhist Order were among the first to experiment with establishing 'Right Livelihood' businesses. From the early days, team-based Right Livelihood businesses have been one of the FWBO's fundamental institutions, along with Buddhist centres and residential spiritual communities; and in the last twenty years many unsung heroes and heroines have laboured hard to bring about a radical change in the nature of work. The enterprises set up in the early days were characterized by a great deal of enthusiasm and vision, but the pioneers often had very little in the way of business knowledge, skills, or capital.

I have now spent eleven years working in the context of team-based Right Livelihood, the last six of them at Windhorse Trading. I began to explore it out of a desire to give of myself more fully in my life and work. In the early eighties I was involved in the development of a Buddhist window-cleaning co-operative that ran for five years. We were very keen to make the business work both financially and spiritually, but we were also rather naïve. Our first major mistake was that most of us chose to go on long retreats during the first year of trading without thinking about the long-term effects on the business. We worked with a number of handicaps. Using a cloth-topped Citroen 2CV to carry five heavy ladders and five workers, one of whom was afraid of heights, were just two of them. Despite the difficulties – and the seemingly incessant rainfall in Lancashire – two members of the team were ordained within the Western Buddhist Order during those years, a measure of the success of the business in spiritual terms. I knew I had found what I was looking for: the beginnings of a deep satisfaction and fulfilment that arose from being able to make a wholehearted commitment to work, and having the opportunity to communicate myself fully to the people with whom I worked.

Six years ago I joined Windhorse Trading, a wholesale and retail business which operates on the basis of team-based Right Livelihood. With a turnover of over £8,000,000 per year, these days we don't have to worry about whether we have made enough money this week to pay our rent. But, like any successful business, ours has grown from small beginnings. It began as a market stall in Camden Town, London, in 1981, run by two members of the Western Buddhist Order with the primary aim of raising money for the FWBO. Before long they abandoned the market stall and went into wholesaling gifts via cash-and-carry vans and selling at trade shows.

The first of Windhorse Trading's Evolution gift shops was opened in Norwich in 1989; today there are seventeen Evolution shops in Europe: fifteen in the UK, one in Spain and one in Eire, which account for over half of the company's turnover. The number of Evolution shops will be increasing at around four shops each year. Each shop, while being part of the wider business of Windhorse, is managed independently by the team of people working in it, in consultation with people working in other parts of the business. This means that Windhorse Trading is effectively seventeen separate businesses co-operating to maximize efficiency, and exchanging ideas and experience. There are now around 170 Buddhists employed in the business full-time. Until 1989 Windhorse Trading was a men's business, but it now includes about 60 women; all the work teams are single-sex. The headquarters is located in Cambridge, where about 70 men and women live in men's and women's communities a few doors away from the Buddhist centre, and ten minutes' walk from the offices and warehouse.

The growing number of Evolution shops is providing an increasingly popular service to people who wish to buy unusual gifts in an aesthetic and friendly environment. Workers in our warehouse and shop teams have many different skills and abilities which they bring to their work. The challenge for a team is to use whatever relevant skills are available and to develop those that are needed to fulfil the team's aims.

Windhorse Trading's Vision

As the business has developed there has been a parallel development in our ideas about the spiritual side of team-based Right Livelihood. The primary aim was to generate money to give away, but it soon became obvious that this was not enough. We needed to work out in detail how to apply spiritual practice in the workplace. For quite some time we thought of Right Livelihood as having two aspects – profit and spiritual development – that were opposed to each other, and we would think in terms of compromise between the two. If spiritual practice was done primarily on retreat – as we assumed it was – the priority was therefore to have as many weeks on retreat as possible while trying at the same time to make as much money as we could. But this, as we have now realized, is a false dichotomy. The workplace can be just as much a context for spiritual practice as any other. More recently we have been exploring how we can lead full spiritual lives at work, as well as making a profit to fund the teaching and communication of Buddhism throughout the world.

Our explorations have led us to formulate three main aims:

(1) To promote the spiritual development of the individuals working in the business.

(2) To generate money to give to Buddhist projects.

(3) To encourage the development of Right Livelihood as a viable path for Western Buddhists.

Guided by these aims – each of which is based on the principle of generosity – we are working to create the conditions for leading a life dedicated full-time to spiritual development. These conditions include working in teams, living together in communities, going on regular retreats, studying together, and deepening friendship with one another.

Teamwork provides a very effective context for spiritual development. Everyone who works in Windhorse Trading is a member of a team which meets briefly every morning before work and also for one or two hours a week to discuss how things are going. These meetings are an important part of the week, giving us an opportunity to explore our ideals about work: to keep alive our vision of why we are doing what we are doing, to explore our ethical practice at work, and to look at our communication and how we are transforming ourselves through our work. In this context we can explore and challenge any views we have about work that may hold us back from engaging fully in what we are doing.

Wherever possible, our teams are single-sex. We have found that the single-sex environment supports us in developing friendships with one another, as well as helping us to cultivate qualities that are usually considered to be the province of the opposite sex. And, where possible, we make sure that there is at least one person on the team with substantial experience of the spiritual life – usually a member of the Order – to support the overall growth of the team.

Spiritual Practice in Team-Based Right Livelihood

There are many ways in which working in team-based Right Livelihood supports spiritual growth. Here I will concentrate on three: friendship, co-operation, and taking responsibility. Spiritual friendship can be a difficult and precious jewel to find. I used to find it very frustrating trying to get to know other Buddhists with whom I neither lived nor worked, only seeing them once a week over a cup of coffee. These meetings were valuable and enjoyable, but they weren't enough. I have found working full-time with a team of women committed to the same project and ideals much more satisfying. Spending time together in this way allows us to see each other and be seen more and more fully. Opening up to others is like being let loose, liberated, like a flower opening out into the full sun. Friendship can be a process of transformation: things that were previously hidden come to light, and can therefore be changed. Yet revealing oneself through work doesn't necessarily mean talking about oneself; one is just as truly revealed, possibly more so, in the carrying out of day-to-day duties. It is my experience that the more I get to know people in all their glory, the more I love them. Spiritual friendship is the developing of a deep awareness of one another, to the extent that we are more and more able to consider our friends' needs as much as our own.

The fact that all this is happening in the midst of running a busy and demanding business makes for a particularly robust kind of friendship: a connection between people which is built on the highest common factor – the commitment of each individual – rather than on the lowest common denominator of personality preference. Again and again I hear different teams saying, 'How amazing it is that we work so well together – we're all so different!' I don't think it's at all surprising.

Co-operation is perhaps the first thing one thinks of when it comes to effective teamwork. Because the word is so familiar, we tend to think that we can get together with a group of people and just co-operate – but this is not so. Co-operation needs to be learned. It is not 'equality' or 'democracy', but a mutual effort to create something. In the context of team-based Right Livelihood, to co-operate means to do whatever is necessary to realize your ideals, and to make your business succeed. Both these aims are crucial, and both of them involve a much wider concern and interest than your own individual wants and needs. Your needs are important, of course, but you see them within the wider perspective of what you are trying to bring about as a team. This idea has a radical effect on day-to-day life. If, for example, things are not going particularly well, rather than complaining or grumbling or blaming someone else for doing something wrong, it demands that we ask 'How can I help to make this situation better?'

I remember very well one of my first realizations about Right Livelihood. I had the idea that I needed good conditions in which to practise as a Buddhist, and I knew that the conditions were only good inasmuch as they provided me with an opportunity to give, to go beyond myself. And yet I found myself in a stalemate with another team member who, I thought, was obstructing my initiative and didn't seem to want to budge. In the midst of my frustration I suddenly felt the strength of my own desires, and saw clearly that the people around me weren't there simply to help me to fulfil them and obviously had no intention of doing so. That was a turning-point for me. From then on I was more able to think 'What can I contribute to the situation?' rather than 'What can I get out of this?'

To co-operate, we need to be resilient. We will at some stage find some people difficult to work with. They will appear to us to be anxious, fearful, even downright irritating, and we will find ourselves reacting to them. Being resilient means being aware that we are feeling inclined to react towards someone, but trying as hard as we can not to act on our negative responses. At times this is very hard indeed. We have to be very patient and very kind. This, indeed, is working creatively. We so often want to be right, and to see others as being wrong. In fact, we not only want to be right; we want to be seen to be right, even proved to be right. But in practising co-operation one's ego really does have to take a back seat at times, and this is transforming. It means having others' interests at heart as much as one's own. To do this is to follow the Bodhisattva path.

The third area I want to mention is that of taking responsibility. My experience of working in a team-based Right Livelihood business is that it stretches me; and when I'm being stretched I'm at the cutting edge of my spiritual practice. Usually this means going beyond what I think or feel I am capable of doing. In other words, the view I hold about myself is challenged. In my work I try to combine the objective needs of the business with doing what I enjoy and am personally interested in. Most of the time I have managed this; but at the same time I often feel stretched beyond what I think I am capable of achieving. There are jobs to be done and responsibilities to be met in order to realize the goals of the business.

Recently I noticed my reluctance to take on yet another area of responsibility. We opened two new shops recently, and the teams needed training in the running of the business. I could see that this job needed doing and mentioned it several times to a friend at work. She didn't hesitate to point out that if it was important, I could simply decide what needed to be done and do it myself. I realized I was trying to get someone else to do something about it, although in many ways I was the best person for the job. I had had the idea that the best person would be someone with previously proven capabilities in this particular area, but on reflection this was obviously not the case. Much of what we are trying to do has not been done before; the best person to do it is simply the one who happens to be in the right place at the right time and is willing and able to take on the responsibility. Every development is a venture into the unknown, and the most important thing is that the job is done. If I can bear this in mind, I am much more receptive to comments about how well or otherwise I am doing the job. The successful outcome becomes more important than whether or not I am seen personally to succeed or fail. Fear of failure is often what prevents us from acting. What a waste!

Feeling a lack of confidence can hold us back from taking new initiatives. Not feeling confident usually relates not to how well we are able to do the job, but to a fear of standing out, of standing up and being counted, of being answerable to others, of receiving criticism and praise, of taking the lead. It's no good assessing whether we feel confident enough to do something; we need to assess our ability using other criteria. Working with other women means that we are reflected back clearly and truly by our colleagues; knowing where we stand, we know how to proceed. What holds me back sometimes is simply the thought that other people will think 'Who does she think she is?' In our women's teams we need to explore the question of leadership by women – and also develop confidence in the value of playing a supporting role where necessary. Teams may have one overall leader, or leaders in different work areas.

Before the Buddha-to-be became Enlightened, as he was sitting on the spot where he eventually gained Enlightenment, Mara (the threatening but ultimately powerless 'devil' of Buddhist tradition) came up to him and asked him what right he had to sit in the place where countless Buddhas before him had gained Enlightenment. The Buddha replied that he had been practising the perfections for countless ages. When Mara asked who his witness was, he called upon the earth goddess to confirm his spiritual practice. I find it useful to call upon my spiritual friends to witness my abilities when I am assailed by doubts or lack of confidence, or when I'm afraid of taking a lead.

These are just three of the many areas in which we can progress spiritually at work. To see whether one's work is effective in this way, it is important to find ways of measuring progress. One way of doing this is to set oneself clear objectives. One may wish to become 'more co-operative' or 'more confident', but these goals may be too abstract to be useful. Specific objectives, both practical and spiritual, open us up to feedback through which we can measure our performance and help us to be clearer about what we are doing. Members of a shop team, for example, may set themselves practical goals: how many new displays they want to achieve in the shop in a week; how often they will dust the shelves, and so on. They may also set themselves 'spiritual targets'. If someone has the general aim of improving her mindfulness, with the help of the rest of the team, she will try to find out which particular aspect of mindfulness she needs to improve. Is it remembering to finish jobs off properly? Is it keeping the counter tidy? Measuring her mindfulness against external standards in this way, she is more likely to succeed in her attempts, or at least to know whether or not she is achieving what she set out to do.

Such practices are not simply a matter of being caught up in mundane details. Our experience is that what people need to do to improve their work seems almost always to be just what they need to work on in their spiritual practice. Setting ourselves targets in this way gives our spiritual life and the life of the business the drive and impetus they need to succeed.

Conclusion

There are two extreme views about working in a Right Livelihood business, both of which are limiting. One is thinking that making money, professionalism, efficiency, and suchlike are anathema to a Buddhist way of life and that working with other Buddhists ought to be about having a laid-back time, not worrying too much about making money. The other is that working in a Right Livelihood business means working hard at menial tasks for little reward.

To avoid these extremes we need to keep a clear sense of purpose. We need to keep alive our ideals, both personal and collective, and make our work more and more an expression of these ideals. In many ways the process of engaging in meditation practice can be applied to engagement in work. Just as Padmasambhava exhorted the three fortunate women, 'Again and yet again work at whatever estranges you from meditation,' so we need to work to stay connected with our vision for our work as practice. In our teams, developing an awareness of why we are doing what we are doing is just as important as the work itself. There is a story of three bricklayers building a wall. Someone asked each one: 'What are you doing?' The first replied, 'I'm building a wall.' The second replied, 'I'm making money to support my wife and children.' The third replied, 'I'm building a cathedral.'

I have said that the principle that underlies all Windhorse Trading's aims is giving. Giving is vitally important because it is the complete antithesis of selfish accumulation. Giving is the first perfection of the Bodhisattva (one dedicated to helping others to become Enlightened). Giving is other-regarding, altruistic, liberating. In short, there is no spiritual life without giving. And one of the things we specifically give, of course, is money. Each person in our business is given as much money as they need to live a relatively simple life, with six weeks' retreat time each year; then our net profit is given away to Buddhist projects and charities which cannot generate their own funds.

By giving our money in this way we are going right to the heart of the means of real change in the world, enabling as many people as possible to commit themselves to Buddhism. We are quite single-minded about this. We focus on giving to Buddhist projects because we believe they enable individuals to change and become happier and kinder, thereby helping to change the world, person by person.

As well as giving money, we also give of ourselves in our communication and dealings with the world. Working for Windhorse, we are in touch with all kinds of people in the wider world who don't share our Buddhist ideals. But the effect of our practice of ethics is significant. There is nothing more inspiring than to see someone actually living out their ideals. That one can be relied upon to speak the truth, to be direct, to be considerate in relation to other people, to have integrity, to hold firm to one's principles and not to compromise them, to co-operate – all this is truly revolutionary. Our interaction with people, whether serving them at the shop counter or making a business phone call, can have a profound effect. Recently one of our shop teams was exploring what each team member saw as the most important function of the shop. The factor that nearly everyone held to be most important was communication with the customers. Our communication, influenced as it is by our ideals, is, we believe – in a small way – changing society, recreating the world according to values that we hold most dear.

In engaging with team-based Right Livelihood I feel that I have found a means of satisfying a desire I believe we all experience, at least sometimes: the desire to give, to contribute to something much bigger in scope than our own immediate lives and influence. The urge to give in this more universal context is beautifully expressed by George Bernard Shaw: 'I want to be thoroughly used up when I die. For the harder I work the more I live. I rejoice in life for its own sake. Life is not a brief candle to me. It's a sort of splendid torch I've got to hold up for the moment and I want to make it burn as brightly as possible before handing it on to future generations.'

Right Livelihood is the practice of unselfish actions as a means of self-development. It produces wealth for the support of Buddhism through skilful, creative means; it is practised by similarly committed people working in true co-operation; and, what's more, it is very enjoyable. In fact, it is thoroughly efficacious, nourishing, and enlivening. Working in this way we are aiming for the goal of every Buddhist life – to gain Insight into Reality – just as much as if we were living in a secluded retreat centre. Our ultimate aim, our hope, is that the Bodhichitta, the supreme desire that everyone should attain Enlightenment, will some day arise within us. In the light of this vision, we aspire to transform ourselves and the society we live in.

Santachitta

Santachitta was born in London in 1953 and qualified from the London Hospital Medical College in 1978. Following her house jobs she went on to train for general practice, taking time out between jobs to travel. She contacted the FWBO in 1980 while working in Brighton and was ordained a member of the WBO in 1990, along with nine other women. She was given the name Santachitta (Peaceful Heart). She has also studied acupuncture and counselling and now works as a part-time family doctor in Brighton. She lives in a Buddhist women's community.

Santachitta

The Service of Humanity

Buddhism and Medical Practice

IT IS A WEEKDAY morning in the busy casualty department of a district general hospital. Suddenly a telephone rings. Several staff stop short. A local ambulance crew is phoning advance warning of a 'crash call'. They are bringing in a man who has collapsed, unconscious, and with no pulse. The resuscitation team is alerted.

I am standing with the others in the team as the automatic doors slide open and the body of a middle-aged man is brought in on a stretcher. Everyone jumps into action as he is wheeled into the resuscitation bay. The anaesthetist intubates the patient, an ECG monitor is connected, a drip is put up, and an efficient attempt at resuscitation is made. For some time we try to bring the man back to life, to re-establish his cardiac function. We fail. Eventually one of the team signals that it is time to stop. It has become obvious that this man cannot be saved. We stop what we are doing, turn off the monitor, and he is certified dead.

This is a routine scenario in any hospital, familiar to many of us from the soap operas on our television screens. Yet this was the end of a person's life; a tragedy for his wife, relatives, and friends; a loss that would cause much pain and grief.

As a junior hospital doctor I often had to deal with such events. I remember walking calmly away from that man to see my next patient, and a colleague commenting how callous and cool we would seem to anyone walking in off the street. That simple remark stopped me in my tracks. I was still relatively newly qualified, intent on following a career in medicine, but already I had become hardened. Death was a familiar occurrence, part of my job. But was the emotional detachment I saw in myself necessary, or even healthy? I suddenly became aware of how my chosen career was affecting me, and how in turn I might be affecting my patients.

I had just started meditating, and was beginning to discover Buddhism, though I could not yet call myself a Buddhist. Already I felt a conflict between my vocation and my desire to pursue the spiritual life taught by the Buddha. Yet why should this be? Surely medicine was Right Livelihood – that is, ethical in Buddhist terms? Was it not concerned with alleviating suffering, both physical and mental? This was the beginning of a conflict with which I was to wrestle for many years.

Right Livelihood is the fifth step of the Buddha's Eightfold Path, which is in turn the fourth of the Four Noble Truths, the first teaching the Buddha gave after his Enlightenment. As it happens, the Four Noble Truths are based on an ancient medical formula used to ascertain the cause and hence the treatment of an ailment. The Buddha took this basic formula and used it to communicate his Insight into the nature of existence and his understanding of human suffering. The four Truths are that there is suffering, a cause of suffering, a cessation of suffering, and a way leading to the cessation of suffering. The Buddha expressed this fourth Noble Truth, the path or way, in many terms. One of the best-known formulations is the Noble Eightfold Path: the path of vision and transformation.

The first step on this path is vision (sometimes less accurately translated 'understanding'). This is not, for most of us, the perfect understanding of a Buddha, but a small flash of insight, an awareness of something higher and greater than us, which is enough to inspire us to set out on the spiritual path. This flash of vision may come about in all kinds of ways. It may arise following some tragedy, loss, or bereavement, when our whole world is turned upside down, and we have to find new meaning in life. It may be a spontaneous mystical experience. It may come through deep reflection, or with increasing life experience.

However that initial vision occurs, the other seven stages of the Noble Eightfold Path are concerned with transforming ourselves and our lives in accordance with it.[82] And one of these seven stages involves the practice of Right Livelihood. In short, it matters how we earn our living. It matters just as much today as it did in ancient India; perhaps it matters more. At the very least, our work should do no harm to living beings. Ideally it should enhance our lives, as well as the lives of others, by being helpful, creative, and rewarding.

Finding such employment is not always easy in our society. But medicine, one might think, seems to fit the description. It is more than a way of earning a living; it is a vocation. It is concerned with the relief of human suffering. To some extent it has a spiritual dimension. Although today it is a secular occupation, the history of medicine is rooted in religion, and the fundamental ethical principles of professional behaviour have remained unaltered for thousands of years.

The Hippocratic oath[83] is thought to have been formulated 2,200 years ago. It was probably a temple oath written by priest-physicians in the temple of Asclepius, the ancient Greek god of healing,[84] rather than by Hippocrates himself. The oath as it stands is obviously dated, but its essence still holds true. In 1947 the World Medical Association produced a modern restatement of the Hippocratic oath known as the Declaration of Geneva. This is the basis for the International Code of Medical Ethics which applies in times of both peace and war. The latest amended version reads as follows:[85]

I solemnly pledge myself to consecrate my life to the service of humanity;
I will give to my teachers the respect and gratitude which is their due;
I will practise my profession with conscience and dignity;
The health of my patient will be my first consideration;
I will respect the secrets which are confided in me, even after the patient
has died;
I will maintain, by all the means in my power, the honour and the noble
traditions of the medical profession;
My colleagues will be my sisters and brothers;
I will not permit considerations of age, disease or disability, creed,
ethnic origin, gender, nationality, political affiliation, race, sexual
orientation, or social standing to intervene between my duty and my
patient;
I will maintain the utmost respect for human life from its beginning
even under threat and I will not use my medical knowledge contrary to
the laws of humanity;
I make these promises solemnly, freely and upon my honour.

This oath was intended to be taken by any doctor on entering the medical profession. Sadly, however, in Britain at least, the Hippocratic oath is no longer taken.

The first line of the oath seems to me to be akin to the vow of the Bodhisattva. A Bodhisattva is an 'Enlightenment being', one who vows to alleviate the suffering of all sentient beings and lead them to Enlightenment, the only true answer to the pain of this world. The Bodhisattva ideal, which flourished in the Mahayana period of Buddhism, is beautiful and inspiring, and embodies the altruistic dimension of spiritual practice.[86]

The work of a true Bodhisattva is not really 'work' but spontaneous play: a bubbling up of creative spiritual energy which is directed through wisdom to the needs of any given situation. It is an imaginative flow springing from a deep understanding of, and desire to alleviate, the suffering of sentient beings. This ideal of a Bodhisattva's activity is a source of inspiration in the work I do, even though it is a very high ideal to which to aspire.

When I became a member of the Western Buddhist Order, one of the lines I recited during the ordination ceremony was: 'For the benefit of all beings, I accept this ordination.' This expresses the altruistic, compassionate aspect of Going for Refuge or commitment to the Three Jewels of Buddhism. I also undertook to practise ten ethical precepts. The first of these is expressed in its negative formulation as 'I undertake to abstain from taking life', and in its positive formulation as 'With deeds of loving-kindness I purify my body.'

The highest aspirations of the medical profession, as originally expressed in the Hippocratic oath, can be seen as a practical expression of the Bodhisattva ideal and an application of the First Precept. But does modern medicine allow room for such ideals?

Like many young people, I was idealistic when I entered medical school. What motivated me was the desire to help people. It is unfortunate that disillusionment often follows. Idealism is lost, swallowed up by the attitudes inculcated by the training. Competition, the desire to succeed, often at the expense of others, and the need just to survive in the environment of a teaching hospital, do much to destroy those early, naïve aspirations. It is hard to keep a sense of perspective in a busy hospital, to see patients as more than interesting diseases or further demands on an exhausted doctor. I am not alone in having felt, at times, resentful of my patients, particularly when I was working in junior hospital posts. The hours are long, the responsibilities great, and the level of anxiety high. This environment is hardly conducive to Right Livelihood, to developing awareness and compassion, which are so central both to the spiritual life and to the practice of medicine.

After that moment in casualty, I realized I had fallen far short of the naïve, unformed aspirations I had held on entering medical school. Of necessity I had built a hard shell around myself to protect me from the suffering I saw around me every day. I could put on a façade of coolness and efficiency, but underneath there was a frightened, unhappy human being, resentful of the pressures and demands placed upon her. Emotionally drained and often physically exhausted, I was not really capable of meeting people on a truly human level. The shell was beginning to crack, meditation was already beginning to weaken my defences, and I was being forced to look at myself. This was the start of a slow, painful process.

I knew I would have to move from a hospital environment into the community if I was to stay in medicine and practise Buddhism. My aim was to work part-time in general practice, preferably with other Buddhists, near an FWBO centre. Around that time I wrote to Sangharakshita expressing my desire to be ordained and to continue practising medicine. He challenged me with the words, 'Medicine is a very demanding mistress, if not an all-devouring monster,' adding that he would be interested to see if I could reduce it to part-time proportions. I took up the challenge, intent on trying to bring these two aspects of my life together. Medicine, I resolved, would be an expression of my spiritual practice.

Having achieved this to a certain extent, I still struggle to achieve a balance between my practice of medicine and my spiritual life, though the two are inextricably linked. Working part-time in general practice has given me the opportunity to work to a higher standard. As a family doctor I do not spend very long with each patient; however, it is possible over time to build up a working relationship. One can gradually put together a picture of each person in the context of their family and friends, and form a far more satisfying relationship than is usually possible in a hospital environment.

The challenge is to respond to each person who comes to see me with the same quality of concern and care, regardless of who they are. This requires a real awareness and understanding of myself and my prejudices, likes, and dislikes. Why do I feel attracted to one patient and threatened by another? What is this person telling me about themself or even myself? What are they really asking of me? Can I give it and is it appropriate? I am painfully aware that I often fall far short of this challenge. I catch myself responding too quickly and inappropriately and the moment is lost. I often find the work stimulating and exciting, although at times it is exhausting and overwhelming.

A surgery is the perfect situation in which to practise metta, unconditional loving-kindness. The Metta Bhavana was one of the basic meditation practices which the Buddha taught. It involves working with one's emotional and mental states, acknowledging them and transforming them into a warm, unconditional love for oneself and for all sentient beings: an outflowing of positive emotion which should extend out beyond the meditation cushion into one's everyday life. This, of course, is very difficult. There are days when one feels positive and the world seems a benign place, and other days when life is a struggle and to change one's emotional state takes a supreme effort. However, Buddhism is very practical, offering valuable tools that can be used to work with oneself, even within a doctor's surgery. In this situation I meet up to thirty people a day, each with their own particular anxieties, fears, or illnesses, together with their joys: the discovery of a pregnancy or the birth of a new child, for example. Can I really empathize, meet the suffering with real understanding and compassion, share in the pleasure? Can I respond appropriately and maintain enough objectivity to assess the problem, diagnose, treat, or refer according to the needs of each patient?

Perhaps the hardest thing of all is to be with someone else's suffering, particularly when there is nothing further medicine can offer: to share their pain and not be overwhelmed by it; to accept their anger and their frustration and understand; not to put up defences and cut off from or deflect that person's experience; not to be overwhelmed by my own sense of failure; to be in touch with my own weaknesses as a human being.

Jung's archetype of the wounded healer, taken from mythology, expresses the importance of this. The idea of a healer who bears wounds or a figure who wounds and heals is common in Greek mythology: one such is Chiron the centaur, who taught the healing arts to Asclepius, the son of Apollo, and who himself was wounded by the poisoned arrow of Heracles. Jung used the image of the wounded healer to demonstrate the conscious and unconscious processes interacting within the psychotherapeutic relationship. He likened the interaction between doctor and patient to an alchemical reaction: both parties are transformed or affected by the meeting.[87]

In the doctor–patient relationship, the doctor is automatically seen as being in a position of power. There is a danger of accepting that position and inadvertently misusing it. A doctor needs to be potent and at times to take control so that the patient may adopt the sick role, but this position must never be abused. At the risk of over-simplifying the matter, I would say that the image of the wounded healer illustrates that every doctor has a potential patient within and every patient a potential doctor or healer. None of us is totally one or the other. It follows that, as a healer, to be in touch with one's wounded, more vulnerable aspects allows the patient to realize their own healing potential.

To deny those aspects of oneself is to operate from a position of strength and power only, putting the patient into a vulnerable position, unable to realize their own potency. Clearly this is the antithesis of the Bodhisattva ideal and the First Precept – the basis of loving-kindness I mentioned earlier. Power in itself is neutral: it can be used positively and creatively when tempered with awareness and concern for others, or negatively, to impose one's will on the helpless patient.

I should now like to touch on some of the more common ethical dilemmas that doctors face. (I am not including the recent upheavals caused by the introduction of market forces into the British National Health Service, which have added a further level of practical and ethical difficulties for many doctors.) Although these dilemmas have to be faced and dealt with by the doctor, their solutions or resolutions are not, I believe, just the responsibility of the medical profession: they are questions that need to be faced by society. I will not attempt to make any judgements, but will try to draw out some of the different arguments.

One such issue for society is that of abortion. The Hippocratic oath, in its updated version, categorically states that a doctor should not induce an abortion in a woman: 'I will maintain the warmest respect for human life from its beginning.' The First Precept taught by the Buddha is the principle of abstaining from killing living beings, or love. But in Britain and many other countries, abortion is legal. There is sometimes genuine conflict between the life of the mother and the life of the child. Whose life does one save? Nearly always it is the mother's. But the issue of abortion extends beyond life and death: the concept of therapeutic abortion includes the threat to the mental and/or physical well-being of both the mother and her existing family. This can be and is interpreted very loosely. Abortion is also offered when the foetus is deformed or handi-capped in some way.

Ultimately the decision whether to have an abortion must lie with the pregnant woman, and in my experience few women undertake it lightly. It can be a very painful and agonizing decision to make. But as a doctor one has to be clear whether one is willing to participate in this practice, and if so whether under certain circumstances and not others. My own practice is to refer women for abortions if that is the decision they reach, having offered them counselling and time to reach that decision. I do not always sign the blue form (a legal document which has to be signed by two doctors who independently agree that termination of pregnancy can be carried out). If I am not happy with the circumstances under which the woman is seeking an abortion, or not confident that her decision is for the best, I will still refer her, but leave it up to the hospital gynaecol-ogists to decide and sign as appropriate. I try to remain as impartial as possible to help the woman reach her decision, but do suggest alterna-tives to abortion, and also point out the emotional and psychological consequences she may experience as a result of having a termination.

In contrast to unwanted pregnancies there is also the rapidly expand-ing area of infertility treatment. There has been much media coverage of this over the years, including debates about *in vitro* fertilization and the keeping of frozen embryos for implantation. Having witnessed the joy of previously infertile couples conceiving and having a child, I feel that this is a positive, exciting area of medicine. However, I do wonder about frozen embryos being kept for years, and their disposal after five years, required by law, if they have not been used. Is this a form of abortion? Where is the consciousness of this being? Traditionally Buddhism says that consciousness enters the being at conception. This is hard to com-prehend in terms of modern fertility treatments. Is the potential human being damaged in some way by being kept frozen in embryonic form for several years? There are no easy answers to these questions.

When working in a special care baby unit with premature or sick babies, there have been times when, as part of a medical team, I have been responsible for keeping alive a child who might otherwise have died, but who ends up severely mentally and physically handicapped, placing a huge burden on their family. What will the quality of life be for that child and that family? Should we be saving lives at all costs? This question applies not only to small infants but to people of all ages, particularly old people.

Ancient Greek physicians saw it as wrong to treat anyone who was terminally ill (not always a clear diagnosis to make). As they saw it, the gods were calling the souls of the dying back and it was extreme hubris to tread on the territory of the divine. But in working with those who are dying or near death, the question arises: when is killing or assisting death a humane form of treatment to relieve suffering? When does one stop active treatment and provide only palliative care? As technology advances, this grey area becomes increasingly difficult to deal with.

Doctors are taught to be heroic: to treat and cure, to save lives. The care of the dying and the chronically ill is less glamorous than curing people and therefore attracts less attention. Medicine is influenced by the ancient Greek tradition of warrior gods fighting disease and death, and the battle-ground metaphor still holds true today. Doctors work on the border between life and death, continually trying to keep death at bay (though these days they are not so concerned about incurring the wrath of the gods). Elisabeth Kübler-Ross has spoken of many doctors' inordinate fear of death: for them, working in the field of medicine is an unconscious way of trying to deny their own mortality.

As part of the medical profession in Britain, I am subtly involved in feeding the denial of death which prevails in our secular, materialistic society. The concept of perfect health lurks in the background, tied up with the desire for longevity, and fed by the exciting and dramatic advances made in medicine in recent years. But the fact is that we all become sick at some time, we all grow old (if we live long enough), and we all die. Nothing is going to change that. We live in a culture where youth is admired and envied. Death has become to a large extent a medical concern and is discreetly dealt with by professionals. Many people reach adulthood, even middle age, without ever having seen a corpse, something unheard of fifty years ago. Yet if we open our eyes we can see the process of birth, decay, and death going on all around us, and even experience it within ourselves. Is this denial of death an aspect of medicine which detracts from its being Right Livelihood in the truest sense? I collude with this denial to the extent to which I cannot face my own mortality.

Working in general practice gives me more opportunities to explore this. Since I am in the authoritative position within the doctor–patient relationship, it is up to me to open the way to allow patients to express their fears and anxieties, to explore what their illness means to them, and maybe, if appropriate, eventually to face their own mortality.

This is very much in keeping with my Buddhist practice. Buddhism is about facing reality, not trying to deny it or colluding with illusions. It teaches us to see and truly understand that all things are impermanent. The positive side of impermanence is that all things change, including ourselves, and we can consciously change and develop for the better.

Only recently I visited a lady in her late eighties who was dying. She had lost her desire to live, and appeared to be declining fast. I asked her how she felt and she asked, 'Am I dying?' I was surprised by how difficult I found it to answer her question truthfully. First I tried to find out whether she was afraid to die, or whether she was ready for death. Then, eventually, I managed to say, 'Yes, you are dying.' She was quite calm and ready to let go. She simply said, 'I want to die quietly and peacefully.' I took that as a request for help; she was in some pain but until then had refused medication. I gave the nursing home a prescription for morphine to make her more comfortable. We both knew it was not going to be long, and she died the next day. I find moments like that challenging.

These are just a few of the ethical dilemmas that face all doctors, regardless of any religion they may follow. Responses to them may differ but the underlying ethical principles are the same.

Another great difficulty for me has been to find a way of working in the medical profession as a woman. During my training the ethos was very masculine: the whole system was set up in a military style. Ward rounds were led by the chief or consultant, followed by a whole entourage of medical and nursing staff. Medical language was often couched in aggressive terms, 'attacking' infections or cancer with chemotherapy, radiotherapy, and surgery. The disease was seen as the enemy within the body which had to be rooted out and destroyed.

The way in which medicine is practised in the West has been strongly influenced by the Cartesian ideal of observer objectivity and the breaking down of the observed into ever smaller parts, to the extent that awareness of the whole is lost. This approach has achieved much, but at a price. As doctors we not only split mind from body; the body is also split into numerous functional parts, so that the patient is in danger of disappearing altogether. The spiritual well-being of the patient is rarely acknowledged.

There have been exceptions to this approach. For example there is the attitude of the medieval physician Paracelsus, who is seen as an example of the complete physician and still holds a great fascination for many. His practice of medicine was imbued with his spiritual sense, and a belief in the interconnectedness of all things (the macrocosm expressed in the microcosm). He is quoted as saying 'Medicine can do nothing without heaven, it must be guided by heaven,' and 'Where there is no love there is no art.'[88] His view is similar to other systems of medicine, such as the traditional Chinese and Indian Ayurvedic systems. These approaches look at health and disease in terms of harmony and balance or lack of it.

However, the archetypal image of the warrior god which underlies the physician is still strongly present in Western medicine. It is difficult for many women to fit in without becoming pseudo-men, one of the boys, compromising their womanhood and all this has to offer. Many women move into general practice or psychiatry; few make it to consultant posts in surgery. I feel that I cut myself off from my more feminine side to survive within the National Health Service. I had an ambitious streak which drove me to prove to myself that I was equal to any man. I chose to ignore that I was different and had other qualities to offer. Through meditation I started to reach and discover more fully those hidden aspects of myself. As part of this exploration I studied and started to practise acupuncture, as well as learning counselling skills to improve the range and quality of help that I could offer people. As I have explored, I have found a deepening satisfaction in my work – and an increasing frustration with the system within which I operate.

Though I do not work in a team-based Right Livelihood context, I am part of a team which on the whole functions well, although if all the members of the team were practising Buddhists things might be even better. There would be a clearer understanding of how we could work together and I would hope that communication among us would be clearer and more direct. I know it would be more challenging for me. I valued the support and friendship of one particular member of the team, who has now died. She was our practice nurse, and was also involved in the FWBO; our relationship was important to both of us. There are a number of doctors committed to the FWBO; from time to time we meet to share and discuss the difficulties and challenges we face, exploring ethical issues and ways in which we can combine our spiritual and medical practice.

My personal journey continues. I have chosen to carry on practising medicine in the context of general practice, but my desire to work more deeply with people is leading me into the area of psychotherapy, particularly Jungian analysis. I may be able to combine this with my present work at some time in the future. In the meantime I continue to wrestle with the difficulties I have described and with many aspects of myself, some of which I would rather not know about. I feel fortunate to be able to work in such a stimulating, challenging form of livelihood, despite the difficulties. There are times when it is frustrating and exhausting; at those times I very much need the support and encouragement of friends and colleagues. I feel privileged to be entrusted with so much by so many of my patients. I need them, I realize, as much as, if not more than, they need me.

Dayanandi

Dayanandi was born in 1954 in a small village near Peterborough, England, the younger (by 15 minutes) of identical twins. Many of her childhood memories are of time spent in a lovely, rambling garden, which her mother created from a wilderness. She studied architecture at London University and worked in London upon qualifying. In 1979 she came across Buddhism at an FWBO meditation class recommended by friends. A weekend retreat soon followed, a turning point in her life. She decided that she wanted to join the Western Buddhist Order and to become a Bodhisattva, and her life continues to be shaped by these ideals. Dayanandi was ordained in 1986.

Dayanandi

Building Tara's Realm

The Story of Taraloka Women's Retreat Centre

IN THIS CHAPTER I want to tell a story. It's the story of the coming into being of a vision; and it's my own story too. Once upon a time, in the early days of the FWBO, we found ourselves with nowhere to hold retreats for women. For some years retreats had been held in a borrowed farmhouse in Norfolk, a rambling place where retreatants were accommodated in barns, vans, and chicken huts. When the owner wanted the farmhouse back, we were sometimes able to borrow Vajraloka, the FWBO's meditation retreat centre for men, but often we hired venues such as public schools for retreats. In such unpromising surroundings we would work to build up a meditative atmosphere during the retreat. But although the gyms and dining-rooms we used were carefully and beautifully disguised with shrine cloths and candles, the use to which they were normally put still seemed to cling to them. At the end of the retreat we would dismantle everything, only to start again from scratch on the next retreat.

It was clear that we needed a permanent place as a focus for our shared inspiration, a place which we could see developing and growing, and which would build up an atmosphere and identity of its own. We would, we felt, develop a collective confidence and strength from seeing something grow in this way.

To begin with, although we had ideas for raising funds to buy a property, there were not enough women Order members free to run such a centre. The very few Dharmacharinis there were then were scattered among Buddhist centres not just in Britain, but in Finland and New Zealand. At the time this seemed an insurmountable difficulty. But there was one Dharmacharini, Sanghadevi, who had a vision of what might be possible, and took on the project, determined that she would succeed.

When I asked Sanghadevi recently about this vision, she said, 'It seemed important that women owned their creative powers and experienced themselves as not only willing but able to take full responsibility for their lives and work. I began to see the establishing of the retreat centre not only as a vital facility, but also as a source of inspiration and encouragement to other women to think more imaginatively in their own fields of interest, and in their own way step into the unknown. It did seem important to have at least one completely single-sex environment open to women: a realm which all women could identify with and draw upon. In the summer of 1981, I was on a solitary retreat in Cornwall, and found myself drawing sketches of barns, speculating about large sums of money, and imagining us having a women's retreat centre. It was then I realized that it would take us years to collect the amount of money we would need. By the time we bought a property, we would surely have some women Order members able to live there.'

Sanghadevi was the chairwoman of a registered charity formed by a group of Dharmacharinis to organize retreats for women. In November 1981 they decided to follow Sanghadevi's proposal and go ahead with raising money to buy buildings for use as a retreat centre. Two years later the entire women's wing of the Order – 21 women at that time – attended a month-long retreat on a small island off the Scottish coast. They discussed plans for the new retreat centre and decided to look for a place which could cater for 25 or 30 women, with a possibility of going up to 50 occasionally. There had been some discussion about a smaller meditation retreat centre but the decision was made in favour of a project of larger scope which would be available to more women. It would be an important step, not only for those women who attended the retreats but also for women Order members, inspired to rise to the challenge it would bring.

The retreat centre project sparked the imaginations of women throughout the movement, and a lot of enthusiasm went into raising money through concerts, sales, vegetarian catering.... By 1985 enough money had been raised to buy a property. Women all over Britain searched estate agents' windows for suitable buildings, until eventually Cornhill Farm, in the Welsh border country, was found and purchased.

It was set in seven acres of land, a mixture of pasture and barley fields in a quiet corner of Clwyd in North Wales, half a mile from a large peat bog created thousands of years ago by glaciation, and now a protected area sheltering rare species of plants and wildlife. The land is bordered by the beautiful, tree-lined Llangollen branch of the Shropshire Union Canal, built to carry slate to England from the Welsh quarries. The property consisted of a long, whitewashed farmhouse, which would be the base for a women's community, and some red brick outbuildings which we intended to renovate and convert into retreat centre buildings. The new retreat centre was named 'Taraloka'.

The team that set up Taraloka consisted of four women: Sanghadevi, Ratnasuri, Kathryn Boon, and Tessa Harding. At 31, Sanghadevi was already an experienced Order member and retreat leader, having been ordained when she was 23. After her ordination she was a key figure in initiating and developing projects for women around the London Buddhist Centre. Her qualities of courage, inspiration, and determination made her an ideal person to spearhead the Taraloka project. She has since become one of the preceptors who ordain women into the Western Buddhist Order.

Ratnasuri's background could not have been more different. She arrived at Taraloka at the age of 62, having been ordained for two years. Her courage and open-mindedness in joining such a pioneering project at that age were admirable. Besides bringing up two sons, she had been a window dresser, a laboratory assistant at a milk depot, and a chocolate factory worker. She also spent four and a half years in the women's army during the Second World War. (Ratnasuri still lives at Taraloka; she is also a preceptor, and still enjoys supporting and leading retreats.)

Born and brought up in Lancashire, Kathryn had spent some years teaching English and music in Germany before meeting Buddhism in the early 1980s. She soon moved to London to help with fund-raising for the retreat centre project and became Taraloka's first treasurer. Very inspired by this new project, she threw herself into it wholeheartedly and was ordained in 1988, receiving the name Kulanandi.

Tessa was ordained the same year, receiving the name Karunasri. She was working as an information officer in London when she became a Buddhist in 1979. Shortly afterwards she changed her life radically, joining a women's residential community and working in a Right Livelihood business, until she joined the fund-raising team for the retreat centre, becoming the charity's secretary. These four women took much of the responsibility for Taraloka's development over the crucial first few years.

They moved in in November 1985, and held their first retreats over Christmas and New Year, after a hectic period of preparation. Women volunteered their skills in electrical work, carpentry, decorating, and spraying for woodworm. Ratnasuri cooked all the meals on a primus stove, as the kitchen was not yet equipped. The new community and their helpers camped out in one room and then another as each room was wired, de-woodwormed, and decorated. Sturdy tables and benches were constructed for the kitchen, a shrine-room was created in the smoky old lounge, and finally everything was ready for the first retreats. The new retreat centre was under way – and so was a new phase for women in the FWBO. It was a time of great expansion and creativity as Taraloka became more and more a focus for women's inspiration, and a model for their achievements.

My own story became interwoven with that of the retreat centre from its very early days. I had the idea of joining the retreat centre community eighteen months before I moved there, before the buildings had even been purchased. I was working as part of a team of women in a Right Livelihood project called Friends Foods, a wholefood shop in Notting Hill Gate, London. My time at Friends Foods was very important to me. Gradually I began to learn how to communicate with people and form friendships. Shy since childhood, I had found this very difficult. Meditation, on the other hand, immediately made me feel at home. When I was meditating I could be fully myself, and my experiences in meditation, especially on retreats, gave me a deepening confidence in myself. But even when meditating I experienced emotional blockage. Joy or very strong love sometimes arose, but I couldn't express these powerful emotions. I felt that I needed to spend more time with other women Buddhists in order to make changes in this area. When a place became available on the Friends Foods team, I left my job as an architect to join it.

Meditation continued to be close to my heart. While I was working at Friends Foods, going on retreat was the highlight of my year. I enjoyed retreats even more than holidays; they refreshed me, whereas I sometimes came back from a holiday feeling less alive than before. When I meditated I experienced myself more clearly and truly, and I found this very satisfying and enjoyable, despite all the accompanying ups and downs. I felt at my happiest on retreat, as I became freer of my lifetime habit of hiding from myself and others.

After a few years at Friends Foods I felt I had made considerable changes in these habits. Perhaps these changes left me freer to consider a new direction in my life. The more I heard about the idea for the new retreat centre, the more inspired I felt, until I realized that I very much wanted to be part of this project. I loved retreats and wanted to spend more time living in that way; and I also felt tremendously inspired by the project and wanted to put my energy behind it. I asked to join the team, and was accepted. I couldn't go straight away, needing to pass on my responsibilities at Friends Foods, and so I missed the first nine months of life at the new retreat centre.

I was newly ordained when I moved to Taraloka in August 1986. Retreats were already running using the basic facilities, and the community was continuing to develop and improve the centre. Excitement and positive pride in this pioneering project overlaid the tiredness and anxiety stemming from its newness and ambitious scope.

Earlier in the year the red-brick outbuildings had been converted to provide the core of the new retreat facilities. Women on working retreats had begun to strip out the barns, removing concrete cattle troughs and cement rendering using pneumatic drills. They did as much as they could without calling in professional builders. This challenged their ideas about their supposed capabilities as women; they found they could do far more than they had imagined. In June the main buildings were converted; women's teams took on one building while professional builders converted the other. The retreat centre shrine-room was converted from a lovely old granary by the women's team, and they put a lot of care into its creation. The following year we laid a beautiful beechwood floor in the shrine-room, beneath which we placed verses and mantras dedicated to the Buddhas and Bodhisattvas, as well as our good wishes to those who would meditate there in the future. By the time I arrived, even though floor finishes were not down and rooms were not painted, the first retreats were being held in the converted barns. We didn't yet have a dining-room or lounge, but it was the height of summer, so we could live outdoors a lot of the time.

About a month after I arrived at Taraloka I was plunged not into the realms of meditation but into an intensive building project to convert the next section of cow-shed into a dining-room. Four of us from the community, with a tight budget and a very mixed bag of skills and experience, achieved the main conversion in four months, so that the dining-room could be used for the large retreats to be held over the Christmas period. The work was a gruelling experience. I had to convert my architectural knowledge into practice and do building work for the first time in my life, and I also felt responsible for the harmonious working of the team. There were many things I didn't really know how to do, and I wasn't always confident enough to ask. The work was hard physical labour, and the weather was cold. The team comprised Luise (now Ratnadevi), who had learned a little about brickwork and concreting in the previous months of work, Elaine, who had similarly learned a little about slating a roof, and Sue, who was a trained carpenter and knew something of electrics. It was a battle against time, during which we triumphed over anxiety and difficult team dynamics, creating a lovely dining-room in the process.

So my early days at Taraloka were not easy. We were all stretched to our limits. At first the emphasis was very much on the practical business of creating buildings and running retreats (we were soon running a year-round programme), and there was little time to spend with one another. This was necessary at the time, but it felt unbalanced. Once the dining-room was finished, and the other rooms were floored and decorated, we had time to take stock. We could now begin to take account of more personal needs, and create a real sense of community among this band of heroic, hard-working, and self-sufficient individuals. This was the beginning of another new phase at Taraloka.

We instituted a community day on Mondays, reducing the working week to four days. This added greatly to creating a sense of community. As we were often supporting retreats at weekends we had previously gone for long periods without having time free to spend together. The programme for our community day has changed over the years, but it has included such activities as 'reporting-in' (a meeting in which community members share their thoughts and feelings), study of Buddhist texts, meditation and devotional practice together, and a period for cleaning the house. It is often a rather full day, but occasionally we have days out together – there have been trips to castles and gardens, and once to a sauna. It's important to relax together, too.

The aims of the project became clearer and more expansive over the first few years. The initial target had been realized and this now gave scope for wider possibilities. Our aims were:

(1) To create a permanent venue for retreats for women set in a beautiful environment conducive to positive mental states and feelings of self-worth; a place where women can deepen their spiritual practice in an intensive, distraction-free situation either by going on retreat or by living in the resident community.

(2) To offer a variety of retreats all year round catering for the needs of women at all levels of experience, including those completely new to meditation and Buddhism.

(3) To provide a place where women can be trained as prospective members of the Order and in the teaching of Buddhism and meditation.

(4) To be a source of inspiration and encouragement to women within the FWBO and beyond; to be a concrete demonstration of what is possible.

Ten years later, we have gone a long way towards the realization of these initial aims. In fact, the women's wing of the Order has now established a second retreat centre for women, called Tiratanaloka (the place of the Three Jewels), specializing in the training of women wishing to enter the Western Buddhist Order. Since Taraloka's inception several thousand women have been on retreat here, and forty or so women have lived in the community, helping to run the retreat centre for periods ranging from a few months to ten years.

At present two teams, of four women each, are responsible for the administration and practical running of the retreat centre, while a council of Order members has responsibility for the long-term direction of the centre both in practical and spiritual terms. We are not on retreat all the time by any means, as we need to give time to our other work, so the leadership of retreats is shared with women Order members from elsewhere. All our events are led and organized by women.

We are gearing up for what I see as an exciting change. We intend to restructure the community. A support team will look after the practical running of Taraloka, while a newly-created retreat team of experienced Dharmacharinis will take on the development of our retreats, including finding better and clearer ways to communicate the Dharma. The retreat team's time will be shared between teaching on retreats, discussing and reviewing retreats back in the community, deepening their personal practice of meditation and Dharma study, and developing friendships within the team and wider community. I would hope that the women on this team will gradually find that they have a lot to give to the whole project in terms of spiritual depth and perspective, becoming its spiritual heart. Over time I envisage Taraloka being profoundly transformed by this change.

This is a natural development from the way we have been working for a number of years. The community shapes the annual programme of events, taking on the task of developing and improving what we offer. Occasionally we go back to basics and ask ourselves such questions as: 'What is a retreat? What are the benefits of coming on retreat?' trying to keep our minds fresh about what we are creating at Taraloka.

Put simply, a retreat gives us time out from our everyday lives, time to look at things from a broader perspective. It is an opportunity to gain greater depth and honesty in our experience of ourselves and of life. We leave behind radio, newspapers, and telephone, let go of our usual roles and responsibilities, and take the rare opportunity to experience ourselves just as we are. This is a new experience for most people. Each retreat has a programme of activities as well as time for quiet meditation and reflection. The day begins with a period of meditation and there are usually other opportunities to meditate during the day. Often there are talks and workshops on aspects of Buddhist practice, opportunities to be inspired and uplifted by the perspective brought by the Dharma. Discussion groups give the chance to ask questions, discuss issues, and share experiences. Retreats can provide a creative context for self-exploration, can deepen our spiritual practice, and bring about self-transformation. People often change a lot during a retreat in a way which seems almost magical. It isn't, of course. Retreats change us because they give us supportive conditions in which we can make the effort to change ourselves.

At Taraloka we run a variety of retreats. There are retreats for those completely new to meditation; study retreats on various Buddhist texts and themes; meditation and ritual retreats; and retreats devoted to cultivating the *brahma-viharas* – love, compassion, joy, and equanimity. There are retreats exploring the arts and spiritual life, and ritual and devotion in Buddhism; and there are working retreats. A wide variety of retreat themes and lengths is provided, to suit as many women as possible. The most popular retreats are those devoted to meditation practice.

Women come from all walks of life and all age groups. I find it moving and inspiring to see women in their early twenties learning the basics of meditation alongside those in their sixties or seventies, finding enough in common to bridge the age gap. Taraloka attracts visitors from Europe, America, and Australasia as well as from all parts of Britain. We place emphasis on making the teaching of meditation and Buddhism practical and readily accessible to Westerners. A retreat is an opportunity to experience Sangha – spiritual community – as a group of women come together, spending time in each other's company, sharing our experience of the spiritual journey with its ups and downs, successes and failures, inspirations and difficulties. We come to see that we have far more in common with one another than we thought.

I have been involved in two more major phases of building work since I came to Taraloka. In 1989, a team of seven women converted a length of barn into a spacious lounge. I organized the project, but this time I made sure that the project worked for the team as much as the team for the project, and I enjoyed it wholeheartedly. I had all the materials and methods organized well in advance, and we brought in professionals to do the areas in which we had no skills (e.g. electrics), or which would exhaust us or take too long (e.g. drilling out the rest of the cattle troughs). Making good use of our skills and acknowledging our strengths and limitations made for a very successful and enjoyable project. We were a cosmopolitan team, with women from France, Germany, Holland, and Britain, and we worked well together, without a sense of anxiety, completing the lounge according to schedule.

We then turned our attention to the gradual transformation of the area around the retreat centre, with most progress taking place on our Landscape and Maintenance retreats. The garden is a really beautiful addition, with its lawn, flower beds, pond, small rockery, trellis and pergola, entrance flagpole, and outdoor shrines. I have lovely memories of sunny days, measuring up the site for the pond and lining up the poles for the pergola. Digging out the pond was some of the hardest physical work I've ever done. We had sunshine every day until the day we were laying the pond-liner in its prepared base. At almost the very moment the liner was settled in the hole, thunder clapped and the gradually darkening skies broke into torrential rain – which filled the pond.

Most recently, we have finished the conversion of the remaining sections of barn outbuildings, a project that provided small bedrooms, a second shrine-room, a study room, a suite of rooms suitable for solitary retreat use, and a bathroom with facilities for the disabled. I did the designs for the conversion, together with architect and Mitra Erica Light. We launched a big fund-raising appeal which raised enough, together with our existing reserve, to fund the building work. This time we decided to have all the major work done by professional builders, leaving only the decoration and external work to be done by women's teams. This was partly because the work was more complex than any we had done before, but more importantly because it could be done quickly so that the retreat centre would be closed for as short a time as possible.

My strongest friendships are with the women I've lived and worked with here over the years. It's been an opportunity to experience the truth of one of Sangharakshita's sayings – that you can grow to become friends with anyone, whether or not you like each other at first sight or feel you have things in common. I've come to value and respect the differences I've seen in others, come to understand them and appreciate their qualities, come to like and even love them as friends.

Having lived and worked at Taraloka for several years now, I feel stronger, more confident, and clearer about my abilities. I have experienced a potent combination of being pushed by the objective challenges of the project and drawn forward by the vision for it and the atmosphere of encouragement which has mostly prevailed. To create a concrete, material counterpart of the archetypal realm of Tara is not the work of a day. It's a practical and spiritual task that requires persistence and generosity of spirit from those involved. It has been hard work but it has drawn more out of me than I knew was there, and I am very glad to have been part of it.

Taraloka has developed very broadly, not only materially but also in a more subtle way. It has acquired what I would call a mythic dimension. The retreat centre's name has played a part in the development of this other dimension. It means 'realm, abode, or place of Tara'. Tara is an archetypal Bodhisattva, the female embodiment of the compassion of the Enlightened mind. She is a graceful and dynamic figure who sits as if in meditation, but with one leg stepping down from her seat. She stretches out her right hand, and we feel that she is moving towards us, moving to help any being who is suffering. The qualities which Tara embodies provide the vision behind Taraloka. Her main quality is compassion, a very active compassion based in transcendental wisdom and springing from a vibrant liveliness and energy. She is also associated with loyalty and devotion.

When the centre was first set up, it had no name. Sanghadevi told me: 'It was as if we had not found what we were yet. Lots of names were suggested and discussed, but none of them seemed quite right. Then "Taraloka" arose in my mind, and it seemed the obvious name. Tara is in a female form, but that form transcends dualism and does not feed any tendency to polarization between the sexes. "Taraloka" evokes a mythic dimension. It's as if Taraloka already exists in an ideal or archetypal world, and we are creating its counterpart on the physical plane. The women who live, work, and go on retreat at Taraloka are building a realm where Tara's influence can be felt. It is a place where women can become more than women. They can become true individuals.'

Taraloka is bigger than its buildings, more than just a place or the people there; it is a very important and precious place in the hearts and minds of those who visit. At its broadest, it is the sum total of everything that has happened to women within its boundaries: the highest visions, the deepest reflections, the clearest insights, the strongest experiences of transformation. An ever-deepening atmosphere of spiritual practice, of stillness and vibrancy, has built up in the shrine-room, and it feels as though this radiates out into the surrounding land.

I look back over Taraloka's first ten years with a sense of achievement and satisfaction. Although there is much more still to do, we have begun to create a 'realm of Tara' whose effects are being felt not only in Britain but around the world. Taraloka is a prototype, and I hope that many more retreat centres like it will be developed in other countries. Now we have achieved some of our earlier aims, the way is open for further develop-ment. We have recently been focusing much more on deepening the spiritual practice of the community, because Taraloka is to a large extent the expression of its resident community. We are also developing and improving our retreats year by year, experimenting with new forms of teaching as well as refining those already well established. It is my hope that Taraloka will always continue to grow and change. May it also continue to be of benefit to those who visit it in years to come. May it become an ever truer expression of the compassion of Tara, of the wisdom of all Enlightened beings.

V Buddhism in Different Cultures

Muditasri

Muditasri was born on the island of St Kitts in the eastern Caribbean, but has lived in England for most of her life. She has worked as a social worker and in social work education for many years, as well as supporting and leading Buddhist classes and retreats. She was ordained in 1989.

Muditasri

Unity in Diversity

A Black Buddhist Speaks

MUCH OF WHAT I WRITE here is drawn from my experience as one of the few black women practising Buddhism in the context of the Friends of the Western Buddhist Order (FWBO) in Britain. In using the socio-political term 'black' (within the context of a dominant white culture) I refer to all people of African and Asian descent who define themselves as black. I also use the term to include people who experience prejudice in this society because their noses are wider and their lips fuller than those of white Europeans. Some women in this latter group have identi-fied with black issues and have chosen to attend retreats advertised for black women.

For a black woman to come to a Buddhist centre in Britain is a leap into the unknown, a stepping out into an area where the only black face present will probably be her own. For most black people in Britain racism is a familiar backdrop against which our lives proceed, and this makes us uneasy about how we will be received by British Buddhists. Generally speaking, white English people are not renowned for ready warmth of temperament. My parents' generation faced reserve and overt hostility when they came to Britain in the 1950s and 60s and attempted to join their white Christian brethren in their cold, joyless churches. The formation of our own churches in Britain began as a reaction to this.

Most women who become interested in Buddhism do so having long rejected Christianity, which, in general, was the religion of their parents. They want a different yardstick by which to measure their lives. In essence they want a new morality. Black women do not generally come to a Buddhist centre in search of friends or yet another social group. For many there are difficulties to overcome, including ignorance and diffidence on the part of white people running the centres, which can hinder their involvement. Black women entering into any new sphere of life in this society face a particular complexity. This complexity is racism.

After spending my first eleven years on the island of St Kitts in the eastern Caribbean, I arrived in England. In 1979, at the age of 31, feeling thoroughly exhausted after a long stint of full-time social work, I fulfilled a long-held ambition to travel to India. I had no other conscious reason than that I was drawn to that country and its people. I also visited Nepal and Sri Lanka. In the course of my journey, as a sense of calm and perspective entered my life, I felt an urge to learn to meditate and a need to find some deeper meaning to my existence. In previous years I had been slightly involved in political activity, but had come to realize that this was not the way for me to gain greater self-knowledge or to assist others in doing so. By the time I made my journey to the East I had abandoned politics as the way forward, and my Christian upbringing had long seemed irrelevant.

My travelling companion and I stood intrigued at the doors of many Hindu temples to which, as women, we were barred entry. Finding a Jain community and standing in its central place of worship was a moving experience. In Sri Lanka we visited a number of Buddhist religious centres but could find no one there teaching meditation. I needed something to help me sustain the calmness I was experiencing, feeling that without some method of meditation it would be impossible to maintain it once I returned to my busy life in London. During our stay in Sri Lanka we spent a couple of weeks in Kandy, and each day our journey took us past a beautiful lake and yet another temple. Then, on the day of the full moon in May, as we approached this temple, we heard the sound of vibrant African-style drumming. My heartbeat was in tune with the pounding drums, and I eagerly asked those gathered around the temple what was happening. They told me that Buddhists were celebrating the Buddha's Enlightenment of around 2,500 years ago, and that we too could join in the festivities. Had we not been invited into the temple I would have been ready to participate anyway, just dancing on the pavement outside. However, I found myself in a semi-darkened room, circumambulating what I was later told was a relic of the Buddha. This was the Temple of the Tooth, a tooth which was said to have been the Buddha's. When I emerged into the blinding sunlight, I knew that I had to find out more about Buddhism, and soon.

When we returned to Colombo, our enquiries led us to a community of monks who formally received us. The senior monk who gave us an audience imperiously barked an order of dismissal to his attendant. This I found jarring and unkind. I remember asking 'What is Buddhism?' but do not remember the answer. However, when I left I was given eight tiny pamphlets about the Buddha's Noble Eightfold Path.[89] Each evening, in our little room in Colombo, my friend and I read and discussed a pamphlet. I was deeply moved and inspired by the Buddha's message, and before we had completed our 'studies' there was no doubt in my mind that I wanted to be a Buddhist, I wanted to follow this path. What I had read was not only moving and inspiring; it showed me that, with effort, it was possible for me to lead a thoroughly human life, beyond anything I had previously imagined. This was what I had always wanted to do.

And so, nine days later, enthusiastic and armed with many questions about how to put these teachings into practice, we returned to the vihara. I have forgotten the answers on this occasion too, but I came away once again with an unfavourable impression of the monk, mainly because he seemed so unkind to his lay attendant. Despite this, I was determined to explore and practise what I had read. As I was shortly to return to London, I would have to find the way forward there. But how? I remembered that some years previously a friend (not a Buddhist or a meditator) had suggested I learn to meditate, and introduced me to a friend of his who was practising Buddhism in the context of the FWBO. I was impressed by her calmness and also by the title of the movement with which she was involved. I was especially struck by the fact that they were 'Western Buddhists'.[90]

Although I am of African descent, I come from a culture which has been Westernized by the cruelties of slavery and imperialism. I have also lived for thirty-five years in England. I am therefore a Westernized woman of African descent wanting to practise Buddhism in the West. From what I had gathered, the teachings of Buddhism were addressed to all human beings irrespective of colour or ethnic background and thus presented a universal path. I reflected that it could be no accident that these teachings had been made available to me, and that the catalyst had been the drums I had heard in Sri Lanka. However, if I was to put into action what I had learned so far, I needed practices which could be incorporated into my busy lifestyle. Above all else, I needed a straightforward meditation practice, free from Eastern cultural accretions, which would help me to sustain my sense of calmness. When I got back to London, I visited the London Buddhist Centre, then the largest FWBO centre in Britain. I found that the people teaching and supporting the classes there were warm, friendly, and willing to engage in open discussion. I was also very impressed by the aroma and welcoming ambience of the place, which suggested that I had at last arrived 'home'.

The people at the London Buddhist Centre in those days were a motley group of middle-class white people – mostly English, plus a few Scots. This didn't concern me so much as the fact that (by chance, as it turned out) I saw no women teachers. In deciding to become a Buddhist I knew before I ever went to the Centre that there would be few, if any, other black people involved and therefore that I was in for yet another experience of going it alone.

How did I know this, and what did it mean to me? Though people of African and African Caribbean descent have lived in Britain since the fifteenth century, it is only since the late 1940s and 50s that we have settled here in large numbers. So we are relatively new members of this society, trying to find appropriate ways of enhancing our self-view against a background of discrimination on grounds of colour. This discrimination can take the form of direct policy: some firms employ no black people at all, while others restrict the posts available to them. Posts where the new employee would be required to deal with the general public are often closed to black people.

If a black person finds work in some sphere other than cleaning, the lower grades of the transport system, and similar manual jobs, they are likely to be the only black person in the vicinity. I was therefore not surprised, dismayed, or concerned to find myself once again in such a situation. This had been my experience since the age of 18 when I left my family and began living almost exclusively amongst white people.

But what effect does this have? What do black women feel on coming to Buddhist centres and finding themselves apparently isolated? As far as I was concerned the main thing was that people were civil. Provided the atmosphere was congenial, I was determined to learn to meditate and follow the Eightfold Path. Having had thirteen years' experience of regularly being the only black person in many settings – in further education, as a social work practitioner at conferences, and so on – there was nothing unusual about the situation in which I had placed myself. I already knew that I was likely to come across well-meaning, middle-class English people who would adopt what I call the 'colour-blind' approach: the attitude that colour doesn't matter.

Confronted with differences or conflict, a black woman is likely to have one of two responses. She can remain silent, seeming to concur with the 'colour-blind' approach, and avoiding standing out. Fear of acknowledging her difference, or weariness of the role of educator, is often at the bottom of this silence. But by responding in this way, the black woman misses an opportunity to express and test her views, and those around her are none the wiser about who she is. This is clearly unhelpful. One of the main reasons for practising Buddhism is to help one gain greater clarity about oneself and the world in which one lives, and you can't gain that kind of clarity by remaining silent. Another equally unhelpful response is the exact opposite. Here, one becomes the centre of attention by highlighting every cultural disparity, thus becoming the group's educator on issues connected with black people and risking conveying the notion that black people are a homogeneous group. Ideally a middle way needs to be found between these two extremes.

In my early days as a Buddhist I watched and listened a good deal. I wanted to avoid the position which, mostly through necessity, I had adopted in my profession: that of repeatedly highlighting, for white social workers working with black clients, how their well-intentioned attitudes and interventions could alienate their clients from the very help they needed. Through reflecting on my past experiences I reminded myself why I was at the Buddhist centre. I was not there to represent my ethnic group, but to find a way to go beyond my present limitations and conditioning. I do not want to understate the significance of skin colour in our society and the damaging effects of racism, but, perhaps for the first time in my life, I began to realize how painful people's lives are, irrespective of colour or cultural conditioning, and how similar we all are, although, paradoxically, we are each unique.

Other black women have had similar experiences. Like me, few with whom I have spoken expected to find other black people at Buddhist centres. An English-born black woman much younger than me, who was contemplating coming to the Buddhist centre, said, 'Meditation is not something black people do – well, not in this country.' However, she did not feel she was embarking upon something completely alien, because she was aware of the reflective, contemplative element in African Caribbean culture.

Until recently, African Caribbean culture – especially on the smaller islands – was not much influenced by the media. On the island where I spent my early years, there was one weekly paper, which was seldom read in the villages, and radios were a rarity. It was, and still is, a culture based on the relational – on relationships. People are generally very aware of their interconnectedness with each other. They are also aware of their surroundings. Owing to limited external input, and the tropical nature of the climate, it is not uncommon at dusk to see many people simply sitting silently observing the mysterious drama of nature, as the day draws to a close and the sun seemingly descends into the ocean, or the full moon rises and lights up a village which as yet has no communal electricity. Such events are a meaningful feature in the lives of many people in a way not experienced in the busy, materialistic West. In this simple manner silence, observation, and contemplation are part of Caribbean culture.

Although my friend was keen to meditate (and she is now a committed Buddhist), she wondered at first whether she would be expected to embrace Eurocentric ideas as well as Eastern mysticism. She soon found that this was not the case. The founder of the FWBO, Sangharakshita, is an excellent translator between East and West, and has always insisted that, even though Buddhism originated in the East, its teachings are relevant to people in the West.

My own experience has been of finding Buddhist connections – sometimes surprising ones – with not only Western but also African Caribbean culture. For example, there was my response to Buddhist iconography. My first encounter with it was in Kathmandu, where the temple walls were intricately sculpted with male and female couples in sexual union. What a strange place for such depictions, I thought. I simply couldn't make sense of it, and got nowhere with my enquiries. Back in London at the Buddhist centre I learned that such figures (known as *yab-yum*) depict the pinnacle of the Enlightened experience – the unity of Wisdom and Compassion – and, surprisingly, have nothing to do with sex.

These yab-yum figures were not in evidence at the Buddhist centre, but other figures were. Among them were archetypal figures known as Bodhisattvas. Upon first sight of one of these figures I was immediately captivated. This was the figure of Manjushri or Manjughosha, the 'gentle-voiced one', the Bodhisattva of Wisdom. He is richly adorned in silks and jewels, as befits a young prince of the Indo-Tibetan tradition. He sits in meditation posture, emphasizing that wisdom springs from meditation. In his right hand he wields a flaming, double-edged sword above his head, and in his left he holds to his heart a volume of the Perfection of Wisdom text. This sword, this compassionate sword, cuts effortlessly at the root of suffering, and similarly cuts away and burns up all wrong views which, if not destroyed, keep us bound to the wheel of suffering. The book at his heart contains the essential lofty teachings on wisdom, whose emphasis is to attack our dualistic way of perceiving the world, and thus point the way beyond dualistic notions of self and other, the conditioned and the Unconditioned, to the Great Emptiness.

After some months of reflection, I began to realize what it was about this figure that had triggered my imagination. When I was a child in the Caribbean, cane-fields were a familiar feature of the landscape. When ready for harvesting they are a tall, thick mass of unruly vegetation challenging the strength and skill of the harvester. This, on a mundane level, seemed not unlike the task which Manjughosha has in hand: that of dealing with this unruly, unending, chaotic world, rife with cankerous falsehoods which, if not checked, wreak havoc on our minds and the world around.

For the cane-cutter two things are necessary to harvest the crop with the least effort; a sharp cutlass and an agile body. And Manjughosha has the sword of compassion and the book of Wisdom, for he is dealing not with plants but with human beings. So strongly was I drawn to what the sword represented that it is only in recent years that I have started to pay attention to the significance of the book. When I was ordained I formally took up the meditation and reflection practice of this figure.

As the years go by, a small but steady number of black women are becoming involved with the FWBO in London. These women yearn to meet and practise with other black women, especially during the early days of their involvement. Many of them have spent years as the only black person in class at school, in further education, or in their profession. They feel isolated and long to share their new experiences with others whose perspectives on life may be similar. Some, finding that their desire to practise, meet, and discuss with other black women is not satisfied, give up or make slow progress. Others forge ahead, having tasted the essence of Buddhist practice. Soon after the first black women's meditation course I taught, one woman enthusiastically went to a retreat at Taraloka, the women's retreat centre in Shropshire, and has subsequently gone on to request ordination into the Western Buddhist Order.

The slow but steady increase in the number of black women interested in practising Buddhism within the context of the FWBO has made it possible for us to organize a number of weekend retreats specially for black women. The main purpose of these has been to provide a forum in which questions about meditation and Buddhist practice particular to ethnicity can be clarified. The retreats have also provided an opportunity to deepen meditation practice and an introduction to some basic Buddhism. We hope also to ensure that those who want to take their interest in Buddhism further will gain the confidence to enter into other activities where, for the moment, they may not be physically reflected. These retreats have fulfilled a need. The challenge is to make sure that Buddhism, not ethnicity, remains the primary focus of such retreats.

As more black women enter the doors of Buddhist centres, like everybody else they bring with them past experiences of pleasure and pain. Some eulogize the benefits of meditation, its healing balm, its power to reclaim that which is best in themselves. They also talk of their experiences of racism at FWBO centres and I find it very difficult to be on the receiving end of such reports, as I cannot comment with honesty and clarity unless I was present at the incidents to which they refer. Even then it's difficult. What I can do is empathize and help the woman to explore the whole incident, and, while not denying that racism may have been a factor, make sure that, besides skin colour, she considers the possible involvement of other factors, such as personality and gender – and also the possibility that she has misinterpreted what was said or done. Most importantly, I encourage her to seek out the individual, especially if they are a member of the Order, and clarify what has taken place. Of course it is not always easy to approach Order members, as they are the objects of many projections, such as being presumed to be perfect and powerful. However, at the end of one such conversation, one black woman said that, unlike most other organizations with which she had been involved, she felt very hopeful about sorting out difficulties with people at the Buddhist centre, and with Order members specifically, because we were all committed to changing ourselves radically. I agree with this, and would add that I have been neither surprised nor daunted by any difficulties I have experienced in the FWBO, whether to do with racism or anything else.

Western Buddhist movements are still predominantly white. White teachers of meditation and Buddhism need to be aware of what is going on in the world, and particularly of the effects of racism on black people. Perhaps, without being effusive, they could be a little more welcoming. It is also important that they do not fall into the trap – especially likely on retreats – of assuming that because there are two black women present they would necessarily like to be in the same study group. However well-intentioned, it is a mistake – and many organizations make it – to presume that skin colour alone will be enough to cement friendship.

But we need to stay focused on Buddhism, for it is this which brings us together and helps us to identify wrong views. The FWBO is a very young Buddhist movement, and people who become involved with it bring with them many wrong views, of which racism may be one, and the idea that all difficulties between black and white people are caused by racism may be another. Such views do not accord with how things really are. Studying and reflecting on Buddhist teachings can, over time, transform these views. In the case of racism, we will be able to see one another as human beings rather than holding on to false notions which derive from suppositions based on skin colour.

The majority of black women attending FWBO centres in Britain are aged 45 and under, so for the most part we are British-born or have lived in Britain for most of our lives. This is an interesting group, historically speaking. We are in the throes of rewriting much of our history, both in this country and in the lands of our forebears. Most of us have been involved in this process through black women's groups, political activity, university education, black consciousness-raising groups, and so on. Activities like these play an essential part in raising black women's self-esteem, enabling us to feel confident enough to explore areas of experience which we would not previously have dared to enter. Meditation is one such area, and this in turn can lead to an interest in Buddhism and the beginning of a spiritual quest.

Many black women have experienced surprise and frustration in connection with language usage. Language is a powerful medium of self-expression, a barometer of the social milieu which we inhabit or want to create. In choosing to call ourselves 'black' we have moved from the slave master's terms – 'nigger', 'negro' – to self-definition. Most people who are happy with the nomenclature 'black' are no more objectively black in skin colour than 'white' people are white-skinned. Labels are powerful.

In the English language the word 'black' is often used to define something which is negative or viewed negatively. It is used, for example, as a synonym for 'dirty'. When we hear of a 'black' day, undoubtedly something awful or evil has occurred. Similarly terms such as 'blacklist' and 'the black arts' have negative connotations. A newcomer to the Buddhist centre may hear the term 'black' used to describe a negative idea or experience, where more awareness and sensitivity would prompt a more creative use of vocabulary. This kind of experience harks back to the negative ideology and myths about black people which date from the fifteenth century onwards. Of course, black women are challenging the alienating use of language, just as are white women and marginalized minorities in Britain and throughout the world. White people sometimes say 'Oh dear, can't we say "blackboard" or "black coffee" now?' but this is to miss the point completely.

My own response is that the term 'black' can be used with clarity and precision, avoiding usage which is potentially derogatory or racist. In adopting this position I do not consider that I am reconstructing the English language. I am simply being sensitive and trying to get my message across to as many people as possible.

Many white people I know – and perhaps some black people too – would argue that language does not change attitude. My experience tells me that the act of changing language is a facet of a wider movement of change, part and parcel of a broader dialogue and a greater understanding and empathy between peoples. The barriers we construct to keep ourselves separate and safe from others serve only to constrict our growth. We live in times in which many people fear using politically incorrect terminology. English is alive and therefore changing. It is important to be clear about the basis for change, to understand what the attitudes and values are that we would like to see changing.

I feel very fortunate as a Buddhist to have a yardstick by which to examine my own actions and those of others. Buddhist morality is a morality of intention in which the state of mind preceding an action is of crucial importance. If I feel hurt by what someone has said, I need to check out whether they meant to hurt me. If not, although I may still feel hurt, hatred – a common response in such instances – has no place in my interaction with them. (In fact, even if they did intend to hurt, to respond with hatred is still not justifiable. 'Hatred does not cease with hatred. Hatred only ceases with love,' the Buddha said.) The hurt I experience can open the way for dialogue from which greater understanding is possible.

The Western Buddhist Order is faced with a challenge, especially as there are only a handful of black Order members in England. White Order members need to develop greater social awareness and sensitivity to meet this challenge. They need to acknowledge and work with their own racism where it exists, just as they do with other aspects of their conditioning. There is no need for guilt, although it seems to be the most common emotion experienced by white people when confronted with the racist atrocities of their forebears, such as slavery, and their own racism. Guilt is a powerful emotion which erodes confidence, stultifies interaction, and in some cases silences the person experiencing it, rendering them incapable of sorting out whatever has given rise to the guilt. Part of our task as Buddhists is to break down barriers, and to do this, frank, clear, kindly discussion is necessary. Silence on a topic which has been taboo for hundreds of years only compounds the situation.

If we are to develop our highest human potential – the prime function of Buddhist practice – we need to go beyond current dogmas and ideologies, however useful we may find them in ordinary life. The notion that human beings are separate entities is one such idea. Such thinking keeps us alienated from one another and, paradoxically, from our true selves. When we begin to raise our level of consciousness through meditation and other Buddhist practices, we begin to see very clearly that our thinking has limited us. With mingled joy and pain we experience the interconnectedness of all living beings. As we practise meditation and ethics, and get into deeper communication with others, we begin to narrow the gap between ourselves and those around us. This is the experience to which all practitioners attest. In time, labels assume less importance because the quest for true individuality, true wholeness, shifts us into another level of consciousness.

When you meditate regularly and begin to incorporate other Buddhist practices (such as the practice of the Five Precepts) into your life, other issues arise. Some of these are more or less the same for everyone, but there are a few which are of particular significance for black people. One of these is the desire to change one's way of life. It is clear why this should be when one considers the background history of black people in Britain, especially those from the Caribbean.

Most of those who left the Caribbean to come to Britain were economic refugees rather than immigrants. They did not intend to settle, but to work for a few years and save enough money to enable them to return to their islands and create a viable standard of living for themselves, their families, and their communities. For the majority this proved impossible. Their ambition, and their willingness to work hard and save money, came up against the vast housing shortage after the war, the low wages, the deadening effects of the English climate, and racism on a scale they could not have imagined until they experienced it. When it became clear that the often-quoted five year plan would not work, many sent for their families and settled in Britain.[91] The black women involving themselves with the FWBO today are the progeny of those early arrivals. We know the problems our parents faced as 'niggers', 'wogs', and 'coloureds' in Britain, which they had been indoctrinated to see as their mother country, and putting it candidly, we are not prepared to suffer their humiliations and we do not intend to re-live their lives. Our migrant parents expect us to fulfil and surpass their own hopes and aspirations. This is very understandable in view of past deprivations, but in Buddhist terms it is not enough. Though we do not wish to disappoint well-meaning parents or guardians, some black women choose to withdraw from aspirations of a worldly or materialistic nature in order to pursue a different goal, the goal of Enlightenment, true freedom.

Few of us can make radical changes in our lives without the encouragement, guidance, and support of others. We especially need others who understand what we are trying to achieve. Some black women who want to tread the Buddhist path naturally feel an urge to change some basic areas of their lives. It is common to want to live, work, and study regularly with other Buddhists, go on group and solitary retreats, and give time and energy to the local Buddhist centre. Some feel a desire to give up their former lifestyle completely while others aspire to modify their present way of life in accordance with the teachings of the Buddha. Whatever she chooses, a woman in pursuit of the transcendental is drawn on by the need to discover her true individuality rather than simply being defined by colour, profession, or family name.

The actions of one black woman of my acquaintance exemplify the sort of changes some women make. After she had been meditating for a while, it became clear to her that to continue her original plan to enter a very stressful, competitive profession would stultify her overall growth and creativity. On completing her degree she therefore decided not to study any further even though her parents would have been very proud of her achievements. She decided to move to a city where she could live with other Buddhists and have easy access to a centre where there were many women Order members. Her father found it hard to understand why she had chosen to discard her education and a potentially secure financial future; when one considers the history of his generation, this is hardly surprising.

Things have been rather different for me. By the time I became a Buddhist I was already qualified as a social worker and was on the verge of buying my own flat. I had also decided to work part-time. So, on finding Buddhism, I already had the time to practise and reflect. It was as if I had created the space in my life before I knew what I would do with it. However, later on, in an attempt to share my life more with other Buddhists and have easy access to a centre, I left my comfortable flat to share with another Buddhist woman. This came as a shock to my non-Buddhist friends, who knew that my childhood in Britain had been dominated by bad housing conditions. I endured my new living situation for six months. Apart from lack of clarity about what my flatmate and I expected of each other, I found the estate on which we lived unpleasant in every way – not least because of the overt racism, expressed verbally and through graffiti scrawled everywhere. For the first time in years I felt unsafe walking around the area in which I lived. Clearly this was not helpful to me, and the level of support I received from my Buddhist friends was far from sufficient. Unlike my more politically aware non-Buddhist friends, none of them ever commented on the racism or its dangers. Perhaps they didn't notice the graffiti or the fascists peddling their propaganda. I was relieved to return to my former home. Perhaps my connections with my Buddhist friends were not strong or deep enough then. But, more than anything, I think they did not understand what the move had meant for me in the light of my history.

At the same time, some of my white Buddhist friends began working in a women's team-based Right Livelihood business. I admired what they were doing, but felt a responsibility to remain a social worker because I felt I could effect greater change in that capacity, offering a perspective to my white colleagues which could make their work with black clients more effective, and acting as a role model for young black people wanting to enter social work. In this I was typical of my generation of black people. Many of us carry an over-developed sense of responsibility to other black people, and to white people too, because some of the opportunities now available to us have previously been denied to black people. I understand the reasons for this sense of responsibility, but it can prove to be a burden which makes the search for true individuality more difficult than necessary. To support our move away from our cultural group – with which, because of racism, we have been led to identify – greater knowledge, sympathy, and support is needed from other Buddhists. I would suggest that white Buddhists try to put themselves in our shoes, reflecting upon when, if ever, they were the only white person among a number of black people, and how this made them feel.

As the Western Buddhist community becomes more culturally diverse this diversity will permeate all aspects of its activities. Even now, I notice that when women of African Caribbean descent become Mitras[92] at the London Buddhist Centre the audience witnessing the event almost always contains members of their immediate and extended families and friends who are not Buddhists. This creates a valuable link between their two 'worlds'.

The Friends of the Western Buddhist Order is a movement united by the Three Jewels – the Buddha, the Dharma, and the Sangha – and its founder, Sangharakshita. Any other factor can be no more than a stepping-stone towards unification, irrespective of the way some groups are marginalized in society at large. As human beings, members of one race, our differences are eclipsed by what we have in common. Let us rejoice, therefore, in our unity, as well as our diversity.

Vijaya

*Vijaya lives in Nagpur in central India. She belongs to the
ex-Untouchable community, which for thousands of years has
suffered untold misery at the bottom of the Hindu caste
system. Many ex-Untouchables have converted to Buddhism
over the last forty years, inspired not only by the Buddha's
rejection of caste, but also by the example of Dr B.R.
Ambedkar, an Untouchable who rose to become independent
India's first Law Minister, and drew up the Indian
Constitution, in which Untouchability was declared illegal.
Despite this, ex-Untouchables are still subject to crippling
social restrictions.*

*When in 1956 Dr Ambedkar converted to Buddhism,
380,000 ex-Untouchables followed suit. His death shortly
afterwards left the new Buddhists without a leader.
Sangharakshita rallied Ambedkar's followers, forging a link
which led to the establishment of TBMSG (Trailokya Bauddha
Mahasangha Sahayak Gana). Today the ex-Untouchable
Buddhist community numbers about 9,000,000 people.*

*In 1980 some British Buddhists formed a charity to fund
social projects run by their partner charity in India, Bahujan
Hitay ('for the welfare of the many'): kindergartens, hostels,
literacy classes, health care, and sewing classes. Vijaya is
responsible for Bahujan Hitay's social projects in Nagpur.
Here she tells her story (which has been translated from
Marathi).*

Vijaya

A Flower from the Dust

From Untouchability to Buddhism

I WAS BORN on 23 September 1968 in Nagpur in Maharashtra, in a large slum area. I had five brothers and sisters: two elder brothers and one elder sister, and a younger brother and sister. My father worked in a textile mill. He had little education, but he taught himself to read and write and encouraged his children to study. We were poor and had to buy second-hand books for our studies, as father often had difficulty in providing them and the other equipment needed for school. But despite the poverty, the atmosphere in our family was happy, and often after the evening meal we would sit talking together for hours.

Like most Indians, my parents favoured their sons more than their daughters. I felt left out as a child, and often did not want to be a girl. When I started to go to school, my reaction against being a girl became even stronger. Indian conditioning and family traditions placed so many restraints on girls; but I knew from an early age that I did not want to give in to these pressures as other women did. An Indian woman's life is strange! After her birth she lives with her father, after marriage she lives with her husband, and finally, in old age, she lives with her sons. I wondered where her independence was, and felt that I wanted to find my own independence and individuality.

On my way to school each day, I used to see a statue of the Queen of Jansi (a historical figure) in the bazaar square. This statue had a strong effect on me every time I saw it. I did not understand why I was drawn to it, but I would stare at it for a long time. The queen was riding a horse, holding a sword in one hand and the reins in the other, and had a smile of victory on her face. She had fought many battles and now sat on the horse, triumphant. I felt very inspired by her and wanted to do something noble with my life, but I did not know what this might be. Even if I had had a sword, I would not have wanted to fight. I realized that I needed to concentrate on my education first, in order to develop skills and become more independent. Then, perhaps, I could work for the welfare of others.

When I was 18, my father suggested that I should get married, but I was unhappy about this, feeling that I was too young. My elder brother intervened, suggesting that I should be allowed to continue with my education and not be married so soon. My father did not have enough money for my education but I got a scholarship, so was able to continue with my studies.

One day my elder brother attended a retreat with the TBMSG and returned very enthusiastic about the Dharma and the movement. I felt very inspired and wanted to find out more about it, so I attended my first retreat with him in 1989. This was my introduction to the movement.

Soon after this retreat my father became very ill. He died in April 1989, and I was very upset by his death. Our material conditions deteriorated without my father's support; my brother left his studies and found a job and we all had to help each other as there was no help from anyone outside the family. I realized the significance of my education and applied myself more seriously to my studies, in order to improve my prospects.

Then suddenly, in June 1990, my younger brother died. The cause of his death was unknown and I went into deep shock. I was distraught and became depressed. My elder brother, feeling deep grief himself, was very kind and supportive. I started to meditate with him. Until then I had meditated occasionally but now I started to meditate regularly and soon my mental state started to improve. I started to study the Dharma, and attended retreats and devotional activities.

On 4 August 1991 my elder brother was ordained as a Dharmachari and I felt very inspired and deeply moved by the ceremony. Buddhism had given me some clarity and stability, both in my struggles to find my identity and individuality, and in my suffering at the loss of my father and brother. Witnessing the ordination of my brother, Dharmachari Amritasiddhi, I realized that I had at last found my own path, my spiritual goal. I wanted to follow this path, and so, on 21 November 1991, I became a Mitra.

I became more involved in the activities of the TBMSG, meeting other women regularly, and in 1992 I joined the women's community,

Shakyaditha, in Poona. I wanted to develop deeper friendships with other women, and also to work in the social projects associated with TBMSG, so I undertook a year's training. This period helped me to understand myself and other women, as we practised the Dharma together, and to find my own individuality.

Returning to Nagpur, I married Dharmachari Amoghasiddhi and continued to work as a supervisor of Bahujan Hitay's playgroups and nursery schools. We were supportive of each other in our spiritual path and our work in the social field. My marriage did not prevent me from following my own spiritual path and on 30 January 1994 I was ordained as a Dharmacharini. I was very happy indeed to make this commitment: that day was the most important in my life.

Soon after my ordination, I became pregnant and I was very happy about it. Unfortunately the baby was still-born at seven months. Once again, I suffered deep shock and grief. I became very depressed and unable to sleep. I could not understand why this had happened to me.

But then, realizing that I could not continue to be miserable, I started to concentrate on my spiritual life again, meditating daily and turning fully towards the Dharma. I realized that I had to let go of the past and concentrate on the future; that there would always be suffering in life, and that I needed to be strong to confront it. I also realized that there were other women around me with similar experiences of loss, death, and deprivation, and they needed support.

I am now involved in women's activities, helping with retreats, meeting individual women to build up friendships. I am responsible for all the social projects in Nagpur, which include kindergartens, sewing classes, adult literacy classes, and the girls' hostel. I am very happy doing this work and want to continue with it in the future.

Prajnamata

*Like Vijaya, Prajnamata is an ordained Buddhist, a member
of the Trailokya Bauddha Mahasangha, as the Western
Buddhist Order is known in India. The two women do the
same meditations, study the same scriptures, and take part
in the same devotional practices. On retreat together they
share the same food and occupy the same living quarters.
This may not appear startling, but it is, in fact, revolutionary.
For Prajnamata was born to Brahmin parents (the highest
Hindu caste). In orthodox Hindu circles the two of them
would be extremely unlikely ever to have met, but if they had
done so Prajnamata would be 'polluted' by the mere
presence of Vijaya. As it is, as sister Dharmacharinis, the
bond between them – and their connection with all the other
women who have contributed to this book – is very close.*

*Having retired as a college lecturer, Prajnamata now
spends her time teaching the Dharma and writing fiction in
Marathi. In 1995 she was the first Indian Dharmacharini to
visit Britain. Her story is taken from a talk she gave at the
women's Order convention held in England that year.*

Theosophy, Death, and Inspiration

The Life and Going for Refuge of Prajnamata

I WAS BORN to Brahmin parents. Traditionally in India, Brahmins were considered to be the highest level of Indian society, and the Untouchables (there are people even below that) were at the bottom. My parents were not terribly orthodox: religious-minded, not devout, but conventional Hindus. I have one brother; my parents were modern enough to limit the size of their family. My father was a doctor. My mother could read and write but, like most women her age, was taken away from school before she reached puberty. That was a very sad thing for her, and she bemoaned it all her life. I was born when she was 21, and I have never got over the fact that in the space of those 21 years things had changed to such an extent that I could get whatever education I desired, but she could not even finish school. She was an avid reader, and instilled the habit of reading into me.

Something very significant happened to me during my school years. When I was about 11 years old, the school I went to introduced the *Bhagavad Gita* as a compulsory subject. The *Bhagavad Gita* is one of the major books of the Hindu religion. It is part of the *Mahabharata* (an epic somewhat like the *Iliad*), which describes the beginning of a major war between cousins. There has been a long history of enmity in their family; one branch of the family has been unjust to another branch, and the branch that has suffered has tried very hard to make known to the other branch what is right and proper. However, they will not listen; so it has come to conflict. All kinds of efforts are made to avoid war, including mediation by the god Krishna himself, but to no avail. War is imminent. Both armies are on the battlefield. Then Arjuna, one of the major warriors on the side of right, throws down his bow and says: 'I will not fight the war because I would be killing my kith and kin.' The *Bhagavad Gita* is the answer that Krishna gives to Arjuna, exhorting him to fight. It is his duty to fight. Every effort has been made to avoid war; everything that was possible has been done, and at this last minute he cannot leave the battlefield, or there will be chaos.

The head of my school was exceptional in that he was not an ordinary orthodox Hindu: he was fired with the zeal of social reform, backed up by his own understanding of Hinduism. He married a widow – which is unusual in India – and he was totally against the caste system. Though he was very well qualified and could have found a well-paid job, he had decided to start a school for girls. I came into close contact with this headmaster, because he and my father were good friends, and I used to spend time with his family as well. And he used to teach the *Gita*. He had a very light touch; he was full of humour. Of course, everybody rebelled against the *Gita*'s being made compulsory, because it was not part of the official curriculum. The schoolchildren soon discovered that it was not relevant from the point of view of their final exam. Almost nobody was sympathetic, but he didn't mind at all. He taught what he wanted to teach. This went on for four years. We learned the *Gita* – or at least part of it – word for word.

Nobody else at school seemed to be influenced by it. Everybody was against it but me. And of course, I was considered crazy. Not only was I studying what was taught in the class; I asked him which other books I could read. The *Bhagavad Gita* influenced me enormously. I would say that it gave me my first contact with the transcendental. For some reason which I do not fully understand, it totally banished from my mind the idea of a personal God. I felt that the transcendental was the highest value, and devotion was due only to it. Very often in India, temples where gods are housed are frequented by people who want things for themselves. I found this totally unacceptable. I didn't think the atmosphere in the temples was truly devotional; I didn't think that asking for things for oneself was putting faith in God. I thought it was wrong to ask God for things for oneself – 'Let me pass an exam, get me out of this difficulty,' and so on. This feeling has remained with me.

I finished my school examinations at a slightly early age. My parents seemed quite interested in educating me, but when I was around 15 they started looking for a boy for me to marry. I had different ideas; I met and married a young man of my own choice at the age of 16. Before a year was out I had a daughter. My household consisted of me, my husband, my father-in-law, my mother-in-law, my father-in-law's mother, as well as a sister-in-law who was 11, a brother-in-law who was 8, and another sister-in-law who was 3. My mother-in-law was of unsound mind, so before long I became the woman of the house. All nine of us lived in a space of about 300 square feet. Water came only at specified hours. In the first years of my marriage the water tap functioned between 11 p.m. and 6 a.m., during which hours we had to fill up our water pots. I cooked for all these people, and you can have no idea of what cooking in India is like: I made heaps of chapattis! So this was my life, which I accepted quite happily and willingly.

I wanted to continue my education. My father-in-law gave me permission to do so, and also gave me the small amount of money required, which was extremely generous of him, and quite out of keeping with the normal traditions of Indian households. So I continued with my education for six years, and acquired a degree and a postgraduate degree in economics. It was hard work. The hard work was more the cooking and looking after the family than studying. My marriage was falling apart and almost came to an end, but my father-in-law wanted me to give it one more chance, so I continued for a little longer. But at the age of 23, with the permission of my father-in-law, I left the house with my daughter. I took up a job as a lecturer in a college, and worked in that capacity until my retirement.

I met my present husband when I was not quite 25 years old. I had not yet obtained a divorce. This used to be a much lengthier process in India than it is now. I didn't know anybody who had divorced, although I'd heard of one or two film stars who had. But I had decided to follow this course so I got a divorce, and married my husband, Ramesh. We lived in Theosophy Hall. As a confirmed Theosophist, he asked me to attend some of the meetings held there. He would never have forced me to follow Theosophy, but he wanted me to give it a try.

So, on the day that Theosophy Hall was inaugurated, I went to a meeting addressed by a Mr B.P. Wadia, who spoke for an hour and a quarter. I find it difficult to describe my experience. I can only say that once again, after such a long time, I recognized the transcendental in his speech. I was sure that this was a man whose knowledge was not just acquired from books. He had realized something to which very few people come in this lifetime. I had never come across anybody like that before. I went to every one of his meetings for some time, and each time came out feeling that I had been transported into another world. I didn't want to talk to anybody. I wanted to maintain my state of mind for as long as possible.

Although his talks had this effect on me, I was wary of being carried away by personal magnetism; and so I read some Theosophical works, especially *The Ocean of Theosophy*. Theosophy has as its devotional books the *Bhagavad Gita*, the Buddha's *Dhammapada*, *The Voice of the Silence*, Patanjali's *Yoga Sutras*, the *Tao Te Ching*, and the *Upanishads*; also extracts from the Bible and the Koran. Theosophy does not repudiate any religion out of hand. It says that all religions were pure in the beginning and that they have been sullied by later practitioners who misunderstood them, or had the wrong motives. I felt that this was a very acceptable philosophy.

I got married to Ramesh in 1961. In 1962 my daughter Karuna was born and in 1966 my son Meher. My husband was a full-time worker with the United Lodge of Theosophists, and he received an honorarium according to his needs. However, sometimes it was not quite enough for a growing family, so I had to supplement the family income. With two small children, and working full-time in a job I enjoyed, my attendance at meetings and my study of Theosophy was limited. But in 1964, Ramesh told me that Sangharakshita, an English bhikshu, was coming to the Lodge to give a lecture. I went to the talk, and again I was taken aback: not by the content of the lecture, but by something beyond its content.

I was completely transported. Sangharakshita was quite young then – around 39, thin, in robes, with shaven head; very intense. You could see his engagement with the Dharma. He did not bother about what kind of impression he was making on people. He was completely at one with what he was saying. It was an experience I will never forget.

I was told that Sangharakshita came down from the Himalayan valley to the Indian plains every summer, and sure enough he appeared and gave another lecture in 1966, but then he didn't come again. When I asked Ramesh what had happened to the English monk, I was told that he had gone to England and he was not coming back. This was a loss, but I was so engrossed in worldly life that I rarely thought about him.

About 1972 I wrote to Sangharakshita. At that time I couldn't say that I was a Buddhist; I had spent so many years of my life studying Theosophy that by now Theosophical ideas were part of my mental furniture. From about that time I actively began to study Theosophy again, but I gradually began to feel that I was going round in circles, and I was not getting as much out of it as I wanted to. It occurred to me that meditation might be an answer. So I asked my husband how to meditate; he told me to sit in a comfortable posture with my back straight, and to fix my mind on *'om'* or a mantra. I tried it. At the first distraction I thought my meditation was over, so I would get up and go away. And I said to my husband, 'I cannot meditate. I meditated for three minutes.' I thought that I needed somebody to teach me meditation in a more methodical manner.

In 1979, one of Sangharakshita's English disciples, Lokamitra,[93] was invited to come to Theosophy Hall and lecture to us. He looked remarkably like Sangharakshita; he talked like him, he was in robes, with shaven head. I felt I had found Sangharakshita again. When I was introduced to him, he just said hello, but I remember saying to Ramesh that in years nobody had given me a look which was so full of goodwill.

On 31 December 1980, Sangharakshita was invited to give another talk in Theosophy Hall, and I took my whole family. I was going to see Sangharakshita again after so many years, and I was looking forward to it with great expectation. I remembered him in robes, thin, intense, visibly engaged with the Dharma. But when he arrived, he wasn't in robes, and his hair was long. He looked like a modern Englishman. And his whole manner had changed – he seemed very calm. This was a bit of a disappointment. But his talk wasn't. He spoke about Going for Refuge. When I had heard him speak before, it was his impact as a person that had struck me, but now it was the content of his talk that was memorable. In the sixties I had been too shy to approach him; but this time I went up to him and said, 'I want to learn to meditate.' He pointed to Lokamitra and said, 'He will make the arrangements.'

It was some time later – March 1983 – that Lokamitra invited me to a beginners' retreat. My daughter and I both went to this retreat. At last I learned to meditate, and I felt transformed; the universe smiled. I was very happy. Of course, I had some difficulties in meditation. Both the usual meditations were taught: the Mindfulness of Breathing and the Metta Bhavana. And, as is usual with the latter, I was told that I had to wish well to my enemies. I scratched my head and racked my brains and said, 'But I have no enemies!' Vajraketu, who was teaching the meditation, said 'What – none?' So I scratched my head some more, and said, 'No. There are people who belittle me, but they are not my enemies.' So he said 'It doesn't matter. You wish them well.' After the retreat, I started to meditate at home regularly; I started to wish them well. And I found it was not possible; they became my enemies! Previously they had not been my enemies, but now, it seemed, they were. So much for the benefits of meditation! But I kept it up; my daughter and I used to exhort each other if we were slack, and we meditated regularly.

I also began to study Buddhism. I read the whole of *A Survey of Buddhism* (Sangharakshita's chief work) with great attention, and I also read *The Three Jewels*. I asked Lokamitra to give me tapes of Sangharakshita's lectures, and I read the *Vimalakirti Nirdesha* in English translation. I listened to a lecture on *The Tibetan Book of the Dead* and tried to read the book but couldn't make anything of it. In short, I read whatever I could lay my hands on, and I went into it all thoroughly and fully.

After I had been meditating for a couple of years I began to feel a little bored with mindfulness and metta. I wanted some other meditations, and – I don't know how – I had heard there were other meditations, and that these were given to people who were ordained. So I wrote Sangharakshita a letter outlining my whole life and my religious beliefs, and said that I wanted to be ordained. Of course, I had no real idea of what ordination meant; I just wanted a meditation. Sangharakshita wrote back saying that in good time I would be ordained. The first step, he said, was to become a Mitra.

My husband is quite sympathetic to my spiritual quest: partly because it is Buddhist, but largely because it is Sangharakshita's idea of Buddhism, and he knows Sangharakshita and has read his books. He himself continues to be a Theosophist; I don't think he will ever overtly become a Buddhist. I respect his spiritual path; I feel that he is spiritually more advanced than I am.

In 1986, my son, who was 19 years old, died in a mountaineering accident. He was a bright young boy, a student at the Indian Institute of Technology. In a routine mountaineering exercise, somebody who was climbing above him fell on him, and they both fell 70 feet. He died; she was all right. This was a terrible blow. I was extremely worried about his after-death state. As I saw the matter then, it was not my loss but his condition that was racking me. His death underlined for me that I didn't own him, I didn't possess him; I couldn't; he was a different human being, bound to go his own way. Of course, nobody wants their children to go that way. I felt that it was not right for me to grieve over my loss, but I couldn't feel that it was wrong to worry about him. Within a few days of his death, I started to read *The Tibetan Book of the Dead* – I remember reading the account of the forty-ninth day on the forty-ninth day after his passing away – and this book made a very profound impact on me. But I was still not free of my worry.

During this period of extreme sadness, anxiety, and worry, the thing I found most conducive to peace was meditation: just these two meditations, Mindfulness of Breathing and Metta Bhavana. Almost every night I woke up in the middle of the night, and I found it difficult to go back to sleep, so I would sit down and meditate. And apart from one occasion, every single time my meditations were peaceful; I was not upset. This increased my faith in meditation considerably.

My daughter had received some scholarships in India, and had gained admission to an American university, so she left for the US two or three months after my son's death, and was there for two years. In 1988, she invited my husband and me to come to the States for her graduation ceremony. On the way home from America, my daughter and I (my husband had gone back to Bombay) spent some time at Taraloka, the retreat centre for women; I also spent some time at the London Buddhist Centre, and a few days in the women's residential communities associated with the London and Croydon Buddhist Centres.

As luck would have it, at Taraloka the study retreat was on *The Tibetan Book of the Dead*. This was still very relevant for me. Here I was at Taraloka, thinking that nobody was feeling as much grief as I was. Two years had passed, so from the point of view of the world I was not in extreme grief; but I must have been extremely upset because I had decided not to mention my son's death to anybody. But, as it turned out, more than half the people on the retreat were afflicted with enormous grief. Day after day I heard such tales of sorrow and saw such evidence of unhappiness that I began to feel that my grief was nothing in comparison. This was quite an eye-opener. When I talked to some of the Dharmacharinis on the retreat, they said, 'Oh, these Western women, they make too much of their grief.' But I felt that this was not so. I was quite touched and upset. I remember many of the women I met on that retreat vividly because of the strong impact it had on me, not only because of what we studied, but also on account of what I heard, and what I must have noticed even without words.

This was 1988. All through this period I was re-reading Sangha-rakshita's books and translating some of them for publication. But until then I had climbed 'the path of irregular steps'.[94] Now I began to tread the path of regular steps. I became a Mitra; I asked for ordination; and finally I was ordained in 1994.

Karunadevi

*Karunadevi was ordained as a member of the Western
Buddhist Order in May, 1993. In 1988 she helped to set up
what is now the Bay Area Friends of the Western Buddhist
Order and the San Francisco Buddhist Center, where she
currently teaches, leads retreats, and is the women's Mitra
Convenor. She is 52 years old and lives in Menlo Park,
California, with her partner and her daughter, who is about to
go off to college. She also has a son, who lives in San
Francisco with his wife. An education administrator by
profession, she is the founder and administrator of a health
centre for teenagers near San Francisco.*

Karunadevi

Women and the Spiritual Life in America

WHAT ARE THE PARTICULAR issues affecting American women who want to embark on a spiritual life, particularly a Buddhist way of life? Further, what are the obstacles to developing awareness and making a commitment to living one's life in accord with Buddhist principles, putting those principles at the center of one's life, and striving to realize transcendental awareness of Reality? A number of issues are specifically related to our cultural conditioning as Americans and as women. Given my very limited experience of other cultures, I cannot say for certain that these issues are not common in other Western cultures as well; and I am fairly certain that some also affect American men, but perhaps in different ways.

Being so large and diverse, the United States is home to many different types of people and ways of thinking. There are regions in which you would be hard-pressed to find a single Buddhist group, and others where, if you did find Buddhists, they would be 'ethnic' Buddhists – that is, people whose country of origin is traditionally Buddhist but who are unlikely to have made a conscious choice to practice Buddhism. If you happen to live in one of these areas and you wish to explore Buddhism or another Eastern religion, you are likely to be thought of as heretical, crazy, or, at the least, eccentric. I can speak from my own experience, having been born and raised in the Midwest as a church-going Methodist, conditioned to conform to the cultural mores of my community and not to rock the boat or do anything to draw attention to myself. Though I conformed to these mores as a young person, I always felt that I was different to others. I felt more at home and more free to explore my own feelings and thoughts in California, which is made up of a very diverse and more tolerant population. Many people change after moving to California; I was no exception. Within two years of moving there in 1967, I was calling myself a radical pacifist anarchist; within seven years I was a vegetarian and had been divorced; and six years later I became a Buddhist. Not that these changes were the fault of California, but California is seen by many as the land of the devil, the corrupter of the wholesome children of the Midwest, the South, and other insular areas.

Nearly all Americans born and raised in this country are conditioned by similar traditional values, even those who have grown up on the coasts and been influenced by newer and less provincial ideas. American society as a whole is predominantly white Judaeo-Christian, and strongly influenced by the Protestant work ethic, rugged individualism, and capitalistic greed. In this society, some of the issues women may encounter in the process of their spiritual development include materialism, individualism, dependence on men, competition with women, deciding on livelihood or career, choosing whether or not to have children, parenting, self-esteem and confidence, taking responsibility, feminism, and spiritual hierarchy, to name but a few.

In this short essay I want to focus on five of the most crucial areas for women exploring a spiritual path in America: materialism, personal responsibility, livelihood, self-confidence and feminism, and spiritual hierarchy and the student–teacher relationship. I will conclude by examining the relevance of Buddhist teachings to our lives as American women. I will draw from my experiences as a practicing Buddhist over the past sixteen years, and my background as an Iowan from a lower middle-class Protestant family.

Materialism and Spiritual Materialism

A by-product of capitalism and the American Dream, materialism is one of the most pervasive causes of spiritual malaise in American society: it is a cause of violence, war, poverty, environmental degradation, and other social problems. Materialistic conditioning has overshadowed such ethical principles as public responsibility, generosity, sincerity, and loving-kindness. Americans are conditioned to want and expect many choices when they seek to buy something, and shopping is an addiction for many. 'Keeping up with the Joneses' has intensified in recent times. Many people desire instant satisfaction and gratification; if a product doesn't give that, they take it back to the store and try another. Likewise, in the area of spirituality, if the spiritual group and its practices don't immediately give the desired results, the temptation is to drop it and try another. This conditioning is one of the many obstacles to taking on a spiritual way of life in an extremely materialistic and cynical society.

In the United States all the major schools of Buddhism can be found, along with many other Eastern and esoteric religions and New Age spiritual groups. Women here, at least on the West and East coasts, have much to choose from if they are seeking a spiritual path. This variety is both an opportunity and a hindrance for a woman choosing to live a spiritual life. It is an opportunity in that she can explore different groups and methods of practice, examine the principles behind them, and choose the group which most clearly resonates with her own temperament and philosophy. But in many cases all this choice can be overwhelming, and she can spend a long time shopping around, getting attracted first to one group and then to another, without delving into any one of them deeply enough to experience its benefits or understand what it is really about. She may also be attracted to a particular religion for reasons other than her initial impetus to find a spiritual path. Sometimes the cultural form and rituals are attractive, or a particular teacher is charismatic, and this distracts her from carefully assessing whether this particular path or discipline is something she seriously wants to take on.

Personal Responsibility

American society doesn't encourage responsibility in the real sense of the word. In the course of interviewing a woman who was applying for a job at the health center where I work, I asked her what she thought were the main problems facing adolescents today. Her response struck a chord with me. She said that teenagers are not invited to be adults. I started to wonder what it would be like to be invited to be an adult. I thought of rites of passage and other formal ceremonies which are not part of contemporary Western society. This is of particular concern for young women, because women are not even invited into the workplace with the same status as men in many places. However, the Dharma invites people, all people, to be adults, to take responsibility for their own lives. Living a Buddhist life means acting from the knowledge and experience that you can change your life, break through patterns of conditioning, change your attitude toward any situation and thereby change your experience of it. Playing the victim, blaming others or our conditioning, and resenting others are no longer justifiable or ethical reactions to circumstances. When these reactions arise, which inevitably they do from time to time, it is important to be aware of these strong emotions, acknowledge them, and allow for the possibility of changing our feelings and attitudes.

Before I met up with the Dharma at the age of 36, I was somewhat immature. I was emotionally dependent on my husband, had low self-confidence, felt trapped in my life as a woman, and blamed it on society, the schools I went to, the part of the country I grew up in, and my Christian conditioning. I did have some faith in my ability to change – with much effort I had already made changes in my life – but I was impatient, and afraid that I might have reached a plateau without a way beyond.

The Dharma and my spiritual friends taught me to see that how I am now isn't anyone else's fault. I know now that it is my responsibility to become aware of how my conditioning is affecting me, and to begin to live in a different way to change the patterns. My parents and teachers did the best they could, based on their own conditioning and levels of awareness; blaming them was only making things worse for them and for me. Reading the Buddha's teachings gave me hope that I could address my problems at another level, not merely the psychological level of coping or analyzing, and not the conditioned, reactive mode of blaming and resenting. I resonated with the transcendental archetypes presented in Buddhism, whose qualities I could develop.

Livelihood and Spiritual Practice

Our work takes up most of our waking life, particularly in America where the work ethic is very strong and the cost of living is high. From a spiritual point of view, I have experienced the immense benefits of making my work a practice of awareness and generosity. At other times it has been a hindrance to practice, and a source of stress and conflict. Since work is so central to our lives, it makes sense for us to use it as an opportunity to address matters related to spiritual life. Responsibility, authority, generosity, self-expression, achieving a balance in our lives, and defining work for ourselves, can all be part of our spiritual practice.

A couple of years before I discovered Buddhism, I made a major career change which greatly influenced my attitude to work. I was an elementary school teacher for twelve years before my second child was born, but I never really took my work seriously; I just did what I saw needed to be done, in quite a narrow way. After my second child was born, I went to work part-time for a non-profit-making work resource center called 'New Ways to Work'. I was a vocational counselor and co-director in a small experimental collective organization which helped people examine their work in the context of their whole lives and society. We stressed the importance of socially constructive work and integrating work with life. We conducted workshops and seminars called 'New Ways to Work and Live' and 'Create Your Own Work'. The most important thing I learned was that work, my work, could have a broader effect on society, and could be a vehicle for social and personal transformation. I also learned that collectivity is very difficult, in fact impossible, without individuality and a sense of personal responsibility. During this time I discovered Buddhism, and this had a significant effect on how I approached my clients and my work.

The agency closed down in the eighties due to lack of funding and I went back to teaching. I taught adults who were high school dropouts wanting to get an alternative to the high school diploma, usually for employment purposes. I did a bit of everything. I began with teaching, then counseling, then administering exams, and within two years I was the manager. But five months after I became the manager I was told that, due to budget cuts, the center was to close down in four months. This is when I really started to take work seriously. With the help of two staff members I started to apply for grants to keep our services alive in decentralized locations, in adult schools, and in jails. We were successful and these programs still exist.

For the next two years I continued to apply for grants for new alternative education programs in other areas of the county. In 1988 I met a woman paediatrician who wanted to conduct a survey of teenage health. This was the start of what is now the Daly City Youth Health Center. It took us two years to get it started and I am still involved as its administrator. This is the largest and most challenging programme I've ever taken on and I know I couldn't have done it without my Buddhist practice. It so happened that I met Manjuvajra, a member of the Western Buddhist Order, two months before I met the paediatrician. As a result of meeting

Manjuvajra I helped to set up a meditation and study group in San Francisco. The beginning of the FWBO in the SF Bay Area coincided with the conception of the health center. The two activities fed each other. Regular meditation, discussing the Dharma, and friendship helped me to create conditions within myself (confidence, concentration, perseverance, patience, to name a few) to move toward and refine my vision for social and personal transformation.

I feel very grateful for the opportunities I have had. There have, however, been difficulties. For me, as for other American women, problems have often arisen as a result of my conditioning. There are two extreme attitudes toward work, both of which result in dissatisfaction and inhibit spiritual growth. One is 'workaholism', a result of compulsion or a desire for money, power, or status, and the other is passivity toward work, usually due to lack of confidence and a desire to be taken care of. The former is unsatisfying because life is out of balance, while the latter also fails to satisfy because one is not sufficiently involved with life.

In America we have been conditioned to define ourselves by our work. 'What do you do?' is one of the first questions we ask when we meet someone. There can be danger in seeing our work as an extension of ourselves, a means to gain self-confidence and meaning. When we over-identify with work, we experience disappointment and a lack of confidence when things don't go the way we want. This results in a roller-coaster ride of highs and lows, without the motivation to develop character, genuine confidence, and happiness based on an understanding of our true nature. It can be difficult to imagine life without our work. This is a sign that we need to look deeper for life's meaning. Often we get caught up in work, habitually and without self-awareness working more and more hours; we can become compulsive or obsessive about it. When we are in this state, we usually feel that there is little time to devote to meditation and other spiritual activities, and we see these as being quite separate from the rest of life.

At the other extreme, when we don't identify with work enough, we perceive it as boring and meaningless. In this state of mind we don't take much personal responsibility or initiative, and may develop a self-deprecating, victim-like attitude towards our work and our boss, which leaves little room for developing confidence and a sense of satisfaction.

If we are bored with work, this is a sign that perhaps we are not engaging enough in it, not bringing enough awareness to what we are doing.

To achieve a balance between these two extremes, we can think of work as an expression of ourselves, a giving of ourselves. Of course, some types of work are better suited to this than others. But whatever our work, if it is reasonably ethical, or at least not unethical, becoming more aware of each action, interaction, decision made, word spoken, will bring more meaning, satisfaction, and balanced effort to our work. Work as a giving of ourselves can take us beyond ourselves, beyond our selfish desires and narrow perspectives. To quote Sangharakshita, 'If we are not prepared to meet the needs of the moment, to put ourselves out, how are we going to take that leap beyond ourselves into the transcendental?'

Self-Confidence and Feminism

American women are probably the most 'liberated' women in the world by feminist standards. However, a lack of confidence and self-esteem hinders, even plagues, many women in both worldly and spiritual pursuits. Our biological and social conditioning still tends to result in passive, unassertive, dependent behavior. Of course, this is not true of all women, and these tendencies have changed a great deal in the last twenty years. However, particularly for women of 40 or over, strong conditioning has affected our confidence and self-esteem. Women of my generation were in their twenties or thirties before feminism and the women's liberation movement became popular. If I hadn't been living on the West Coast in the early seventies, it would probably have been another decade before my life was affected by it.

By contrast, the younger generation is showing more confidence and initiative. Young women have more opportunities, especially in establishing careers and taking leadership roles. But to be confident in a worldly sense is not the same as spiritual confidence, which needs no external validation to be sustained. As I see it, this need for validation is linked to our biological conditioning. By biological conditioning I do not mean determinism; I mean conditioning which can be worked with and changed in the same way as social conditioning. Since our bodies and minds are inextricably interdependent, it stands to reason that some behavioral characteristics are linked to our biological bodies as women. Those characteristics include, of necessity, receptivity, nurturing, passivity, preoccupation with the body, and dependence on others. The women's liberation movement, using consciousness-raising techniques to help women see that they could change, had a revolutionary effect on women's lives and their place in society. However, in spite of the very valuable opportunities and lessening of discrimination which resulted from this movement, for many women it did not lead to higher consciousness, but to an angry, 'victim' mentality.

The Buddhist approach to developing higher consciousness means taking personal responsibility for change through greater awareness of oneself and the world. This is the antithesis of anger and seeing ourselves as victims. We enter the realm of this 'higher evolution' (as Sangharakshita has called it) when we know that we can change the patterned, instinctual characteristics which govern our actions, and that it is up to us to assert ourselves. We can be at the leading edge of our behavior, using awareness as our guide.

With this kind of confidence and self-assertiveness, the so-called 'feminine' characteristics can be transformed. A passive receptivity can be transformed into being open to learning, aware of one's strengths and weaknesses, and of each moment as a new moment full of potential for growth and change. Nurturing can be directed towards ourselves and all living things as impartial generosity and loving-kindness, without the need for recognition or return. Paying attention to the body can become the practice of mindfulness of the body in meditation and in daily life, a conscious way of integrating body and mind without the hindrances of pride or complacency. And dependency can be transformed into a positive dependence on the truth, and on our spiritual friends and teachers.

There is no biologically conditioned characteristic that cannot be transformed, if we are prepared to make the effort – which includes being convinced of the necessity for and possibility of change.

Spiritual Hierarchy and the Student–Teacher Relationship

The idea of hierarchy is sometimes difficult for American women to understand and accept. Our conditioning in an individualistic society, as well as misunderstandings of feminism, have made hierarchy appear, at first glance, to be synonymous with patriarchy, characterized by the dominance of a male teacher and the submission of the students. There have been abuses of women and men in the name of spiritual hierarchy, and some of these have occurred within Buddhist groups, in the United States and elsewhere. So it is essential that we understand what the benefits of spiritual hierarchy are and how such a hierarchy is meant to function in a Buddhist context.

To begin with, we need to make sure that we are truly receptive. If we accept that it is possible to change our lives and that spiritual growth, Enlightenment even, is possible, then the idea that some people are more developed than others falls into place. There is a continuum of growth and we are at one place or another on that continuum. We need to accept and take responsibility for our place on the continuum. This means being a learner, or student, receptive to those who have greater awareness; it also means communicating our awareness as best we can to those who may be able to learn from us.

Another problem related to spiritual hierarchy is quite the opposite. Instead of being resistant and unreceptive to spiritual teachers, some women have assumed without question that their teacher is enlightened and can therefore do no wrong. In some cases this has led to extremely painful experiences. This delusion has been detrimental to the spiritual development of the student, and to whole sanghas. Spiritual teachers have a responsibility to ensure that this kind of delusion does not arise, constantly checking to see that they are not assuming power over their students.

Students, for their part, must take responsibility for checking their motivations, feelings, and understanding about their teachers' teachings and about their relationship. A number of issues can arise. For example, the development of intimacy between teachers and students is a positive and necessary quality in the relationship, but unless clear boundaries are set, this can be misconstrued or can trigger feelings of sexual attraction. Students may also take on teachings blindly without thinking them through for themselves. This can lead to misunderstandings and resentment if students find that they don't agree with their teacher at some point in their process of learning. The most beneficial way to take up a new teaching or principle – the way advocated by the Buddha himself – is to accept it provisionally and allow the truth of it gradually to emerge through experience. Faith or confidence in a teacher can be balanced with clear discriminating thinking.

The key to overcoming both of these extreme reactions to spiritual hierarchy is open communication and friendship with more than one person in a sangha. The founder of the Friends of the Western Buddhist Order, Sangharakshita, has placed great emphasis on spiritual friendship. He has presented two types of friendship, described as 'horizontal' and 'vertical'. Vertical friendship is a friendship in which one person is clearly more aware and advanced spiritually than the other. This can be the classic guru–disciple relationship, or simply a friendship in which one person has more experience in the spiritual life than the other. Horizontal friendships are equally important to spiritual development. We need friendship with people who have about the same amount of experience as we do; we can learn a lot from such friends, and they can give us a lot of practical support for day-to-day personal change and spiritual growth.

Friendship helps us progress in many ways. It can help us overcome our individualistic conditioning, our selfish tendencies, and the worldly use of power and manipulation in relation to others. Communication with others who have a vision for their lives in common with ours is rewarding, although at times challenging. We begin to experience real connections with other individuals, and to transcend our view of ourselves as separate beings at the center of the universe. In this way, friendship is revolutionary.

Conclusion

When I first came across Buddhism, it was extremely important to me that it was presented in such a way that I could relate it to my immediate situation. I desperately wanted to change the way I related to myself and the world. Buddhism caught my interest from the start, but some of the teaching was mystifying and strange, and I doubted whether I had the intellect to understand it fully. I found it painful and confusing to confront the causes of my suffering, and needed a lot of direct teaching from my spiritual mentors before I understood how to apply the Dharma to my conditioned patterns, and stick with it. It was also important for me to see the effect of the spiritual life on my friends, to hear them talk about their difficulties, and see them change.

I was first introduced to a non-sectarian, Western approach to Buddhism by Lama Govinda. I first met him through reading his books; it was a couple of years before I met him in person. I resonated deeply with his writing; his words touched something within me that felt ancient and sacred. I also read other Buddhist books. No one taught me to meditate; I picked it up through reading and was able to still my mind and follow my breath. My practice initially was introspective reflection, the foundations of mindfulness in everyday life, and some visualizations. I did not join any Buddhist group at that time.

After a few years, wanting more structure, I began to seek out a Buddhist group with whom I could practice, and people with whom I could study. I went to Vajrayana, Zen, and Vipassana groups in the area, but I didn't feel an affinity with any of them. Their practices didn't seem practical or of immediate use, and I wasn't drawn to friendship with the people.

It was during this search that I met Manjuvajra, who had come to Stanford University to give a talk and a meditation workshop. I learned that Sangharakshita and Lama Govinda had been good friends and colleagues in Kalimpong in India, and that they had very similar views on the Dharma. I went to the talk and the workshop where I learned the Metta Bhavana meditation and a specific structure for the Mindfulness of Breathing – after eight years! I was very excited. The next month, three of us started a small weekly meditation and study group. That summer I went to Aryaloka, the FWBO retreat center in New Hampshire, where I learned devotional practices, studied and meditated, and finally found an outlet for the immense gratitude and devotion to Buddhism which I had felt for a long time. I also began to build up enough confidence to ask questions and speak about the Dharma to my new spiritual friends.

I have a sense that a continuum of karmic connections has led me to where I am now, the first American woman to be ordained as a member of the Western Buddhist Order on US soil. But I am similar to other American women who wish to awaken something within. The most important elements in the presentation of the Dharma to American women are that (1) it has a tried and true basis in tradition, (2) it is easily translatable to our modern Western lives without a predominance of Eastern cultural trappings, (3) the people in the groups are friendly, welcoming, and encouraging, (4) communication about meditation and life issues is encouraged and exemplified, and (5) the pitfalls of being a part of a group are openly acknowledged and discussed.

These elements are present in all FWBO centers. Clearly this type of friendly, straightforward environment is important, not only to American women, but to all people interested in the spiritual life. Though there are issues arising from specific cultural conditions that women must address in their process of spiritual development, I have found that in general the similarities of women practicing Buddhism, whatever their cultural background, outweigh the differences. I have experienced this in my contacts with women in the Western Buddhist Order from other countries, such as the United Kingdom, Germany, Australia, and New Zealand. When I visited India recently, I also experienced such similarities. I stayed in a Buddhist women's community for a couple of weeks. Naturally I was aware of the totally different culture and way of life. But I was also quite amazed by the similarities I encountered. The most important basic issues, such as gaining confidence and receptivity, taking on responsibility, being friendly, and having a genuine resonance with Buddhist principles, were the same. My experience is in accord with the ancient truth: that the very act of being a Buddhist and following a way of life committed to the Three Jewels of the Buddha, Dharma, and Sangha, creates a common ground of being that goes beyond all conditionings.

notes

CROSSING THE RAINBOW BRIDGE

1 See Sangharakshita, *Vision and Transformation: An Introduction to the Buddha's Noble Eightfold Path*, Windhorse, Birmingham 1990, p.82.
2 Sangharakshita (trans.), *The Dhammapada*, unpublished.
3 Karma literally means 'action', but more precisely in Buddhist usage it refers to volitional action and represents just one type of conditionality, i.e. that which is under our conscious, volitional influence. We could think of ourselves as a stream of karmic tendencies that moves through this life (and from one lifetime to another), with new karma (actions) being added all the time, karma that influences the course of that stream.
   For a fuller discussion of karma, see Sangharakshita, *The Three Jewels*, Windhorse, Glasgow 1991; and Sangharakshita, *Who is the Buddha?*, Windhorse, Glasgow 1994, pp.99–121.
4 Sangharakshita, *The Ten Pillars of Buddhism*, Windhorse, Birmingham 1996, pp.73–74.

JOURNEY TO THE INNER REALM

5 T. Leggett (comp. and trans.), *First Zen Reader*, Charles E. Tuttle, Rutland, Vt./Tokyo, Japan, 1960, p.131.
6 The traditional antidotes to the five hindrances are:
   (1) Cultivate a sky-like attitude.
   (2) Cultivate the opposite quality.
   (3) Consider the consequences of allowing the hindrance to increase unchecked.
   (4) Suppress the distraction.
   (5) Go for Refuge.
   For more information on the antidotes, see Kamalashila's excellent handbook *Meditation: the Buddhist Way of Tranquillity and Insight*, Windhorse, Birmingham 1996.
7 Sangharakshita, *Human Enlightenment*, Windhorse, Glasgow 1993, p.50.

Searching for the Truth

8 For a fuller account of this story, see Sangharakshita, *Who is the Buddha?*, Windhorse, Birmingham 1994, pp.79–83.

9 H. Saddhatissa (trans.), *Sutta Nipata*, 'Kasibharadvaja Sutta', Curzon Press, London, 1985, p.10.

10 Sangharakshita, *A Survey of Buddhism*, Windhorse, Glasgow 1993, p.33.

11 For a full translation of the *Ti Ratana Vandana* ('Salutation to the Three Jewels') see *FWBO Puja Book*, Windhorse, 1990. See also *Digha Nikaya*: 'Mahaparinibbana Sutta', v2.9 in Maurice Walshe (trans.), *Thus Have I Heard*, Wisdom, London 1987, p.241.

12 Quoted in Sangharakshita, *A Survey of Buddhism*, Windhorse, Glasgow 1993, p.109.

13 For a fuller description of these 'upside-down views' (the *viparyasas*), see Sangharakshita, *The Three Jewels*, Windhorse, Glasgow 1991, chapter 11.

14 Susan Murcott, *The First Buddhist Women*, Parallax, Berkeley 1991, p.38.

15 Thomas Byrom (trans.), *The Dhammapada*, Shambhala, Boulder 1995, chapter 9.

16 Shantideva, *Bodhicaryavatara*, translated by Marion Matics, Allen & Unwin, London, 1971.

17 Mrs C.A.F. Rhys Davids, *Poems of Early Buddhist Nuns*, Pali Text Society, Oxford, 1989, p.21.

The Great Miracle

18 The canonical version of the story of Kisa-Gotami is to be found in the *Therigatha (Psalms of the Sisters)*, Pali Text Society, vol.I, p.106. The Dharmachari who gave the talk on this occasion, however, recommended the version in Marie Beuzeville Byles, *Footprints of Gautama the Buddha*, and this is still one of my favourite accounts of the life of the Buddha.

19 Sangharakshita, *Going for Refuge*, Windhorse, Birmingham 1997, p.19.

20 For detailed and very beautiful accounts of Buddhas and Bodhisattvas, see Vessantara, *Meeting the Buddhas: A Guide to Buddhas, Bodhisattvas, and Tantric Deities*, Windhorse, Glasgow 1993.

21 A full description of the nature of puja is to be found in Sangharakshita's *Ritual and Devotion in Buddhism: An Introduction*, Windhorse, Birmingham 1995.

22 See Sangharakshita, *The Taste of Freedom*, Windhorse, Glasgow 1990, pp.30–31.

23 ibid., p.32.

24 Published as Sangharakshita, *Great Buddhists of the Twentieth Century*, Windhorse, Birmingham 1996.

From Womanhood to Buddhahood

25 The Metta Bhavana is a meditation practice that assists the development (*bhavana*) of universal loving-kindness (*metta*).

26 Subhuti, *Women, Men, and Angels*, Windhorse, Birmingham 1995, p.25.

27 Subhuti, *The Buddhist Vision*, Rider, London 1985 (also Samuel Weiser, Maine 1985), pp.136–137.

28 The Bodhisattva Manjushri takes the following vow, among others: 'When I have attained enlightenment, any woman who is afflicted by the hundreds of various disadvantages of womanhood and who wishes to be liberated from being reborn as a loathsome female should bear my name in mind, and she will no longer be reborn in the female state, right up until enlightenment.' From *Bhaisajyaguru-vaiduryaprabharaja Sutra*, Nalinaksha Dutt (ed.), *Gilgit Manuscripts*, Government Research Department, Srinagar 1939, 1:27.

'May all women constantly become men, strong, heroic, intelligent, and learned.' From *The Sutra of Golden Light*, trans. R.E. Emmerick, Pali Text Society, London 1979, p.17.

For an excellent overview of early Buddhist attitudes towards women, see Alan Sponberg's chapter on 'Attitudes toward Women and the Feminine in Early Buddhism' in *Buddhism, Sexuality, and Gender*, edited by José Ignacio Cabezòn, State University of New York Press, New York 1992.

29 The Buddha's advice to the Kalamans, when asked how to judge whether teachings were false or true, was: '… do not be satisfied with hearsay or tradition.… When you know in yourselves: "These ideas are unprofitable, liable to censure, condemned by the wise, being adopted and put into effect they lead to harm and suffering," then you should abandon them.… When you know in yourselves, "These things are profitable, blameless, commended by the wise, being adopted and put into effect they lead to welfare and happiness," then you should practise them and abide in them.' From Nanamoli, *The Life of the Buddha*, Buddhist Publication Society, Kandy 1978, pp.176–177.

30 Craving, ill-will, and delusion (or ignorance) are known as the three *akushala mulas* or unskilful roots.

31 See Note 3.

32 Buddhism tells us that the root of our suffering lies in our ignorance of the true nature of Reality, which is that all things are conditioned and therefore empty of inherent existence.

33 Gampopa, *The Jewel Ornament of Liberation*, trans. Herbert V. Guenther, Shambhala, Boston 1986, p.16.

34 ibid., p.18.

35 'All beings are endowed with Tathagatagarbha [Buddha nature]. Just as butter exists permeating milk, so does Tathagatagarbha permeate all beings.' *Mahaparinirvana Sutra*, cited in Gampopa, op.cit., p.2.

36 *Duhkha*: the feeling of suffering or unsatisfactoriness that arises from the tendency to cling and grasp at things that are impermanent.

37 Unsatisfactoriness, insubstantiality, and impermanence are the three *lakshanas* or marks of conditioned existence.

38 Shantideva, *Bodhisattvacharyavatara: A Guide to the Bodhisattva's Way of Life*,

trans. Stephen Batchelor, Library of Tibetan Works and Archives, Dharamsala 1979, ch.III, v.10, pp.21–22.

39 Sherrye Henry, *The Deep Divide: Why American Women Resist Equality*, Macmillan, New York 1994, pp.136–143 and 168–170; Alison Landes, Carol D. Foster, and Cornelia B. Cessna (eds.), *Women's Changing Role*, Information Plus, Wylie, Texas 1994, pp.35–37.

40 A Yogachara expression used to describe Insight into the true nature of Reality. For a more in-depth discussion, see Sangharakshita, 'The Turning About in the Deepest Seat of Consciousness' in *The Meaning of Conversion in Buddhism*, Windhorse, Birmingham 1994.

41 Subhuti, *Sangharakshita: A New Voice in the Buddhist Tradition*, Windhorse, Birmingham 1994, p.170. For a more detailed exposition of Sangharakshita's view on this topic, see Sangharakshita, *Transforming Self and World: Themes from the Sutra of Golden Light*, Windhorse, Birmingham 1995, pp.114–122.

42 *Samyutta Nikaya*, I, p.32; *The Book of Kindred Sayings*, trans. C.A.F. Rhys Davids, Pali Text Society, Oxford 1993, I, p.45.

43 In the lecture 'The Need for Spiritual Hierarchy', Clear Vision Trust video, Manchester 1994.

44 Sangharakshita, *The Inconceivable Emancipation: Themes from the Vimalakirti Nirdesa*, Windhorse, Birmingham 1995, p.13.

45 From the story of the encounter of Soma (a Buddhist nun) with Mara (a mythic personification of evil), in the 'Suttas of the Sisters', *Samyutta Nikaya*, I, pp.128–129. *The Book of Kindred Sayings*, op.cit., I, pp.161–162.

46 Sangharakshita defines the crucial situation as 'a situation of crisis into which one deliberately plunges oneself … in which one is forced, compelled to change … in which one must either develop or die.' See taped lecture no.107: 'The Symbolism of the Cremation Ground and the Celestial Maidens', Dharmachakra Tapes, Cambridge 1972.

47 The move from suffering to faith to joy constitutes the first three links of the twelvefold spiral path of conditionality leading to Enlightenment. For an explanation of this teaching see 'The Spiral Path' in Sangharakshita, *A Guide to the Buddhist Path*, Windhorse, Birmingham 1996, pp.88–95.

FEMINISM AND BUDDHISM

48 Mary Wollstonecraft, *A Vindication of the Rights of Women*, Penguin, Harmondsworth 1982.

49 John Stuart Mill, *The Subjection of Women*, Longmans, London 1870, p.147.

50 From her correspondence.

51 *Dakini*, no.12 Winter 1993 (Manchester Buddhist Centre).

MOTHERHOOD: FROM MYTH TO REALITY

52 Julia Vellacott, 'Motherhood in the Imagination', in *Balancing Acts – On Being a Mother*, ed. Katharine Gieve, Virago, London 1989, pp.197–198.

53 Elisabeth Badinter, *The Myth of Motherhood*, trans. Roger de Garis, Souvenir Press, 1981, p.149.

54 ibid., p.119.

55 Carol Wallas LaChance, *The Way of the Mother*, Element Books, 1991, p.xii.

56 ibid, p.117.

57 Tsultrim Allione, *Women of Wisdom*, Routledge & Kegan Paul, 1984, p.19.

58 Susie Orbach and Louise Eichenbaum, *Bittersweet: Facing up to Feelings of Love, Envy and Competition in Women's Friendships*, Century Hutchinson, London 1987, pp.49–50.

59 Nini Herman, *Too Long a Child: the Mother–Daughter Dyad*, Free Association Books, 1989, p.323.

60 Rita M. Gross, *Buddhism after Patriarchy: a Feminist History, Analysis, and Reconstruction of Buddhism*, State University of New York Press, Albany 1993, p.236.

61 Vessantara, *Meeting the Buddhas*, op.cit., p.177.

62 ibid., p.226.

63 Vellacott, op.cit., p.196.

64 Herman, op.cit., p.328.

ABORTION – A BUDDHIST VIEW

65 Glanville Williams, *The Sanctity of Life and the Criminal Law*, Faber, London 1958, p.219.

66 Roger A. Paynter, 'Life in the Tragic Dimension', in Baird and Rosenbauch (eds.), *Ethics of Abortion*, Prometheus Books, Buffalo NY, p.5.

67 I.B. Horner (trans.), Suttavibhanga, *Vinaya Pitaka* I, Luzac, London 1966, p.144.

68 Martin Willson, *Rebirth and the Western Buddhist*, Wisdom, London 1987, p.74.

69 Hans Ten Dam, *Exploring Reincarnation*, Arkana, London 1990, p.171.

A NOBLE RELATIONSHIP

70 From George Meredith, *Diana of the Crossways*.

71 Virginia Woolf, *A Room of One's Own*, Harcourt, New York 1929, p.88.

72 Vera Brittain, *Testament of Friendship*, Virago, London 1980, p.2.

73 F.L. Woodward (trans.), *Some Sayings of the Buddha*, The Buddhist Society, London 1974, p.138.

74 Sangharakshita, 'Benevolence and Compassion', from Gampopa, *The Jewel Ornament of Liberation*, unedited seminar.

75 Sangharakshita, *The Jewel Ornament of Liberation*, Questions and Answers, unedited seminar, 1985.

76 Sangharakshita, *The Ten Pillars of Buddhism*, Windhorse, Glasgow 1989, p.68

77 Janice Raymond, *A Passion for Friends*, The Women's Press, London 1986.

78 Robert Bly, *Iron John*, Element Books, Dorset 1991, ch.1.

79 Erich Fromm, *The Art of Loving*, Unwin Paperbacks, 1978, p.72.

80 Stanton Peel and Archie Brodsky, *Love and Addiction*, Abacus, 1977.
81 Sangharakshita, *Jewel Ornament of Liberation*, Questions and Answers, unedited seminar, p.163.

THE SERVICE OF HUMANITY

82 Sangharakshita, *Vision and Transformation*, op.cit.
83 The Hippocratic oath:

> *I swear by Apollo the physician, and Asclepius and Health, and All-heal, and all the gods and goddesses, that, according to my ability and judgement, I will keep this Oath and this stipulation – to reckon him who taught me this Art equally dear to me as my parents, to share my substance with him, and relieve his necessities if required; to look upon his offspring in the same footing as my own brothers, and to teach them this Art, if they shall wish to learn it, without fee or stipulation; and that by a knowledge of the Art to my own sons, and those of my teachers, and to disciples bound by a stipulation and oath according to the law of medicine, but to none other. I will follow that system of regimen which, according to my ability and judgement, I consider for the benefit of my patients, and abstain from whatever is deleterious and mischievous. I will give no deadly medicine to anyone if asked, nor suggest any such counsel; and in like manner I will not give to a woman a pessary to produce abortion. With purity and with holiness I will pass my life and practise my Art. I will not cut persons labouring under the stone, but will leave this to be done by men who are practitioners of this work. Into whatever houses I enter, I will go into them for the benefit of the sick, and will abstain from every voluntary act of mischief and corruption; and, further, from the seduction of females, or males, of freemen or slaves. Whatever, in connection with my professional practice, or not in connection with it, I see or hear, in the life of men, which ought not to be spoken of abroad, I will not divulge, as reckoning that all such should be kept secret. While I continue to keep this Oath unviolated, may it be granted to me to enjoy life and the practice of the Art, respected by all men, in all times. But should I trespass and violate this Oath, may the reverse be my lot.*

84 See Sangharakshita, *The Drama of Cosmic Enlightenment*, Windhorse, Glasgow 1993, pp.194–195.
85 International Code of Medical Ethics, amended version adopted by the 35th World Medical Assembly, Venice, October 1983.
86 See Sangharakshita, 'The Bodhisattva Principle' in *The Priceless Jewel*, Windhorse, Glasgow 1993; Sangharakshita, *Wisdom Beyond Words*, Windhorse, Glasgow 1993, pp.241–50.
87 C.G. Jung, *The Practice of Psychotherapy*, vol.16, *The Collected Works*, Routledge & Kegan Paul, London 1954.
88 C.G. Jung, 'Paracelsus', in *The Spirit in Man, Art and Literature*, vol.15, *The Collected Works*, op.cit.
    Further Reading: Glin Bennet, *The Wound and the Doctor: Healing, Technology and Power in Modern Medicine*, Secker & Warburg, London 1987.

UNITY IN DIVERSITY

89 See Sangharakshita, *Vision and Transformation*, op.cit.
90 See Sangharakshita, *Buddhism and the West: The Integration of Buddhism into Western Society*, Windhorse, Glasgow 1992.
91 See P. Fryer, *Staying Power*, Pluto Press, 1989.
92 Mitra (literally 'friend'): someone who has decided that they want to pursue the Buddhist path within the context of the FWBO. This step is marked by a simple ceremony.

THEOSOPHY, DEATH, AND INSPIRATION

93 Lokamitra, one of Sangharakshita's senior disciples, a key figure in the setting up of the TBMSG, which is carrying on Sangharakshita's work among the new Buddhists of the ex-Untouchable community. He has also set up a thriving social work wing, Bahujan Hitay, whose many projects are run by Indian Order members.
94 See Sangharakshita, *A Guide to the Buddhist Path*, op.cit., pp.117–122.

index

The Windhorse symbolizes the energy of the enlightened mind carrying the Three Jewels – the Buddha, the Dharma, and the Sangha – to all sentient beings.

Buddhism is one of the fastest growing spiritual traditions in the Western world. Throughout its 2,500-year history, it has always succeeded in adapting its mode of expression to suit whatever culture it has encountered.

Windhorse Publications aims to continue this tradition as Buddhism comes to the West. Today's Westerners are heirs to the entire Buddhist tradition, free to draw instruction and inspiration from all the many schools and branches. Windhorse publishes works by authors who not only understand the Buddhist tradition but are also familiar with Western culture and the Western mind.

For orders and catalogues contact

WINDHORSE PUBLICATIONS
11 PARK ROAD
BIRMINGHAM
B13 8AB
UK

WINDHORSE PUBLICATIONS
P.O. BOX 574
NEWTOWN
NSW 2042
AUSTRALIA

Windhorse Publications is an arm of the Friends of the Western Buddhist Order, which has more than sixty centres on five continents. Through these centres, members of the Western Buddhist Order offer regular programmes of events for the general public and for more experienced students. These include meditation classes, public talks, study on Buddhist themes and texts, and 'bodywork' classes such as t'ai chi, yoga, and massage. The FWBO also runs several retreat centres and the Karuna Trust, a fund-raising charity that supports social welfare projects in the slums and villages of India.

Many FWBO centres have residential spiritual communities and ethical businesses associated with them. Arts activities are encouraged too, as is the development of strong bonds of friendship between people who share the same ideals. In this way the FWBO is developing a unique approach to Buddhism, not simply as a set of techniques, less still as an exotic cultural interest, but as a creatively directed way of life for people living in the modern world.

If you would like more information about the FWBO please write to the

LONDON BUDDHIST CENTRE
51 ROMAN ROAD
LONDON
E2 0HU
UK

ARYALOKA
HEARTWOOD CIRCLE
NEWMARKET
NEW HAMPSHIRE
NH 03857   USA

It's hard to imagine that Taraloka is a place for heroines! With its wide open skies, and set in the rolling plains of the Wales–Shropshire border, it seems an obvious place for quiet reflection, for meditation, for meeting friends and making friends, for gentle walks and beautiful sunsets – it is all of this and more. It is a place where, for the last twelve years, women have been creating the conditions for the unexpected to arise. Being on retreat we can discover for ourselves the creativity that gives our lives a deeper meaning and significance, and where better to discover it than at Taraloka, the Realm of Tara – the Realm of Compassion?

If you would like more information about the Taraloka Retreat Centre for women, please write to

TARALOKA
CORNHILL FARM
BETTISFIELD
WHITCHURCH
SHROPSHIRE
SY13 2LD   UK

also from windhorse

SRIMALA
BREAKING FREE
GLIMPSES OF A BUDDHIST LIFE

This is the remarkably honest, moving, and often very funny story of a woman's journey to spiritual freedom.

Srimala was ordained within the Western Buddhist Order over twenty years ago by Sangharakshita. In this book the challenges of combining motherhood with a spiritual path are laid bare. So too is Srimala's struggle to transform her sexual relationships – to break with the romantic myth and her dependence on men, and to move towards celibacy and contentment.

Srimala is no ordinary Buddhist practitioner. She constantly goes beyond herself, throwing off her doubts and lack of confidence until she reaches a point where she is ready to ordain other women – and in doing so, make Buddhist history.

176 pages, with photographs
ISBN 1 899579 03 6
£8.99/$17.95

PADMASURI
BUT LITTLE DUST
LIFE AMONGST THE 'EX-UNTOUCHABLES' OF INDIA

In 1982 Padmasuri, an English nurse and midwife, arrived in an Indian shanty town to help establish a medical project. Padmasuri was a Buddhist whose teacher had worked at the heart of the mass conversion movement, when millions of 'untouchable' Hindus turned to Buddhism. Now she was to see for herself the realities of life for people whose mere touch was regarded by tradition as spiritually polluting.

Surprisingly her response was to give up nursing in favour of Buddhist teaching. This narrative charts her progress as she helps her friends discover dignity, strength, and freedom on the Buddhist path of individual and social transformation.

216 pages with photographs
ISBN 0 904766 85 3
£9.99/$19.95